Library of
Davidson College

WAYS TO SELF RULE

The Author

George Fischer has been a professor of sociology at the City University of New York since 1969. He teaches in the sociology doctoral program of CUNY's Graduate Center. He also coedits a left New York paper for self rule, *Against the Grain*.

Born in 1923, of a Soviet mother and American father, the author grew up in Berlin, Moscow, and New York. He graduated from the University of Wisconsin in economics, and went on to Harvard to earn a doctorate in history and a Junior Fellowship. He then taught for sixteen years at Brandeis (in history), Cornell (in political science), and Columbia (in sociology).

Prior to the present book, George Fischer wrote or edited five scholarly books and nine monographs. Those works dealt with social change and politics in Russia as well as the United States.

In *Ways to Self Rule*, the author takes a fresh look at steps toward full democracy that he probed and wrote of in the last ten years. Here he draws on marxism and anarchism but moves beyond both.

WAYS TO SELF RULE
Beyond Marxism and Anarchism

George Fischer

AN EXPOSITION-UNIVERSITY BOOK

Exposition Press   Hicksville, New York

FIRST EDITION

© 1978 by George Fischer

All rights reserved, including the right of reproduction in whole or in part, in any form or by any means, electronic or mechanical, including photocopying, recording, or by any information storage and retrieval system. No part of this book may be reproduced without permission in writing from the publisher. Inquiries should be addressed to Exposition Press, Inc., 900 South Oyster Bay Road, Hicksville, N.Y. 11801

Library of Congress Catalog Card Number: 78-58556
ISBN 0-682-49132-2

Printed in the United States of America

To those with whom I practiced and theorized in the last ten years—

Socialist Scholars Conference
City University of New York
Alligerville
Against the Grain
Old friends from Moscow

CONTENTS

Introduction	A DECADE OF CHANGE	11
One	QUESTIONING SCIENCE	27
	Science, Ideology, Self Rule	29
	Questioning versus Taking for Granted	38
	Ideology as Argumentation	48
	Rules of Ideology	56
	Science as Fetish	65
Two	CHOICE IN SOCIAL SCIENCE	75
	Great Power Sociology: The United States and USSR	77
	Limits of Academic Critics	82
	Passive Object or Active Subject	86
	Bureaucracy or Self Rule	89
	Thinking Concretely or Analytically	96
Three	REFORM OF URBAN COLLEGES	109
	Too Much Change? Or Too Little?	114
	What's New So Far	124
	A Gap in Broad Skills: Self Rule	133
	Liberals Stop Halfway	138
Four	AGAINST ALL BOSSES	153
	Antiauthoritarian and Anticapitalist	153
	New York: Whose Crisis?	154
	Lessons of City University	159
	Second Thoughts on Mao's Death	162
	Skokie: For Nazi Rights	168
	Neighborhood Populism	171

Five	**SELF RULE OR 1984**	178
	The Idea of Self Rule	178
	Marx plus Bakunin: Right Grasp, Wrong Way	181
	Beyond Scarcity, Beyond Industrialism	186
	From Natural to Conscious Community: Beyond Civilization, too?	189
	Original Accumulation of Community	195
Six	**FUSING MEANS AND ENDS**	215
	Beyond a False Choice	216
	Both Individuality and Community	218
	A Mixed System	222
	No Fetish, No Sacred Cows	227
	Risking a Bad Choice	231
	Epilogue: Here and Now	234
INDEX OF NAMES		241

WAYS TO SELF RULE

INTRODUCTION

A DECADE OF CHANGE

The middle ground is a notoriously exposed, dangerous and ungrateful position. The complex position of those who, in the thick of the fight, wish to continue to speak to both sides is often interpreted as softness, trimming, opportunism, cowardice.

—Isaiah Berlin,
Fathers and Children

All of my life can be read as a chain of encounters with self rule as I use the term in this book: modern people themselves in the course of everyday change and struggles producing direct, participatory democracy that starts and ends with free individuals and face-to-face communities in all spheres of life. At least as a dream, if all too seldom as a reality, that vision of self rule runs through the fifty-five years of my life.

Communist in Moscow, Liberal in Ivy League

My chain of encounters with self rule starts with a youthful decade as an establishment communist in Stalin's Moscow. The encounters go on through two Cold War decades as an establishment liberal (and Russian Expert) in the Ivy League. They come to a head in the past decade—the late 1960s through the late 1970s—as an antiestablishment radical working in and on New York City (and a Russian Expert no more).

Ways to Self Rule deals with this last decade. For me, it differed a lot from all I had done and known up to then.

As a young communist in Moscow and an anticommunist liberal in the Ivy League, I had stayed close to the views and ways of my parents. Both of them were highly political, cosmopolitan, progressive. Both were writers, lecturers, autobiographers, public figures. And not strongly Jewish Jews: Bertha Markoosha Fischer (1888-1977) and Louis Fischer (1896-1970).

That meant, in all those years in my mother's land of Russia and then in my father's land of America, a life within the establishment dominant in that time and place. By and large, I as well as my parents lived by prevailing ways, ties, and views. With some doubts and zigzags, to be sure, but not more than that. Into my middle age then, past forty, I questioned parts of life now and then—not least my uneven enjoyment of it—but seldom life as a whole, or my work and politics.

The stormy 1960s changed all that.

By and by, step by slow step, I came to leave the establishment. I questioned much more of life around me and of my own life. I tried quite a few things I would have scorned or feared in the past. That led to many more zigzags and doubts than ever before. It led me too, though, to a much more conscious, active search for new ways of living and thinking and doing things.

Moving Left the Last Ten Years

By now, by the end of that decade, my search brought me some guidelines and some choices. From the climactic years of the late sixties to the gray, dour years of the late seventies, some things fell into place in my self and in my thoughts. This book tells of my thoughts, and in that way bears on the rest of my life.

Yet to make sense of what I single out here, and how I deal with it, the reader should see my decade of search and change as one whole. How I lived from day to day shaped what I thought and taught and wrote. In that sense, this book adds up to a theoretical, intellectualized mirror of shifts and struggles that took place in my life as a whole, before and during the writing.

In other words, the present book is not a record of detached thought or depersonalized research. While I tackle some classic issues of scholarship and academic life, I do so not as an aloof observer but as someone out to find and spell out stepping stones toward a new life. In the course of writing, I thus took as little as I could for granted other than my search itself—my search for some choice in life other than the established, prevalent, dominant ones I had stuck to most of my life.

In tangible terms, two new things in American life launched my search and change of the last decade: the New Left in the realm of politics and the counterculture in the realm of the personal and of lifestyle. At the time, no sharp line set off the New Left and the counterculture. That held true for my own life.

In terms of this book, New Left plus counterculture led me to delve into my own realm of work: the university, science, social science, the human and political sides of education. In practice, that meant more and more of an involvement in trying to cut down on the hierarchy, the bureaucracy, the authoritarianism rampant in all of our higher learning.

At peak points in these years, my first involvement took the form of active support of the 1968 student strike at Columbia. Then, when I lost my job there with the strike, I helped to found a far-reaching undergraduate experiment in open learning for a cross section of urban students at the mammoth City University of New York. CUNY's College of Staten Island housed this program, called Integrated Studies.

After a honeymoon of a couple of years, the program ran into the usual share of official and internal troubles. I then spent two years—with a lot of mixed feelings—in the corporate-like Central Office of City University. There I made a national study of college-wide urban experiments in some way like our own Integrated Studies. Chapter three sums up the study I wrote for

CUNY's top brass; here I mute less than I did at the time my stress on self rule and a critique of liberal innovators for stopping basic reforms at a halfway point.

Old Work, New Method

These practical engagements brought with them, and in turn were fed and fueled by, big new questions about the underlying assumptions of my own work: science, my current field of sociology, formal learning.

Here my link between practice and theory took me into byways that seemed and felt far, far away from politics, New Left, counterculture. To make clear how I speak in this book, I need to tell something of this big part of my change.

In all my years in an establishment, be it communist or liberal, I had bought the official view of how to understand life, people, politics. What mattered the most, I held with that view, was content, substance, what facts and schemes people learned and had faith in formally, explicitly, systematically.

Now that changed. I turned to a whole new mode of analyzing how people act from day to day. I did so through specialized, quite technical critiques by phenomenologists and analytic philosophers, and by nonpolitical, procedural critics in sociology (who called themselves symbolic interactionists and ethnomethodologists).

We must give pride of place, I came to feel, not to the established and the dominant—to the concrete, the factual, the positively sure—but just to the reverse. We need to shift our focus from description and logic, from logical induction and empirical deduction, to analysis—analysis in depth.

When we look for facts and laws, we tend to look for things that are fixed and certain, that could not be otherwise than they are. By contrast, I would use what I see as an analytic method. I try to look for the processes by which we produce these apparent facts and laws in our everyday lives. Then I ask, how does it make sense to us when we do this? And what do we assume would *not* make sense when we do this?

So the main thing I start with is to look for things that go on which are hard to see at first glance. In our day-to-day lives, we take a lot of things for granted: objects, needs, rules, definitions, prohibitions. When we assume these things, we allow our actions to be restricted by them. So we tend to reproduce the already existing way of life they express. With an analytic method I look for these ways people take for granted and connect them to the "facts" and "laws" we see around us. A lot of what "has to be" is what we happen to keep doing over and over.

The second main thing I try to do with an analytic method is to look for things that aren't but could be. I look for all the unmentioned options, the things we implicitly assume to be impossible every time we assume something else to be true. So I talk a lot about what would make a different way of life "conceivable." What would we have to take for granted in order for a different form of life to become intelligible, sensible, ordinary?

There are two different ways by which things change. They roughly correspond to these two different aspects of an analytic method.

First, in our everyday activities we take things for granted and thus reproduce what already makes sense to us. But these separate activities we all engage in add up to a totality. So that sum changes as we all change little by little, as we see the everyday world changing in big ways and little around us.

Second, when we think about what we assume to be necessary and true, and start wondering about what else might be possible instead, we consciously change our day-to-day actions in ways that change the world we live in. As this adds up, we see that we take a different world for granted and that other things now appear sensible and possible to us.

Seen whole, this method fits well the alternative culture and politics of the sixties. For both questioned what had been treated as a given. Both stressed how people lived and changed—in short, produced—their life from day to day.

This shift in how to view the underlying assumptions of my own work made a lot of difference in how much all of me changed. For now it came to be more than a shift from one set of concrete facts and schemes and certainties to another, from liberal to radical politically, from mainstream to critical in terms of modes of analysis. Now the focus for me moved from what outside observers and authorities made of life to how people themselves (including observers) improvised, negotiated, and produced whatever we did.

The new sense of people themselves exercising each and every day a choice in life—limited by their environment but all-important all the same—is of course, as I note in chapter one, a close kin to self rule writ large. That's how little known critiques by a few philosophers and sociologists did a lot to boost the other shifts in my own life.

If nothing else, all this changed how I speak of self rule in this book.

As much as I can, I stay away from a concrete, positive scheme of past, present, or future. In its place, I speak in terms of what might make sense—what might seem possible, intelligible, conceivable—to people in the everyday life of our own time and place. In lieu of In or Out schemes, in short, I aim at a set of underlying assumptions or grounds or auspices that could add up to a particular new form of life I call self rule.

Just as the game of chess stops being that if you change any one of its main rules, the same goes for a form of life. Hence I do spell out what rules I think it would take to make for the form of life I speak of. But the rules I dwell on are those people will put to work as they come to share new desires and definitions of reality in the course of struggles against the status quo, and in this way produce a new form of life. Thus they are open-ended, contingent rules not at all like the unquestioned, immutable laws of nature or Order that both advocates and most critics of the status quo lay claim to.

This approach leads me to pick no one basic, constitutive rule of this "game," be it the end of capitalism or the state, patriarchy or empire. Instead, I try to account for—make analytically intelligible—half a dozen such underlying assumptions or grounds in chapter five. In the book's last chapter, I display five more on a quite different plane. Together, I see some such set of grounds making self rule conceivable for our time and place.

My case, in sum, rests on whether it makes sense to the bulk of people in the course of their everyday lives, shifts, and struggles. If our times make it intelligible and conceivable for them, then a direct, participatory democracy makes sense as a possibility. If not, then no amount of concrete schemes will make a bit of difference.

My reading of the technical critics of science thus shaped all of this book. It made me stress possibilities rather than trends, underlying assumptions or presuppositions rather than claims to science or truth or objective knowledge. In ways I hope the reader will see soon, I speak of grand old themes in a new key.

This link between my everyday life or practice and a new view of my work comes out in the first half of this book. More specifically in chapter one and more broadly in chapter two, I say a good deal about how the technical critiques helped me to move away from my unquestioning past. The reader will see how these critiques do show a link to my work at large, and to the New Left and counterculture at their best.

In *chapter one,* a co-author and I question science as a sacred cow, as the main myth or religion of our time. We do so by means of a systematic juxtaposition between science and ideology. The Problem of Ideology we speak of stands out as an old weak spot for those who sanctify science.

Chapter two looks at social science in general, and sociology in particular. The goal is to spell out a choice for antiestablishment academics who want to go, as I do, beyond both the dominant structure itself and what most academic critics settle for in or near that structure.

Chapter three in part supports and in part criticizes reforms liberals made a few years back in metropolitan public colleges. Few radicals did either at the time. Too often slighted, the higher learning of urban America includes of course my own place of work, the City University of New York.

A long leash sets off the United States from the short leash of

Russia. And of late all sorts of shifts made for more leeway at the fringe and even the core of higher learning. Still, we have yet to free American college students—not the least the "new," first-generation ones of our big cities—from what seems to me our academic blend of kindergarten and machine. In place of the status quo, I offer a few possible or actual alternatives that in one way or another help students learn by means of a lot of self rule. I have tried to give that sort of alternative for a decade now to my own undergraduate and doctoral students.

Intertwined with my practical involvement in questioning and changing academic life, a second encounter ran through all of this decade. The second encounter brought me close to the main left currents of a volatile, fast-changing time.

In a loose, sporadic way I served as a middle-aged "camp follower" (a term of derision used by conservatives at the time) of the youthful New Left and its battles. I gave funds and cheers to the Students for a Democratic Society, *Studies on the Left,* New University Conference, as well as Black Panthers and Young Lords.

My first active link took the form of selecting and publishing some papers of the Socialist Scholars Conference, a wide mix of left academics, intellectuals, and other radicals: *The Revival of American Socialism* (New York: Oxford University Press, 1971). The life of the Socialist Scholars Conference came to an end by the time *The Revival of American Socialism* saw the light of day. In the late sixties, though, as I broke my ties with the Ivy League, I spent a good deal of time with people active in the group. It was a child of the left upswing in the mid-sixties, and I found its core group steeped in the ways and lore of those years—years in which I myself changed at a slow pace and struggled little outside of my head and work.

In this way, in and near academic life and through my putting together a book, the Socialist Scholars Conference made public my turn to the left.

Like this group, the New Left as a whole dissolved at the turn of the seventies. Its life had been short, unstable, and with little shape to it. Yet it still strikes me as remarkably vital and influential in its turn away from Old Left orthodoxies and from the dominant gulf between public and private sides of life.

After that, I came close to both of the main left currents of the mid-seventies, marxism and anarchism.

Neither Marxist nor Anarchist

This book as a whole shows that, in all sorts of ways, I drew a good deal from both. Yet in the end I came out neither an anarchist nor a marxist. I joined no group and at no point liked to be called one or the other. For while I found each current tempting and suggestive, my own past as well as the present made both seem to me too limiting, too problematic, too set in their ways.

Why?

All through the book, the reader will find more of an answer than I can give here. In brief, the answer differs a great deal for the two left currents.

Marxism I grew up with from my early decade in Moscow. There Marx loomed huge over Soviet schoolchildren like me as the primal father and sponsor of leninism and of Stalin. Ever since my change in World War II from a young communist to a liberal anticommunist, I see leninism—authoritarian marxism—as one of the most rigid, mechanistic, and inhuman creeds and practices of our time. To this day, my feelings on this run as strong as ever. The readers will find echoes of this deep rejection here and there throughout the book.

True, I gained from this authoritarian, leninist kind of marxism more than the glimpse of 1984 that makes me keep my back to it. Much of what I want and like now goes back to the political baptism of Moscow in the thirties.

For the rest of my life, I gained from it a romantic, utopian faith in revolution—and in grand change and a good life. I gained a sense of dedication from people who shared this vision, as against the fascists of the left who each day kill more of the dream. I gained a sense of The People as the great master of their own fate.

I gained a yen for a large, all-embracing scheme that makes sense of the past, the present, the future.

This double bond to my Moscow youth let me feel close to, or at last not closed to, some active, devout members of a communist party or sect. At least when I met them face to face, one on one. I went through that the most in the 1960s, in Moscow.

Up to the Soviet invasion of Czechoslovakia, I went back once a year or so to my old, still beloved hometown. I did so as part of my work as a Russian Expert—and out of a lot of nostalgia. On all those trips, I saw and liked a great deal not only plain Muscovites and dissenting intellectuals but some Good communists. By my own definition, Good communists shared much more the vision of my youth than they did the base for 1984 that people like Lenin and Stalin built in my mother's land.

These new Soviet ties helped to bring back all that still linked me to my far past. So did half a dozen close old friends from Moscow, now in the West; in the last ten years, I wrestled a good deal with their views of capitalism, socialism, and democracy.

None of this changed or cut down my rejection of leninism as an ultraauthoritarian practice and creed. On the contrary, in time my close collaboration in the mid-sixties with top sociologists in both countries led to me see short-leash Russia and long-leash America as fraternal, nonidentical twins. By this I did not mean the "convergence" toward a Western kind of democracy that some Cold War intellectuals had urged. I raised doubts on the plausibility of such convergence in a book of 1968, *The Soviet System and Modern Society*; less directly, I did the same in my two early books: *Soviet Opposition to Stalin* (1952) and *Russian Liberalism* (1958). The convergence I had in mind was a clearly authoritarian one.

Though my old friends from Moscow did not share that view, I came to see my motherland and fatherland as twins in their statist modes of thought as well as their imperial might. (I speak of this link in the first section of chapter two.)

Up to a point, as the 1960s re-radicalized me, my grand old faith did make more sense than it had in my two Cold War decades as an Ivy League liberal. Up to a point, too, that old red side of me made more sense in the course of a Columbia-sponsored project of cross-national research; that project gave me a glimpse in depth of a Yugoslavia run more by Good communists than Bad ones.

In the past decade, I looked to a new, opposing form of marxism to give me this good side of my young baptism without all its brutality and dogmatism. That opposing form of marxism came to the fore in Eastern and Western Europe and then in the United States after World War II.

Antiauthoritarian and antiorthodox, this opposing form goes by the name of critical or neo-marxism, or of Dialectical critique (to set it off from the orthodox unmasking and predicting called Scientific marxism). In my recent search, key neo-marxists like Herbert Marcuse and Juergen Habermas gave me for a while a new view of life, a new intellectual and political home.

In the end, though, I found even this antiorthodox, antiauthoritarian form of marxism too wed to underlying assumptions that no longer made sense to me. The same held true for Marx himself, a unique figure who still stands out in my imagination and my teaching more than anyone else. For ten years in a row at Columbia and then City University, for example, I taught a course or doctoral seminar just on Marx and the rich play of his thoughts.

In each case, the stress on a grand old scheme came to put me off. So did the continuing stress on science, on industrialism, on a more or less traditional class struggle and work ethic, on a revolution in the form of seizing and using an existing state structure. And the stress only on the end of capitalism as the cure for most human ills—as against all the linked but autonomous hierarchies like the state, patriarchy, empire, as well as capitalism.

To be sure, all sorts of revisions and variations mark the critical marxists and Marx himself. Still, quite a few things about them did not seem to me to fit our time and my own life.

The grounds for my doubts in neo-marxism and Marx I saw plain only in the midseventies. At that time, I gave myself for a couple of years to extensive, enthusiastic reading and thought on anarchism, for the past century and more the one big rival to marxism on the left. With much less of theoretical integration or depth, anarchists spoke to me all the same in a way even the most antiauthoritarian marxism did not.

Starting with the New Left, which Paul Goodman is right to call an offspring unaware of its parentage, the anarchism of our time made vivid a revolutionary faith quite different from marxism in what it loved and what it cursed. If Marx and his disciples stressed either social justice or rational efficiency, anarchists dreamed of instant full democracy from the ground up. They put their faith in a close bond of free individuals and free communities, not as an end goal but here and now. They did the same when they saw the private and public as two sides of the same coin.

For me anarchism at its best laid bare, too, the implicit and at times hidden layers of unquestioned dogma and authoritarianism even in the least orthodox side of Marx and marxism. And while marxists tied most human evils and suffering to a single form of society and economy—capitalism—anarchists made the state their pet hate. No matter what social form or creed a state served, anarchists saw in it the main scourge and foe.

In my own changing life, I found that kind of anarchism much closer than any marxism to what I now did in my teaching and my writing, and in my private life as well. I have in mind a rejection as much as I could of any authority from the top down (not least my own as teacher or father or lover). I have in mind a doubting and probing of assumptions on which rest views that tempt me. And a strong hate of academic hierarchy and the hypocrisy that goes with it, which all too few of my established and marxist colleagues in the academy seem to share with me.

Yet with anarchism, as with marxism, some things kept me from joining up, from taking in hand its black flag of revolution any more than I did the red flag of marxism.

I said already that anarchism spoke much more to my soul and spirit, Marx and neo-marxists to my mind. In any such comparison, the anarchist corpus of thought seems thin. Worse than that, with a few notable exceptions—Paul Goodman and Murray Bookchin stand out, as do Ursula LeGuin and Colin Ward—anarchism in our time seems to dwell on past saints and holy texts and sacred places even more than does marxism. While a few like those I just named deal with the here and now, I found most anarchists I met and read to dwell much more on the past. They speak no end of Proudhon and Bakunin and Malatesta and Kropotkin and Emma Goldman—of their nineteenth-century words and works— of the sainted CNT syndicates (or labor federation) before and during the Spanish Civil War—of Makhno in the Ukraine after 1917—of our own Wobblies before World War I.

In short, the anarchist faith and schemes—most of all hate of the state and of marxism—seemed to fill the whole bill for me no more than did Marx or the critical marxists. So I write here as neither a marxist nor an anarchist, but as a student and friendly critic of both.

At the end of chapter two, I stress that a full choice for antiestablishment academics cannot leave out a base for life and work outside of the academy itself. Since I found no such new base in groups with either an anarchist or neo-marxist stand, this left me in a quandary: how do I bring my own practice in line with that notion of mine?

Decade's Mix: Self Rule

For five years, I lived most of the time in Alligerville, a small hamlet south of the Catskills. Those years let me search for ways to find a base outside the academy. I did get to know up close and like the rural working people near whom I lived, and some young countercultural professionals in the same countryside. For me this meant a novel and rare sense for how all sorts of people live and think from day to day. Close though it got, this link did not lead to the kind of practical engagement that I sought.

I found that engagement only when I moved back to New York in the midseventies. Just then a left paper got launched in the city, *Against the Grain*. Ten or twelve people made up the collective, a team of equals, that put out the paper. Politically, the collective turned out to be a mix of anarchists, antiauthoritarian marxists, and independent radicals like myself.

A noble task stood out: to fuse product (a paper) with process (producing it as a team of equals). *Against the Grain* gave me a base for all-around work outside the ivory tower—political, organizational, and intellectual work—for which I had called and searched for some time.

In turn, though, what I did from day to day in *Against the Grain* faced me with a new theoretical challenge. I met it by and by. At least I started to. The second half of this book shows how I did that.

I made clear in the *Against the Grain* collective that I did not share in full either the anarchist or the marxist kind of antiauthoritarianism. Hence the question came to me as well as to others: what would you put in its place? The same question grew out of my wish not to dwell on the political flag the paper flew, libertarian socialism (see the first section of chapter four). If I claimed this term was neither clear nor convincing, what would I put in its stead?

These practical questions led me to the main term of this book. In lieu of words from the left or the academy, I chose a term old and plain: self rule. The same goes for the book's title, *Ways to Self Rule*.

What I say on self rule as such will be found in the last three chapters.

Chapter four brings together short pieces from *Against the Grain*. All deal with current issues, from polemics on Mao and on Nazis marching in Skokie to my praise and doubts of a new neighborhood movement. And all grope for a clear, whole mode that lets you think and talk of self rule—self rule of a left, anticapitalist kind—without an all-out tie to marxism or anarchism.

Chapter five is the book's most general and comprehensive. In terms of ways to self rule, it should be read as my cornerstone.

Here I try to draw on the best of anarchism and of marxism, as well as my own thoughts, to put the current prospects of self rule in a broad historical frame. Just as in chapter one I questioned science by juxtaposing it to ideology, I set off self rule from 1984. I see these as the main possible futures of our time. In those terms, I analyze step by step how self rule may be conceivable and hence possible for us.

Chapter six takes up the case for self rule where the preceding chapter leaves off. From my practical experiences in and around *Against the Grain,* I found it useful to deal with ways to self rule in terms of a classic distinction, that of means and ends. In our paper's collective, and all through the left, people tend to equate that distinction with a single choice. The choice sets off sectarianism from opportunism, or passivity from absorption by The System.

I argue that this choice, one between extremes, is a false one. In its place, I presuppose a fusing of ends and means. From this recipe flow four others for ways to self rule. Together, the five recipes make up the book's last chapter.

I might sum up the past decade's mix of practice and theory in terms of which political tags I would use for myself as of now, and which I would not.

I feel at home with the tag of radical, and of The Left. I like even better a tag of independent radical, and independent left. Or, negatively put, as both anticapitalist and antiauthoritarian. And I might not mind at all tags like populist (for a fair share and role for all the people) or libertarian (for a life free of outside authority). Or, in my sense of self rule, a revolutionary reformist.

On the other hand, the gods that failed me in the past still rule out the tags communist as well as liberal. All I have said so far rules out marxist and anarchist, too.

At least for now, I don't want to call myself a socialist either. Here I feel more troubled and not quite sure, but clear all the same:

(a) If I would not call myself an anarchist or a marxist or a communist, what grounds does that leave for a socialist?

(b) It matters to me a lot that, in the United States as against most of the world, the term socialism itself means to most people something alien and (except maybe as a nice utopia) unpalatable or unreal.

(c) Little now done in this country by people who call themselves socialist quite makes sense to me. That goes for a host of authoritarian, leninist sects no more than for those who seek a home in or near the Democratic Party—or as plain old (or new) populists—but who won't part with the flag of socialism.

As I write this, halfway between the great sixties and the year 1984, no such tags may make sense any more. All the same, for now I feel at home on some middle ground of the left.

True, as I do not hide in this book, part of me craves to find and settle down with one grand scheme plus a group on the left that shares with me this one scheme. Still more, though, I feel at home in what Isaiah Berlin in the Introduction's epigraph calls "the complex position of those who, in the thick of the fight, wish to continue to speak to both sides. . . ." In my case, that means a middle ground between marxists and anarchists. And, still more, a middle ground between radicals and all the people in the United States whom left politics leaves cold these days. Be they liberals or individualist libertarians or just plain mortals.

If in 1971 *The Revival of American Socialism* made public my turn to the left, here I speak for the first time of how I came to choose a middle ground within the left. This same ground lets me now conceive of self rule the way I do.

In all, this book tells the reader how I put in theoretical terms the main practical issues I grappled with in a decade of more or less active, conscious change. A second task, as I have said, was to start giving one more choice, at least a first step to a choice, both to the communism and liberalism I left behind and to those antiauthoritarian anarchists and marxists whose ways to self rule I share up to a point but not past it.

The glimpse I give the reader of this book of my past, and specifically of my mix of practice and theory in the last ten years, in no way comes close to a full treatment of self rule or my own life. I hope to write a good deal more fully and systematically of my idea of self rule, and perhaps of my own life as well. For now, I share with the reader some of both.

ONE
QUESTIONING SCIENCE

Science shows an old weak spot when we look at the Problem of Ideology. The problem consists of a persistent dispute over the possibility of drawing a clear line between science (or objective knowledge) and its opposite, be it distortion, cover-up, bias, or plain error.

The traditional view is that ideology amounts to just such departures from scientific truth or objective knowledge about social reality. However, deep disagreement on the issue marks social science in general and sociology in particular in the United States. Up to now, the dispute ran between the predominant positivists and relativists like Mannheim. Positivists believe that a properly applied method akin to natural science will produce objective knowledge; relativists see little or no hope for objective knowledge due to the historically limited situation of any scholar or observer.

The Problem of Ideology rests in the fact that this dispute has not been resolved. Nor, in our view, can it be resolved in the terms in which it is traditionally posed. We take this view because both parties to the dispute treat the problem on a concrete level, as against the analytic level that we emphasize in this essay.

As we show below, a concrete treatment of ideology limits itself to the content and structure of ideas about social reality. Our main criticism of this kind of concrete treatment is that most social scientists fail to question, and hence take for granted, the

---

First published, by Helen Margaret McClure and George Fischer, as Monograph B-1085, Bureau of Applied Social Research, Columbia University, New York, July 1969. Revised version, by George Fischer and Helen Margaret McClure, republished here by permission from *Comparative Theory of Opinion Makers* (London: Sage International, 1978), two volumes, edited by Bogdan Denitch.

very concepts they themselves use to make sense of the reality they observe. In the subject at hand, for example, people may disagree over what the concept of ideology means, or what leads various forms of it to occur. Yet they fail to ask the more basic question: how is the phenomenon of ideology possible in the first place? It is this question that we address throughout the essay.

To ask how the phenomenon is possible means to treat the Problem of Ideology not on a concrete level but on an analytic level. This entails examining the process and procedures by which either sociologists or members of any collectivity come to treat an activity as ideological. Dealing with the problem analytically demands that the construction of social reality be viewed as an active process in which all members of a given collectivity take part. Thus the analytic approach assumes that what people come to treat as reality is an ongoing achievement rather than an objective structure—object-like, external, "out there"—the content of which observers can treat as given.

Recent criticisms of U.S. sociology in general suggested to us a new way of dealing with the Problem of Ideology. For the emphasis on a close kin of self rule—the active participation of all members of a collectivity in constructing and reconstructing social reality—we drew from both the dialectic of cultural marxists and the phenomenology of Schutz and Garfinkel. The distinction between concrete and analytic methodologies we owe most directly to the sociological work of McHugh and Blum.[1]

All these criticisms contribute to our emphasis on how the phenomenon of ideology is possible in the first place. This emphasis means grounding ideology in the underlying form of life or everyday practice. Such everyday practice by active, knowing subjects "determines" a concept (the object known) in the strongest possible sense: it generates the concept and thus makes it possible. In short, concept derives from the form of life. It is not something people merely learn or incorporate passively.

This essay, then, dwells on process rather than content—the ongoing practical activity, experience, and creativity that goes into producing and reproducing our particular (or any other) form of life. In further contrast to the concrete methodology, we do not deal in causal terms with why ideology occurs. We do not seek factors to explain the types and incidences of it. Nor do we make overall generalizations about observable, empirical phenomena. Except for a few examples, nothing is said about any particular country or concrete social structure. At this point in time, we feel, one can only make progress with the Problem of Ideology in terms of the analytic as opposed to the concrete.

I. SCIENCE, IDEOLOGY, SELF RULE

To shed light on ideology we look at its relationship to another phenomenon, that of opinion making. By closely examining opinion making as well, it seems to us, one can learn more about the Problem of Ideology than by looking at ideology in isolation.

Ideology is one of the most widely discussed and disputed concepts of modern sociology. By contrast, little or no systematic attention has been paid to the concept of opinion making. To be sure, one can find a good deal of sociological literature on the activity this concept deals with, the purposive and socially organized ways of forming opinion. But the literature tends to draw on no analytical construct at all. Or it makes use of such other concepts as personal influence or manipulative propaganda. Hence much needs to be clarified before the concept of opinion making can be used effectively. As will be seen, the same holds for the concept of ideology.

Ideology has been viewed as an important phenomenon in the realm of public or political discourse in Western industrial countries during the nineteenth century and the early part of the twentieth. In the past decade, however, some leading Western sociologists argued that we are witnessing an end of ideology in the West. By this they meant that systems of ideas and beliefs about the organization of society, particularly radical political ideas or utopian thinking, have lost their power to motivate and mobilize people for political action.

At the same time that ideology allegedly declined in importance, preoccupation with public opinion and opinion formation moved to the fore in the realm of political discourse. That is, the major thrust of attention and effort by those contending in the political arena has of late been directed toward mobilizing public support or favorable opinion on specific issues or candidates. The imagery in public discussion has not revealed, until the last few years, a felt necessity to fashion whole new or alternative ways of organizing society, nor to elaborate systematically and explicitly the basic assumptions and beliefs about the existing social order.

A parallel pattern can be seen in the development of social science, most of all in the United States. There has been a shift in scholarly attention from concern with broad systems of ideas to analysis of the substance and formation of opinions. As Mannheim, Merton, Mills, Mueller, and Wolff point out in different ways, American research in the sociology of knowledge has centered more and more on mass communication and studies of public opinion.[2]

This parallel between the imagery in public discussion and the orientation of scholarship suggests that some kind of relationship exists between ideology and opinion. As they are commonly defined, too, the two show a tie. This is true at least in the sense that ideology is usually defined as a whole system of beliefs about social organization. Opinion, on the other hand, tends to be seen as a single belief, view, or judgment. Prevailing usage of the term implies that a single belief (an opinion) is seen as part of a larger set of interrelated beliefs (an ideology) about social reality.

In sociological literature, the concept of ideology has become so confused and muddled that many scholars in the field now doubt whether it can be systematically analyzed. What is the nature of this muddle? What seems to be the source of it? And can one find some common core of meaning in the sociological literature, once the confusions are laid bare? At least on the surface, much of the muddle has to do with sharp divergences on the nature of ideology and on criteria for setting it apart from other things.

On the nature of ideology, to be sure, the literature shows tacit agreement that ideology refers to some sort of system of ideas, beliefs, and values about social reality. Beyond that vague notion, though, specific formulations differ a great deal. The divergence takes place along at least two axes or dimensions:

1. scope—the range of phenomena which ideologies are presumed to cover;
2. function—evaluations regarding the consequences of ideology for what people do.

In terms of scope, ideology has been used to refer to a wide range of phenomena. The phenomena run all the way from very specific rationalizations or justifications of their own activities by occupational groups (Dibble, Sutton),[3] to broader political programs and social movements (Bell, Bendix)[4] and, at the outer limit, to comprehensive world views or outlooks (Mannheim, Shils, Habermas).[5] In evaluating its functions, ideology has often been denounced as false consciousness, distortion, and bias (Marx, of course, and, of late, Halpern, Glazer, Lichtheim, and contributors to *Socialist Register* and *New Left Review*).[6] On the other hand, some writers have treated ideology as inevitable and essential "shared conventions of meaning" (Madian)[7] or "systems of interacting symbols" which make "otherwise incomprehensible social situations meaningful" (Geertz).[8]

As Geertz notes, those who regard ideology as false consciousness and the like see its main function as justifying vested interests of established or contending groups. This is the interest theory of ideology, rooted in the marxist tradition. Theorists at the other end of this pole see ideology's primary function as providing meaning in problematic situations, thus making action possible. This strain theory of ideology goes back to Durkheim and Parsons.

On another level, one finds confusion regarding the relation of ideology to attitudes. Some sociologists attempt to study ideology by means of opinion surveys. To them, it is "a particularly elaborate, close-woven, and far ranging structure of attitudes" (Campbell, also Converse).[9] Other sociologists reject this way of defining and studying ideology. They do so on the grounds that it ignores the broad context of ideology, the structure of general categories of thought (Danziger).[10]

The confusion surrounding how ideology can be distinguished

from other things grows out of these varying and sometimes seemingly contradictory notions about its nature. Most writers assume that ideology could and should be set apart both from science, philosophy, religion, and myth, as well as from the culture of a society and its dominant or central value system. The various ways of distinguishing ideology stress either some abstract properties of a thought system or the sphere of activity with which it deals, or its structure.

Parsons provides a prime example of the abstract type of classification. He makes distinctions in terms of logical sets of properties of thought systems: empirical versus nonempirical frame of reference, and cognitive versus evaluative emphasis regarding beliefs.[11] In line with these distinctions, ideology as well as science, religion, and philosophy fit into a fourfold table:

		EMPIRICAL FRAME OF REFERENCE	
		+	−
COGNITIVE	+	science	philosophy
EMPHASIS	−	ideology	religion

Other writers make distinctions in terms of the sphere of activity with which ideology is presumed to deal. Most writers stress the sphere of politics. They tend to treat political beliefs as ideology, and other thought systems as nonideological. Yet not all sociologists accept this distinction. Bensman, Dibble, Smith, and Strauss[12] speak of ideologies that members of occupations hold; Schurmann and Thompson[13] point to ideologies of organization; and Goode[14] calls some sets of ideas and beliefs about family relationships "ideologies."

The most elaborate attempt to use structural characteristics to differentiate ideology from other thought systems has been made by Shils (note 5). He distinguishes ideology from outlooks, creeds, programs, systems, and movements of thought in terms of categories like explicitness, systematization, demands for closure and conformity. Unlike the rest, ideologies seek the total transformation of society, either by conquest or withdrawal. As Shils defines them, ideologies are espoused by alienated groups and deviate from what he calls the central value system of a society.

Between ideology and the central value system lie the other types of thought systems. All of its structural characteristics make ideology an extreme type for Shils, and empirically rare. This approach, of course, runs counter to many of the views just cited. Thus quite a few writers see ideology as not at all deviant or dissenting. They see it, on the contrary, primarily as a set of rationalizations for maintaining the position of established or ruling groups (dominant or centrally located groups, if you will). From that point of view, ideology is very closely identified with the central value system or dominant culture.

Together, all of these views support the initial point made: at least on the surface, the sources of confusion about the meaning of ideology have to do with diverging notions about its nature and how it might be differentiated from other things. And the sociological literature, by and large, treats the concept most unsystematically. Rather than trying to put forth one more such formulation here, it makes sense to shift our attention from the usual question—what is ideology?—to a very different one: how do sociologists come to call thought systems ideological? What assumptions and inferences do they make when they invoke the concept? As a first step in attempting to answer this question, we ask: what do sociologists seem to treat as distinctive features of the situations to which they apply the term? Initially, then, we look for common usages and common analytic themes in recent writings on the subject. This should reveal whether there are some common grounds on which current meaning of ideology rests. The literature shows widespread agreement on three distinctive features:

Legitimation

Sociologists seem to agree that ideology is concerned with legitimation—the justification of group action and its social acceptance. This holds whether writers speak of rationalization of vested interests, attempts to "maintain a particular social role"

(Halpern, note 6), or "justificatory, apologetic . . . activity concerned with establishment and defense of patterns of belief and value" (Geertz, note 8). In each case, writers treat as a primary issue the legitimation of how an activity is socially organized.

When the basic assumptions underlying a social arrangement seem to be seriously challenged, the resulting need for legitimation may well take the form of concern with the sacred. It has been observed many times, moreover, that when (as in modern societies) religious world views lose their credibility and widespread appeal, nonreligious world views like marxism and fascism, or outlooks like nationalism, might replace religion and serve its traditional legitimating function. It is not surprising, therefore, that some authors describe ideology as a secular religion (Bell, note 4; Shils, note 5). Indeed, Shils holds:

> Ideology, whether nominally religious or anti-religious, is concerned with the sacred. Ideology seeks to sanctify existence by bringing every part of it under the dominion of the ultimately right principles. The sacred and the sacriligious reside in authority, the former in the authority acknowledged by ideology, the latter in that which prevails in the "wicked world," against which ideology contends.[15]

Power Conflict

All of the sociological literature links ideology to conflicts between people seeking or holding power. But some writers have in mind power in a narrower sense, others in a wider sense. In the narrower sense, these terms refer to a society's formal distribution of authority and resources that by and large takes place within one realm—the sphere of politics. In a broader sense, power and politics involve any sphere of activity, and all of its aspects that deal with the allocation of rewards. While writers are apt to use the terms in the narrower sense, most of them agree that power conflict is always at stake in ideological disputes, whether or not those involved expressly acknowledge that dimension.

For example, Goode (note 14) says that "the ideology of

the conjugal family is a radical one." In terms of the usual sociological interpretation, this means that the organization of activities in the conjugal family (such as the right of individuals to choose their own spouse and place to live) imply basically different power relationships from those associated with the traditional ideal family structure. Conjugal family values thus threaten established power relationships and vested interests in traditional societies.

Along the same lines, paradigm debates in natural science show how the power or political dimension is present in such conflicts. There the controversy is over the legitimacy of problems and procedures that scientists single out. One can readily see how paradigm debates amount to struggles for authority, recognition, and dominance within a scientific discipline. A new paradigm, by questioning old practices and putting forth new ones, threatens vested interests and established hierarchies within the discipline (Kuhn, Mulkay).[16]

These examples make clear that what are seen as ideologically formulated power conflicts may involve nothing less than the survival of a group. For the issues at stake in many an ideological dispute are of fundamental importance to a group's ability to keep or gain a place under the sun.

Style of Argument

Many writers note that quite a special rhetoric, and a heightened affect, mark the argumentation that takes place in the realm of ideology. The large amount of affect is often linked to the threat to group survival, and the concern with the sacred. The rhetoric is seen to be highly explicit, relatively systematic, as well as dogmatic and rigid. At least two reasons may account for the distinctive rhetoric.

First, the fundamental importance of the assumptions at issue to the very survival of a group creates a strain toward more articulate explication of assumptions that mark the group alone, in order to reinforce solidarity and agreement among its members. Conversely, there might be a tendency to articulate the assumptions that are shared—or that are compatible—with those contained in rival thought systems. In this case, explicitness is a tactic that seeks to persuade, to mobilize support, or to convert outsiders.

Second, any explication of the assumptions and ideas implicit in a mode of organizing activity is likely to disguise the vague quality of these assumptions and ideas when they are used in practice. For the sake of clarity and contrast, then, a description of the elements of such modes of organization will give an impression of far more rigidity, dogmatism, and so on.

Underlying these common themes which emerge from sociological discussions of ideology is a general tendency of writers to address themselves to ideas and assertions in terms of their content. The usual approach has consisted of attempting to show how the content of ideas or thought systems may be related to or dependent upon the life situations or class interests of those who espouse them. Thus Mannheim tried to argue that liberalism, conservatism, chiliasm, and socialism reflect or correspond to the interests and experiences of different types of classes or groups in society. This tendency to focus on content persists to the present and can be seen, for example, among those who engage in the End of Ideology debate. The dispute has been, in effect, over whether life experiences and interests have changed in postindustrial Western societies in such a way that certain substantive ideas or theories (namely, revolutionary thinking) have become less appealing, if not irrelevant, to the kinds of groups which were formerly apt to promote them.

The emphasis on content, and the way in which writers treat it, is linked to one more common theme that can be seen in the literature. Whether ideology is seen as distortion, illusion, bias, or as a source of meaning in problematic situations, the view prevails that ideology is not—or is something other than—what participants or observers accept as objective knowledge (or science or truth, as the case may be). Hence sociologists have seen the term as relevant to situations in which someone's treatment of ideas as knowledge or truth—that is, as infallible and objective—is being questioned or challenged, either implicitly or explicitly. Or it is regarded as a substitute for knowledge to which people turn in anomic situations.

This usage of ideology forms one basis of what writers often call the Problem of Ideology, and most of the muddle and doubts about the subject can be traced back to it. Of all the attempts to spell out the Problem of Ideology, and then to solve it, that of Mannheim is probably the most comprehensive and best known. Most writers today reject the solution, and Geertz has called the persistent dilemma Mannheim's Paradox.

Mannheim's total conception of ideology contains the notion that all thought "is bound up with the life situation of the thinker." More comprehensively, all categories of thought, modes of arriving at knowledge, and notions of what constitutes truth are, in his view, determined by the social structures in which they are produced. Hence all knowledge is "ideological" in the sense that it is partial or limited by the historical context from which it is developed.

The question for Mannheim was, to what extent and how might this kind of relativism be overcome? His answer singled out intellectuals. He held that insofar as they become detached from their positions of social origin they are freer to transcend the limitations of situation-bound perspectives. By developing procedures which would enable them to correct each other's limited or partial knowledge, these detached intellectuals could achieve a comprehensive objective corpus of knowledge. What Mannheim failed to see was that, as and when some intellectuals detached themselves from their social roots, they would make up a new collectivity of their own—and that membership in this new collectivity would lead as inevitably to situation-bound perspectives as does membership in any other collectivity.[17]

Many scientists bridle at the relativism contained in Mannheim's formulation. Yet they seem to accept the notion that knowledge that can be shown to be situation-bound is not objective because it is biased. Since most writers are skeptical of Mannheim's solution, as he stated it, the dilemma or paradox remains. The clash between historical relativism and a more or less absolute, timeless view of objectivity expressed in Mannheim's Paradox—that clash stands. If taken seriously, this dilemma would undermine the treatment of ideology as something intrinsically distinct from objective knowledge.

The muddle surrounding the meaning and use of the concept ideology derives, in our view, from these two tendencies. Despite their recognition of this dilemma, most writers seem to assume that a clear line can be drawn between ideology and objective knowledge. And they tend to address themselves to the content of ideas in attempting to make the distinction. No one has shown as yet, however, just how this might be done. At issue in most recent writings is only which side in a dispute should be viewed as ideological and not objective, and as objective and not ideological. Labeling something ideological has thus amounted to little more than a debunking activity; someone exposes what he or she sees to be the bias, error, or evaluation in the substantive assertions of another.

That is why the Problem of Ideology remains a troubling one to quite a few scholars in the field who do take Mannheim's Paradox more seriously. From this troubled sense flow the widely expressed doubts about whether the concept of ideology should be used at all.

II. QUESTIONING VERSUS TAKING FOR GRANTED

The sociological literature on ideology shows that people invoke the term when also at stake is what someone treats as knowledge—as a taken-for-granted unquestioned definition of reality. Most of the difficulties encountered in these sources, it would seem, stem from two tendencies already noted. Sociologists treat ideology as something intrinsically different from truth or objective knowledge. And they are apt to focus on the content of ideas. This section responds to the first of these tendencies, and the next section to the second.

A question implied earlier must be considered here. How can an observer use the concept without having to make implicit assumptions or explicit claims as to what constitutes truth? How can one study ideology, in other words, without getting into the exceedingly difficult domain of epistomology? If to deal with ideology we must await settling the problem of the nature of truth,

Mannheim's Paradox is bound to haunt and thwart any attempt. For there will remain countless logical problems and the grave risk of bias in the observer's own view of truth and, hence, of what he or she calls ideological.

The shift of focus proposed here seems to offer a way out of this dilemma. Instead of being concerned with how or whether ideology can intrinsically be distinguished from truth (or from objective knowledge), one asks: how do people come to treat these notions as distinguishable? This means inquiring (as we did in Section I about ideology) how both of these notions are possible sociologically; how observers can treat them as sociological phenomena in the course of their work. This approach to the questions above would be concerned with what passes for knowledge, as against ideology, in a given collectivity. Collectivity here stands for anything ranging from a group—a set of people who interact with each other more or less regularly—to a culture, in the sense of a speech community whose members use the same language.

The analysis involves not the substance or content of ideas as such, but the procedures by which members of any collectivity are able to treat things as either knowledge or ideology. The problem here, therefore, does not consist in seeking to explain ideology by looking for factors or variables external to it which might account for it. The usual *What* questions about content and causal *Why* questions are replaced with *How* questions about methods and procedures used by members of a collectivity—not least a collectivity made up of observers, of people who study other people.[18]

Analytically, to describe procedures whereby a collectivity establishes or "authorizes" knowledge means to describe how the activity of producing and using knowledge is socially organized, how social structures come to be known in common. The focus becomes the procedures that are actually used to establish knowledge as warranted and socially accepted and, hence, in a given setting, as objective. By thus shifting the focus, one sidesteps the impossible concrete question altogether. One no longer asks whether any substantive proposition is true or false. One asks, rather, how people can call it true or false. Here the sociologists who might use the term ideology in their work must be just as much an object of analysis as the social situations and activities they discuss.

To focus the analysis on procedures by which a sociologist or anyone else is able to treat something as ideology rather than objective knowledge is not simply to rely on the formal rules of science that can be obtained by reading any standard textbook. It entails going beyond this to observe the assumptions and procedures that "everybody knows without having to think about." It means looking for the practical solutions and decisions that scientists make in the course of coping with the practical problems of research. These "solutions in use" can then be compared to those of the members of collectivities being observed, because such members, or common-sense actors, are not only the object of the sociologist's research. In daily life, they too are concerned with what they can treat as objective knowledge. Like the sociologists, they need to be clear just what warrants further inference and action on their part, as they deal with their practical problems.

Knowledge, as we use the term throughout, is not limited to the formal scientific corpus of knowledge or the esoteric knowledge of intellectuals that has usually been the focus of interest in the sociology of knowledge. It refers, rather, to any skills, information, procedures, or norms that any actor (scientist, intellectual, man on the street) draws on as he or she engages in any activity. In this sense, anyone has a stock of knowledge and uses it in different ways depending on his or her interests and purposes at any given moment.

What anyone treats as knowledge are those aspects of reality which he or she can take for granted without question until proven otherwise. To take something for granted as knowledge means to accept it as not seeming to require further investigation or inquiry. It is treated as given, even though it may not be fully understood. Complete understanding is not deemed necessary for the purpose at hand. Should one's purpose shift, however, what had previously been taken for granted may then be questioned. One may need greater understanding in order to deal with the practical purpose of the moment. Such questioning, however, takes place within a wide range of things that are taken as given in the way they have been handed down.

What is taken for granted as knowledge, as opposed to what is questioned by members, is a central issue for our conception of ideology and opinion making. It points to a basic contrast between the two, a distinction that will pervade our entire analysis. The notion of opinion making implies that the organization of some human activity and the knowledge about it are taken as given or treated as true. In this case, consensus regarding the system of interrelated assumptions and ideas that define the activity are taken for granted. Disagreements and differences that arise in such situations are treated as differences of opinion on specific issues within the same framework of shared assumptions.

The notion of ideology, on the other hand, implies that the modes of organizing some activity are not taken as given. In this case, consensus on basic assumptions that define it cannot be taken for granted. Disagreements and differences come to be treated as ideological; the views of opponents and defenders of the existing organization are treated by at least some contenders as "ideology."

The contrast between ideology and opinion points to a fundamental similarity between them: something is being questioned when either of these terms is used. If nothing were at issue, presumably, there would be no felt need for the making of opinions or for conflicts over modes of organizing activity. Hence it should be asked here: how is it that people take some things for granted and question other things?

In his essay, "The Well-Informed Citizen," Schutz has dealt with this question. He sets up three ideal types or constructs—the expert, the man on the street, and the well-informed citizen. These types describe varying attitudes toward knowledge that different types of activity seem to involve. Schutz outlines how these types differ in their readiness to take things for granted and to question by introducing the notion of relevances. Relevances refer to those aspects of knowledge that members assume they must take into account in contemplating a course of action or engaging in it.[19]

Two kinds of relevances are singled out by Schutz. Intrinsic relevances are aspects of knowledge that must be considered as a consequence of one's chosen interests and purposes. Members treat them as within the realm of control or choice. By shifting one's interest one can modify the relevances intrinsic to it. Imposed relevances are those aspects of the world that members assume must be taken as they are. They are imposed by events beyond our immediate control, and we have no power to modify them by our spontaneous activities unless we somehow transform them into intrinsic relevances. In the words of Schutz, here is how these three types differ in their use of knowledge and thus in their tendencies to take things for granted:

The Expert

> The expert's knowledge is restricted to a limited field but therein it is clear and distinct. His opinions are based upon warranted assertions; his judgements are not mere guesswork or loose suppositions.
> . . . The expert, as we understand this term, is at home only in a system of imposed relevances—imposed, that is, by the problems preestablished within his field. Or to be more precise, by his decision to become an expert he has accepted the relevances imposed within his field as the intrinsic, and the only intrinsic relevances of his acting and thinking. But this field is rigidly limited. . . . The expert starts from the assumption not only that the system of problems established within this field is relevant but that it is the only relevant system.

The Man on the Street

> The man on the street has a working knowledge of many fields which are not necessarily coherent with one another. His is a knowledge of recipes indicating how to bring forth in typical situations typical results by typical means. The recipes indicate procedures which can be trusted even though they are not clearly understood. . . .

> The man on the street "lives, in a manner of speaking, naively in his own and his in-group's intrinsic relevances. Imposed relevances he takes into account merely as elements of the situation to be defined or as data or conditions for his course of action. They are simply given and it does not pay to try to understand their origin and structure. . . . He will not cross the bridge before he reaches it, and he takes it for granted that he will find the bridge when he needs it and that it will be strong enough to carry him."

The Well-Informed Citizen

> The ideal type that we propose to call the well-informed citizen (thus shortening the more correct expression: the citizen who aims at being well-informed) stands between the ideal type of the expert and that of the man on the street. On the one hand, he neither is, nor aims at being, possessed of expert knowledge; on the other, he does not acquiesce in the fundamental vagueness of a mere recipe knowledge or in the irrationality of his unclassified passions and sentiments. To be well informed means to him to arrive at reasonably founded opinions in fields which as he knows are at least mediately of concern to him although not bearing upon his purpose at hand.
> . . . The well-informed citizen finds himself placed in a domain which belongs to an infinite number of possible frames of reference. There are no previous ready made ends, no fixed border lines within which he can look for shelter. He has to choose the frame of reference by choosing his interest; he has to investigate the zones of relevances adhering to it; and he has to gather as much knowledge as possible of the origin and sources of the relevance actually or potentially imposed upon him. . . . Thus, his is an attitude as different from that of the expert whose knowledge is delimited by a single system of relevances as from that of the man on the street, which is indifferent to the structure of relevance itself.[20]

It should be stressed here that this typology represents for Schutz types of knowledge and not types of people. This is another way of saying that these are varying uses of knowledge or types of activity. As Schutz puts it, "each of us in daily life is at any moment simultaneously expert, well-informed citizen, and man on the street, but in each case with respect to different provinces of knowledge." It would thus be inappropriate to view these as concrete types of people and to draw pejorative conclusions about one type and elevate another. Instead, what should be borne firmly in mind is that, at any given time, each of us uses knowledge in these different ways.

We show our competence as members by knowing what factual claims and uses of knowledge are relevant, warranted, or socially accepted in what setting. Usually people know, in other words, when it makes sense for them to act as an expert, or as a well-informed citizen, or as a man on the street. And if, for example, they act as an expert in a situation where others expect them to act as a man on the street, they will probably be negatively sanctioned—that is, be treated as pretentious, pedantic, boorish, or some such thing.[21]

As Schutz's typology illustrates, all of us question some aspects of the world that others may take for granted as knowledge. And, as our interests and purposes shift, we come to question things that we ourselves had previously accepted as knowledge. Questioning, in this sense, means to treat knowledge as problematic. There are at least two ways in which members might be observed to treat knowledge as problematic. These are crucial for this work and for its conception of ideology.

Knowledge becomes problematic all the time—for one, as people in the course of everyday life face the problem of choosing. The choices lie between alternative courses of action, and usually these options are treated as acceptable by the collectivity of which one is a member. In this case people are apt to raise particular kinds of questions: Which aspects of their stock of knowledge are relevant to their practical purposes at hand? Is this knowledge adequate for dealing with the problem? Do they lack the relevant knowledge altogether? This kind of questioning, we presume, takes place within the realm of taking for granted all those procedures for treating things as knowledge. And the choices that people make in such cases are part and parcel of their routine coping with practical tasks.

The second way in which people treat knowledge as problematic has to do with questioning whether something that is asserted as fact or objective knowledge can indeed be acted upon or warranted as such. Questioning the factual status of someone's assertion of fact amounts to question him or her as a competent member of the collectivity in which he or she acts, scientific or otherwise. For under "normal" circumstances, when someone is treated as a competent member, other members assume that he or she has followed the legitimate or sanctioned procedures in arriving at the stating of something as fact. They assume that if they were in his or her place, they would be able to reach the same conclusion as he or she. They take the competent member's word, and do not check up on how he or she arrived at the assertion.

To treat a member's assertion or claim that something is fact as problematic, then, means that others question whether he or she indeed followed the appropriate procedures. This is the same thing as questioning his or her competence as a member. The problem in this case is not that of choosing between things that are recognized as legitimate options. It is rather whether the member has conformed to a procedure or rule that the collectivity does not treat as a matter of choice, but as a required feature of order.

Challenging the competence of a member, we would expect, is a disruptive phenomenon. For order and stability in any context or collectivity are maintained insofar as people can take for granted the activities or procedures that are criteria of membership. It makes sense to suppose, therefore, that any action that calls taken-for-granted procedures into question (that is, action that is taken to violate them) will produce an unusual or special kind of response. Members have categories (and indeed even rituals) for dealing with such violations. Actions that go against legitimate or morally required procedures are treated as "crazy," "criminal," "heresy," and so on. And such treatments of violations seem to be accompanied by all sorts of explicit justifications for so categorizing the "offenders."

Indeed, when people treat knowledge as problematic in either way, one is apt to observe more explicit talk or argument about what would otherwise not be specifically discussed, because it tends to be taken for granted. In such situations two kinds of disputes may emerge. One has to do with opinion making and the other with ideology. Dispute, disagreement, or discussion among members over alternative courses of action, all of which they treat as legitimate, seems to fit the imagery of what is going on when the term opinion making is invoked. Discussion or dispute over whether a member or group of members have followed what a collectivity treats as the legitimate procedure for asserting something as knowledge appears to fit the situations where the term ideology is used.

The distinction between ideology and opinion making just developed points to a suggestive resemblance on an analytic level. Analytically, the difference between ideology and opinion making is similar to that between knowledge and belief.

There is no need here to get embroiled in the philosophical and epistomological difficulties of this distinction.[22] Despite these difficulties, there seems to be agreement among writers that when something is treated as knowledge, the question of truth is irrelevant. The issue of truth has either been settled because people have been convinced by the evidence that further inquiry is unnecessary, or the truth of the matter is taken for granted (it has not been questioned). Writers also tend to agree that what passes for belief can be judged true or false in terms of what members treat as evidence or knowledge. Until something that is a matter of belief comes to be treated as knowledge, members recognize that it is open to investigation or further proof. Belief, then, is opinion which may or may not be warranted. Knowledge is fact—something that warrants further inference or action. Hence it is frequently observed that knowledge is treated as something about which members are certain, and belief retains an element of uncertainty.

This leads us to recommend, as a strategy for analysis, investigation as to whether it could be observed that members treat disputes, which we have called ideological, in such a way that an observer could say that what passes for knowledge, in the relevant collectivity, is at stake. In the case of what we call opinion making, on the other hand, the task would be to see if members treat the issues as matters of belief.

Even in this initial form, linking ideology to what passes for knowledge, and opinion making to belief, makes possible some inferences from the sociological literature. If people treat knowledge as giving much more authority to concepts of reality than do beliefs, we may assume that some of the traits of ideology noted by observers will not apply as much to opinion making. This might well be the case for all three common themes in the literature listed in Section I. Things warranted in a collectivity as knowledge or fact provide far more legitimation for a social arrangement than things treated as mere beliefs. This suggests, by the same token, that although opinion making is apt to involve power conflict, it should usually be less threatening to group survival than ideological activity. If this is the case, then the style that marks ideological disputes—its special rhetoric and affect—should not be as prominent in opinion making. With less at stake when mere opinions are at issue, relatively speaking, we can expect opinion making to seem less rigid, for example, or less concerned with the sacred.

To summarize, we have argued that the difficulties encountered when ideology is treated as something intrinsically different from truth or objective knowledge can perhaps be avoided if the Problem of Ideology is rephrased as a question of how members of any collectivity organize or use what they treat as knowledge.

The basis for this essay's overall distinction has been made clear, we hope, by elaborating the notion that although ideology and opinion making are related, in that something is at issue when the terms are apt to be invoked, they also differ analytically: the issue of legitimacy is attached more to ideology, which bears on objective knowledge, than to opinion, which has to do with beliefs. In the terms Mao used in his essay, "On Contradictions" (1937), ideological argumentations deals with antagonistic contradictions while opinion making deals with nonantagonistic contradictions.

Beyond that, a key point stands out here. As people themselves produce and reproduce the social structure they live in from day to day, they do so through an ever-present dialectic, a struggle of opposing tendencies. The dialectic pits questioning that social order against taking it for granted.

III. IDEOLOGY AS ARGUMENTATION

It makes little sense, we have argued so far, to assume that either the people involved or the observer can always take for granted what is "real," or a fact, or "objective" knowledge. As analytic constructs, ideology and opinion making convey the opposite notion—that members of the same collectivity can be observed to be unclear, and sometimes to disagree, about matters of knowledge and belief. When they do disagree, we shall stress in this section, they negotiate with each other about what they can treat as real, or as knowledge. In this continuous negotiating process or dialectic, argumentation stands out as an important means. Ideology and opinion making, it seems to us, might best be analyzed as forms of argumentation.

In this context, we need to ask now: what makes it possible for members to agree? What enables them to treat something as objective knowledge? To ask this question, it should be noted, is another way of raising the classic problem of what makes order possible. Order means, of course, that members are able to treat events as intelligible, sensible—in short, meaningful. Order becomes problematic for people to the extent that they know too little in common to be able to agree on what is real or on how to interpret a given phenomenon or situation. To describe how people come to know things in common is to begin to describe how order and objective knowledge are possible for them.[23]

Knowing things in common and being able to agree about what is real are not matters of shared knowledge of content or substantive agreement. Not only the observer, but each member as well, enters any situation with his or her own quite unique perspective on it. Like the observer, any member brings to it a biography that cannot possibly be shared in full with any other member. And both observer and member have interests or purposes not held in common with others in the situation. In view of the different perspectives members have by virtue of their positions in a situation and their unique private experiences, any substantive knowledge that is shared is not—from the point of view of the observer—a basis for order or agreement among members. It is rather epiphenomenal; shared knowledge itself presupposes orderly procedures whereby members are able to reach substantive agreement or share knowledge of content. For if managing in an orderly fashion in an unfamiliar situation depended entirely on the sharing of substantive knowledge, most of us would flounder much of the time.

Knowing things in common as a basis for order, rather, has much more to do with knowing what procedures members of a collectivity or culture draw on in order to cope with a given problem. In his essay on The Stranger, Schutz makes clear the endless variety of "recipes" or "solutions in use" the outsider must learn as he or she seeks to become a member.[24] And the most basic of these are not, by and large, spelled out, codified, or made explicit at all. A member or an observer gains that "knowledge" when he or she finds out what a collectivity treats as fact, as being what it appears to be, in short, when he or she "learns the rules."

It is this kind of knowledge of rules that constitutes members' common-sense knowledge of social structures. Members come to know these rules or structures in common, regardless of the unique aspects of their own biography. To ask what makes it possible for people to treat something as real or objective, then, is to ask what are the rules by which they construct and maintain their common-sense knowledge of social structures.

Among sociologists who now stress rules, the idea tends to vary in meaning or its meaning is left unclear. Since the idea of rules is central to this essay's whole conception of ideology, it should be spelled out somewhat.[25]

When the term is used here, it refers to all the methods, procedures, or recipes that members of a collectivity need to know in common about relevant social arrangements and interactions; the term refers to the organized, patterned, or "structured" ways of doing things in which they are apt to take part. Rules, in short, are standards or criteria which enable people to act together. In that sense, rules underlie (or could be inferred by an observer to underlie) each and every social activity; all activity can be said to be guided by rules. And since membership in a collectivity depends on knowing its rules, it makes sense to conclude, as we just did, that these rules constitute members' common-sense knowledge of social arrangements or structures.

It follows that even the most mundane everyday activities are guided by rules. This is not to say, however, that people must be literally conscious of their ways of doing things as rules. The opposite is apt to be the case. Yet people do respond to rules. They are able, when asked, to give reasons or explanations of their actions, which are intelligible or sensible to others. And such reasons or accounts are only sensible or meaningful to the extent that members know rules in common. These rules, for example, include the rules of language, of grammar and usage. They are what members treat as the "normal," morally sanctionable, or conventional ways of doing things—of managing everyday practical affairs.

A distinction has been made between two kinds of rules: constitutive and preferential rules. Constitutive rules are the basic, required features of a given activity. They are the means by which members are able to define that activity. To writers who discuss constitutive rules they are, by popular analogy, like the "rules of the game." That is, they define the game. They enable people to identify or categorize an activity as one thing rather than another.

Preferential rules are discretionary. They are choices or options with which members may or may not comply, once constitutive rules are taken for granted. Thus there are constitutive rules which must be followed in, say, playing chess, doing scientific work, or courting a person. But in each case members recognize alternative ways of engaging in the activity. That is, they treat all of these alternatives as more or less appropriate. The activity can still go on and be identified as such, no matter which preferential rule one may choose to follow. Whereas constitutive

Questioning Science

rules enable members to categorize (or identify) an activity, preferential rules are means of characterizing (or describing) attributes of this category or identity.

Constitutive rules are not ordinarily observable. In commonsense activity, unlike games, people do not usually think in terms of constitutive rules. If asked about them, they have difficulty telling you what they are. This is the case because constitutive rules are the ones taken for granted. Ordinary routine activity would never proceed smoothly if the people involved had to question continually the rules that define such activity, or consciously attend to them.

The results of breaching constitutive rules experimentally indicate that self-conscious preoccupation with these rules, and their questioning by common-sense actors, is empirically rare in natural (or nonexperimental) situations. We can infer this from the confusion and anger that subjects in experiments show when constitutive rules are violated, and from how much they resist recognizing such violations. For violations of constitutive rules may invite nothing less than redefinition of reality.

While preferential rules have not been studied to the same extent, one could assume that self-conscious discussion and attention to them is a more frequent and less disruptive empirical phenomenon. Since people treat preferential rules as acceptable alternatives within the bounds of a given activity, it seems plausible that common-sense actors find it neither unusual nor unnatural to question, discuss, and evaluate their adequacy, efficiency, or appropriateness. As against violations of constitutive rules, violations of preferential rules, we assume, are not likely to threaten knowledge held in common.

The concept of paradigms in natural science, developed by Thomas Kuhn (note 16), is quite parallel and compatible with the notion of rules as we use it here. And the way he describes what goes on in periods of "normal science," as compared to crises or paradigm conflict, illustrates the distinction we have made between treating constitutive versus preferential rules as problematic.

Paradigms are not highly explicit or articulated rules. They are, rather, models (in the sense of examples of actual practice or scientific achievements) that set the broad boundaries or outer limits within which the collectivity—the scientists in a given field—can treat certain ways of formulating problems and doing research as consistent and proper. They can be seen as rules that organize how knowledge is produced in a field.

In periods of normal science, basic assumptions about the legitimacy of problems and methods (the constitutives rules underlying the paradigm) are taken for granted. They are not problematic because members of the scientific collectivity agree on what is appropriate. Hence there tends to be little dispute which could be seen to challenge the constitutive rules that define the paradigm. In times of crisis the situation changes; the adequacy of the paradigm itself comes to be questioned.

Even in times of normal science, a certain kind of debate goes on. Since paradigms are open-ended and contain unresolved problems and ambiguities, there is much room for debate over residual ambiguities and application of rules. In this case, however, we would presume that what is at issue are alternative ways of proceeding within the context of taking the constitutive rules of the paradigm for granted. Through such discussion and debate the paradigm gradually becomes elaborated and articulated, as problems are either solved or ruled out as beyond the scope of the paradigm.

The notion of rules, as it has been sketched thus far, does not provide sufficient means for describing how order is possible. Several questions remain.

Is it inevitable that people will follow a rule, or do so correctly or competently? How do members decide correctness or competence? Are rules complete? Do they cover all the possible contingencies that people may face in a given situation? Are rules precise or is there much vagueness, ambiguity which members in some sense acknowledge and, more than that, manage?

Experimental studies by Garfinkel and McHugh indicate that these questions point to problems that common-sense actors face all the time. Order is not entirely, it would appear, the result of following fixed, shared rules which may exist prior to action in any situation. And competence, it seems, is not mainly a matter of knowing such fixed rules. Competence has mostly to do with one's ability to manage in spite of the vagueness and incomplete nature of fixed rules, to the extent that they exist at all. And, beyond that, it entails creating rules where they may not exist.

In the face of all this, how is it that most of the time people can and do take for granted their common-sense knowledge or order? One answer lies in the notion of trust. In brief, trust refers to the idea that members do not ask for full information, clarity, or consistency in every situation they encounter. It means that where explicit rules are lacking they accept and use definitions of situations that are vague. Members assume that they and others will act and interpret such action in ways that can be mutually comprehended, despite the vagueness of knowledge.

To put it somewhat differently, where the meaning of an event is unclear or open to alternative interpretations, members assume that a pattern exists and can be discovered by means of what has been called the "documentary method." This term refers to a rule of common-sense thinking. The rule involves treating a given event or appearance as pointing to (or "documenting") an underlying pattern. People relate their prior knowledge or interpretations to present events or appearances in order to discover some identical pattern. Moreover, they assume (or trust, if you will) that further clarity or patterning can be discerned by waiting for future events in the situation. That is, one waits for something later in order to understand what was meant before. Meaning is assigned by testing and revising prior knowledge against present and future events. Thus the sense of an event is to a large extent retrospective. Interpretation emerges in an ad hoc manner.

Trust and the documentary method "work" much of the time. They are possible insofar as common-sense actors take for granted a number of assumptions about the world, which Schutz and Garfinkel have listed as the constitutive features (or rules) of the "natural attitude" of daily life. Since these features have been discussed in several basic sources cited in this section, they need not be repeated here. The important point to be noted is that members respond to these constitutive features or rules as morally enforced requirements for competent membership. Shared knowledge, therefore, is possible to the extent that the natural attitude serves as an enforceable ethic.

It should now be clear that common-sense knowledge as a condition of social order is very much an ongoing accomplishment or achievement. The sharing of rules and agreement about what is real or what an event means must be continually managed, adapted, brought up to date. To posit shared norms as a precondition of order is to beg the question rather than to answer it.

Part of the task of managing order has to do with coping at points where trust, common-sense knowledge, and the documentary method are not sufficient. This is to say, when knowledge or meaning have become problematic for members. In such situations, as we have indicated before, members cannot take their common-sense procedures entirely for granted. We would expect to observe more questioning and more self-conscious attention devoted to deciding what will constitute common understanding of an event. Where alternative interpretations of a situation are made explicit by members, we would presume, knowledge, common understanding, or "agreement" must be negotiated. In this sense, negotiation refers to any of the activities in which members might engage in order to produce agreement when knowledge is treated as problematic.

Negotiating activities could include descriptive statements, explanations or reasons, or argumentation. Argumentation, in this view, would occur if members were not satisfied with the other types of communication, or if they assume other members would not be. Ideology or opinion making ought to be found, then, if members do not treat a description as adequate, or an explanation or reason as a good or acceptable one. For ideology and opinion making can be seen as those forms of argumentation which imply that members have failed to agree by other means or that they anticipate the possibility of disagreement about what they will treat as knowledge or belief, respectively.

It might be suggested here that a distinction between constitutive and preferential rules may be, in part, an accomplishment or product of argument itself. The idea of the documentary method, which was discussed earlier, indicates that many of the rules to which members can be said to respond are not fixed prior to interaction, but are worked out or "managed" in the course of interaction. To the extent that this is so, and to the extent that argument has to do with knowledge that is treated as problematic, the constitutive as well as preferential rules, which could be said to define order in a situation, may well be produced or be clarified in the process of argumentation. This is not to say that the participants in the argument need be explicitly addressing themselves to the defining of rules. It suggests, rather, that by examining argumentation the observer can discern more easily than in nonproblematic situations how members go about constructing and maintaining order. By inference, he or she can thus observe the construction and enforcement of rules.

Like description and explanation, argumentation is a form of discourse, of more or less extended communication by means of language. It differs from the other forms of discourse in that it seeks more actively and explicitly to persuade, to get people to take some course of action (if only the action of assent or not opposing). In other words, argumentation is the purposive use of language to justify, interpret, gain support or adherence of others to some point of view. Arguments can be highly elaborate and systematic, or just the reverse. Here it does not matter which it is. What matters is that ideology and opinion making can be described as argumentation or as attempts to persuade through the use of language.

To persuade people, all sorts of action are used, of course, other than argumentation by means of language. Many of them are often more effective. Physical coercion is a case in point. So also are the psychological or symbolic techniques of conditioning.

Language, furthermore, is not always used for discourse. By itself, for instance, a blessing or a curse (such as Nixon's expletives) does not constitute discourse. Nor do slogans like "Up against the wall, motherfucker" or "No more bullshit" or the antiabortion "Right to life." The use of language amounts to discourse only if the talk is more or less extended. In turn, discourse takes the form of argumentation only if it seeks to convince someone to act in a certain way. A blessing, curse, or slogan must be part of such discourse if we are to classify it as argumentation.[26]

To describe ideology and opinion making as forms of argumentation in the way we have proposed should help to avoid some of the confusion that has resulted from the prevailing tendency to focus on content when discussing these terms. We have argued that knowledge, as a condition of order in any context, does not consist in substantive agreement. What passes for objective knowledge depends on whether or not members can assume that someone's substantive assertion of fact is a product of what the collectivity treats as legitimate or warranted procedures for making such assertions. Hence what people call knowledge, or what they might call ideology or opinion, is much less a matter of the content of an assertion as such than of how members treat it.

Ideology and opinion making as sociological constructs, therefore, might best be seen as ways of describing how people argue or question when matters of knowledge or belief are at issue. In this way sociologists can use these concepts without departing from the common core of meaning usually attached to them. At the same time, this would avoid the pitfalls and polemics that result from relying exclusively on the substance of ideas and assertions, as is the practice of concrete science.

IV. RULES OF IDEOLOGY

So far, we have formulated a general rule for describing how ideology and opinion making are possible as sociological phenomena. This means that we have attempted to make explicit, at least in general terms, the assumptions and procedures that we go through, as observers, in order to use these constructs to describe what members of a collectivity do. Describing such operations of the observer, the reader should note, is the same analytical process as showing how the observer makes inferences about what the rules are that govern whatever activity he or she is studying.

The rule generated up to now, our overall conception, can be summarized by two points:

1. Ideology and opinion making are constructs that can be used to describe argumentation or questioning about matters of knowledge and belief;

2. the two constructs can be distinguished from each other by observing which form the argumentation or questioning takes.

In this last section, we seek to specify the general rule put forth so far, and thus make it more accessible to observation. In specifying this rule, no attempt is made here at either completeness or finality. On the contrary, what we offer are no more than a very few specifications. They illustrate the kinds of things an observer might look for or, at best, hypotheses to be tested. We first say a bit about possible features of argumentation in general, and then turn to some hypothetical constitutive rules for differentiating ideological argumentation from opinion making.

Common-Ground Rule

A perhaps self-evident and yet most fundamental rule underlying argumentation, we would presume, is that there must be some common ground. As a minimum, any argument requires a common language that all parties understand, even though they may not completely agree on usage or interpretation. That is, there must be some initial premises that all parties accept as fact.

One often observes situations in which one party may say, "I'm not sure that this is true, but let's assume that it is for the sake of argument." This illustrates a significant corollary of the rule: when parties do not agree about what they will accept as fact, part of the process of negotiation may well include this kind of "pretense of agreement" that makes further communication possible. That constitutes, in effect, a reassertion or refurbishing of common ground.

The Rule of Assuming a Problem Exists

The other side of this initial observation points to another touched upon already. A required feature of argumentation is that a matter of belief or knowledge be problematic in the sense discussed earlier, and that members treat it as something that could lead to disagreement. This means that open disagreement would not be necessary for this rule to be operative. All it would require is that members assume the possibility of disagreement and act as though it were there or at least imminent.

Other forms of discourse, which we have linked to the notion of negotiation where discrepancies and ambiguities occur, may resolve whatever is at issue before it reaches a stage of anticipated or open disagreement. It is also possible that disagreement may be so sharp or deep that no argument takes place at all because the participants no longer see themselves as members of the same collectivity. This is another way of saying that the first required feature of argumentation, the common-ground rule, is inoperative in the situation.

Two-Parties Rule

Closely related to the first two constitutive rules is a third. There must be at least two parties to an argument. This rule would not require, however, that both parties be literally present. A writer may address herself to a more or less anonymous or even imagined other party, anticipating possible disagreement with a case she is attempting to make. She would thus be engaging in argumentation even though the other party or parties are not there participating in an active dialogue. Similarly, a woman often argues with herself. The two-party rule also applies to this case; in some sense, the woman treats herself as two parties.

The following example points to a situation in which neither open disagreement nor an active second party is visible. Yet, one party, in this case the state, could be described as engaging in argumentation. The state, in effect, treats the whole population as the second party.

One sees in the United States continuous effort in schools, the mass media, and other organizations to reaffirm established definitions of reality such as the superiority and vitality of the American Way of Life. That active campaign goes on, year in and year out, although no element in the society can be said to press a challenge that comes anywhere near to matching this campaign in scope or intensity. The Soviet Union, based on party state capital as against our monopoly state capital, provides a still more striking example. Despite the lack of any significant vocal challenge, the state keeps up intensive argumentation at home to reinforce its own definition of reality.

In the example just given, and generally as well, the lack of a commensurate opponent may go back to Repressive Tolerance, as Marcuse argues is the case in the United States, and to its Soviet counterpart of Repressive Denial.[27] In each case the two-party rule would seem to apply, as would the problem.

Undoubtedly there are many other constitutive rules underlying argumentation which could be observed in our form of life. A number of possible preferential rules could be suggested as well. What is of specific interest here, of course, are those rules which might make it possible to distinguish ideology and opinion-making analytically. In the context of argumentation as a general category these would be preferential rules. In terms of each type of argumentation, however, they would be constitutive rules. Insofar as such constitutive rules do set one type apart from the other, they should not turn out to be required features of both.

What follows are procedures which one might expect to find as required features of argumentation that takes the form of ideology, but not of opinion making. We suggest and discuss briefly four hypothetical constitutive rules for ideology.

Asymmetry Rule

To identify and describe our main distinction between ideology and opinion making, the asymmetry rule is crucial. For it conveys how an observer might be able to decide whether what is at issue in argumentation is treated by members as knowledge or belief. That is, the observer should be able to distinguish the two forms of argumentation by attending to the way people argue about the issue at hand.

Ideological argumentation could be described as asymmetrical in the sense that one or both parties in the argument can be observed to treat its own position as absolute or infallible. Its position, from its point of view, could not be otherwise. There are no legitimate options. Thus each side treats its own position as a matter which is closed to further analysis or investigation on its part. The opponent is simply wrong. A party to this kind of argument may indeed be pressed by an actual or potential opponent to justify its claim. This does not mean, however, that it questions the objective-warranted status of its own assertions.

Opinion-making argumentation, on the other hand, is symmetrical. By and large, both parties can be observed to treat their assertions as fallible, as matters of choice. It is recognized that it could be otherwise. Further analysis, additional evidence, or convincing argumentation could lead either party to change its position. In short, the matter is treated as open to further investigation.

The asymmetry in ideological argumentation can also probably be observed by attending to what members appear to expect or sanction as an acceptable outcome or solution. Complete conversion or winning over of the opponent, we would assume, would be the only acceptable solution in the case of ideology. Here again opinion making may be more symmetrical in that both sides acknowledge the possibility of convergence. This form of argumentation would seem to rest on the assumption that the argument can be resolved by both parties' coming together. Each side is assumed to be open to compromise or some modification of its position.

Related to this asymmetry rule is our view that when an observer can infer that what is at issue in a situation documents a constitutive rule of order, the argument is ideological. Opinion making, on the other hand, can be seen as argumentation about issues that document preferential rules. For the most part, such argumentation occurs when constitutive rules are taken for granted, but when members disagree about alternative ways of proceeding within the framework of shared assumptions.[28]

In line with the asymmetry rule, the distinction between constitutive and preferential rules may also have implications for differences in rhetoric or style between ideological activity and opinion making. Where members treat constitutive or preferential rules as problematic, their style of communication and treatment of other people may turn out to differ in ways such as these:

a. If preferential rules are at issue, but constitutive rules are not, members of the relevant collectivity are likely to treat the issues as resolvable (because they are matters of opinion) either by elite-level Rational Discourse or by mass techniques of verbal persuasion.

b. If constitutive rules are at issue, the people involved (both opposers or violators of the rules and those not violating them) are likely to treat each other and the issues at stake as less accessible to the usual discourse or mass techniques. Other types of action are likely to accompany verbal arguments, like confrontation, disruption, use of force, and the labeling of violators as beyond the pale of ordinary social life.

For instance, the widespread protest movements of our own time tend to be seen by those in authority as violating the constitutive rules of politics. Such action is defined as outside the bounds of legitimate channels of political life. Initially, those who disrupt are considered as hooligans or anarchists or parasites. The tendency is to assume that these violators cannot be brought around in ordinary ways. This justifies treating them as "criminals" or "patients" who must be punished or isolated. As this clash around constitutive rules keeps up, the protesters come to be seen as revolutionaries and as "subversives" or outright traitors. That warrants still harsher treatment.

In the eyes of the protesters, dialogue and action through established channels is presumed to be useless. For this reason, radicals are apt to define extra-legal confrontation as legitimate political action, and elite-level Rational Discourse as little more than a hoax. Increasingly, from their point of view, all of this justifies disruption, civil disobedience, or even armed struggle.[29]

Membership-Denial Rule

The preceding example points to another constitutive rule of ideological argumentation, which distinguishes it from opinion making. Opinion making, as noted, does not tend to question the competence of an opponent to be a member of the collectivity. Ideological activity does just that. For it revolves around the issue of whether another member has followed legitimate procedure when he or she treats something as fact, rather than mere belief.

As could be seen from an earlier example, much of current argumentation in United States politics has to do with established elements denying membership to all-out opponents, and vice versa. Those in authority seek to deny membership by isolating or punishing the opponents. Opponents in turn try to do the same by the much more limited, and quite different, means open to them. They thus may use a great deal of obscenity in relation to sanctified objects and rituals, and disparage policemen and other officials as "pigs."

In another sphere, mainstream sociologists in this country argue that political activism lies outside the sphere of science; they often deny jobs (which here means membership) to those who go against that view. Young radical scholars contend just the opposite, and question seriously the competence of their established elders. And in the Soviet Union the growth of sociology in the 1960s took the form of a lot of argumentation about who belongs in this new sphere of activity and who does not.

Denial of membership can also be observed in arguments in the natural sciences. Wilhelm Reich, the initially marxist psychoanalyst, offers a striking example when he turned to his later work on bodily energy. Another striking example has to do with Immanuel Velikovsky, also a psychoanalyst, and his book, *Worlds in Collision* (1950). A storm of controversy broke out over Velikovsky's book even before it was published, and the dispute went on for some time. The theory contained in this book challenged some of the most fundamental accepted notions in astronomy and related sciences. Throughout, established astronomers and other natural scientists rejected this theory because they did not accept the methods and procedures used by Velikovsky as legitimate. They would not take his theory seriously because they could argue that he lacked the proper credentials of membership. Few of these critics dealt with his actual arguments. Many did not even read his book. Instead, they wrote it off by assuming that he must not have conformed to warranted procedures for putting forth new claims to knowledge or challenging existing ones. At issue here, as in all ideological argumentation, was the kind of denial of membership that we would not expect to find to be a constitutive rule of opinion making.[30]

The Rule of Talking Past Each Other

Another possible rule underlying ideological argumentation follows closely from implications of the two rules just discussed. It is also a specification of the common-ground requirement for argumentation in general. When an argument is ideological, the parties can be observed to be talking past each other. This should be the case precisely because the parties do not agree on the warrant for treating what is at issue as knowledge. Hence the very criteria of adequate membership are at stake. While they must share some common ground in order to even talk, in part each party is using different procedures for asserting something as fact. They also probably recognize different categories of things as acceptable evidence.

One can thus possibly observe that each party treats the assertions and responses of the other as irrelevant to the points they are trying to make, or at least as not directly addressed to these points. This should be far more visible in ideological argumentation than in the case of opinion making.

Alternative-Structure Rule

If it is correct that an observer should be able to show that constitutive rules of order in a situation are at issue when ideological argumentation is going on, this implies another required feature of ideology. One of the parties must be observed to be using a framework of assumptions that imply an alternative social structure. Indeed often in such disputes one side is explicitly challenging what it takes to be the existing order and is actively advocating an alternative social structure (or recognized and different constitutive rules). The other side, then, would presumably be in the position of defending and seeking to maintain the existing order or the present commonsense knowledge of social structures.

One can conceive of situations, of course, when both parties are attempting to define an alternative to what they treat as the existing structure. In that case, however, although the participants may have some common "outsider" assumptions, one of these parties probably treats the other as retaining more of the constitutive assumptions of what both would treat as the established structure. Thus the alternative-structure rule might describe not only disputes between In Groups and Out Groups, but among Out Groups as well.

Argumentation is important for an existing structure, too. Presumably it serves to further the process of negotiation involved in maintaining and managing order within the framework of taking constitutive rules of the existing structure for granted. When these basic rules are challenged either explicitly or implicitly by the actions of opponents, defensive measures like cooptation, repressive tolerance, and overt repression are apt to be used in our form of life. These measures amount to trying to buy people off or to squelch them before they can develop effective alternative structures. Confrontation and disruption are recognitions of the defensive measures and attempts to undermine them. The counter tactics seek to accelerate the process of crystallizing alternative structures by maintaining and sharpening argumentation and counteracting (or exposing) cooptation.

Argumentation may be especially important for newly emerging structures. Dissident collectivities probably need to develop a common, shared corpus of knowledge that is distinctly theirs if they are to maintain themselves. Common understanding of a different sort from that which prevails is a life and death matter for them. The question for further study here would be, what is the minimum requirement of distinctive common-sense knowledge for sustaining an alternative structure?

By definition, observers would not apply the alternative-structure rule of ideological argumentation to opinion making.

There the dispute occurs within the context of both parties' taking for granted the same required features of life.

In terms of questioning objective knowledge, none of the rules of ideological argumentation we put forth as illustrations—asymmetry, membership denial, talking past each other, alternative structure—are concrete. None of these rules address themselves to the content of any ideas. Instead, the rules above help us to describe the day to day process by which members of any collectivity deal with the issue of drawing a line between truth and error, or objective knowledge and ideology.

V. SCIENCE AS FETISH

In our time and place, when either everyday actors or social scientists attempt to draw this kind of line, ideology would seem clearly to stand out as the obverse of the predominant view of science. This predominant view of science permeates not only established academic life but everyday life, too. The result is a deep faith in the truth-giving powers of scientific concepts and methods, as now conceived, among most people. The strength of that faith can be seen in the extent to which the vocabulary of established medicine and social science appear in everyday conversation.

In this historically specific context, people tend to treat science as the concrete, positive, absolute basis of all objective knowledge. And by and large people trust such impersonal, depersonalized knowledge more than they do their own self or collectivity. In short, truth comes to be wed to the predominant view of science: like commodities, concrete science acts as the fetishism of our time.

By the same token, people treat ideology as the other side of the coin, as that which lacks a scientific basis. In line with our analysis, then, the Problem of Ideology is at one and the same time the problem of science as it now functions. Ideology turns out to be the Siamese twin of a concrete, taken-for-granted science.

Our whole analysis may suggest that this way of defining and sharply dichotomizing science and ideology appears to be grounded in a particular historical actuality. One might be able to extrapolate the nature of this reality by looking back to the extensive review of social science literature, presented in Section I of this essay. The literature reveals that the modern dichotomy between science and ideology rests on at least these key features: first, the need to legitimate dominant or competing social arrangements; second, conflict over vested power; third, a strong, heightened rhetoric or style of argument.

To us, these features point to a hierarchical and repressive form of life. More specifically, these widely held views of ideology suggest not a welcome differentiation between people and groups, but a form of life possessive, competitive, and aggressive to an extreme. Along with ideology, this form of life elevates a concrete science to great heights. In turn, concrete science provides supposedly objective findings that legitimate power and control by the few over how most of us live and work.

A final question: How can we solve the Problem of Ideology? How can we solve the trouble people experience, in the midst of our scientific age, in sorting out truth from error? Needless to say, the hierarchical and repressive form of life that makes it possible in the first place is not at all apt to transcend the Problem of Ideology. A solution calls for a quite different form of life, one which would make possible a different form of science.

The analytic approach explored in this essay shows the way to what the alternative may be. Most of all, the analytic approach forces our attention back to the very active part people play in reproducing the social structure they live in from day to day. In all sorts of ways, we see people go back and forth between taking for granted and questioning features of everyday life, depending on how they treat their interests and purposes at hand. We see a ubiquitous struggle as well as unity of opposing tendencies, an everyday dialectic between questioning and taking for granted.[31]

A hierarchical, repressive form of life tends to obscure this close kin of self-rule—the active role we all play—and persuades us instead that we are powerless in the face of reified conceptions of dominant social arrangements. An alternative form of life, much more egalitarian and libertarian, would free people from treating as given any of the limiting, alienating arrangements of our time.

In an egalitarian and libertarian form of life, science would cease to be a fetish akin to commodities, a human-made thing that seems to lie beyond the realm of what people do from day to day. A new science would stress as an ongoing achievement by all people the everyday dialectic between questioning and taking for granted, which concrete science now glosses over. To be sure, people will continue to take for granted some features of daily life. So will science. However, we would expect an egalitarian and libertarian form of life to generate a science that gives primacy to the analytic or questioning, while the concrete or taken-for-granted is always treated as provisional.

To put this another way, a concrete science gives first place to a set, unquestioned Kingdom of Necessity; an analytic science (or critique) will do the same with an ever-problematic, ever-questioned Kingdom of Freedom. To repeat, what people take for granted (and the study of it) will not disappear altogether. But the orientation does shift. The orientation shifts from how people make do with Necessity to how people can and do change with Freedom. In all forms of life we can think of, a new science is apt to look for the struggle as well as unity between these opposing tendencies, the everyday dialectic of taking for granted and questioning.

Now the opposite holds true. Only a sharp decline in hierarchy and repression might solve the Problem of Ideology. An egalitarian and libertarian form of life could make irrelevant the dichotomy we brought out, between a concrete, taken-for-granted science and "unscientific" ideology as its Siamese twin.

ACKNOWLEDGMENT

Our thanks to Alan F. Blum, Peter McHugh, and Trent Schroyer, as well as Allen H. Barton, Bogdan Denitch, Liivi Joe, Phyllis Sheridan, and Madeline Simonson.

NOTES

1. On cultural (or critical) neo-marxists, see note 8 and related text in chapter two of this book. We cite key works on the phenomenology of Schutz and Garfinkel here, in notes 18 and 23. On the distinction between concrete and analytic methodology, most suggestive is sociological work which its authors brought together and developed since we first wrote this essay: Alan F. Blum, *Theorizing* (New York: Humanities Press, 1974); Peter McHugh et al., *On the Beginning of Social Inquiry* (Boston: Routledge and Kegan Paul, 1974). On form of life, Derek L. Phillips sums up the use of the term in chapter 8 of *Abandoning Method* (San Francisco: Jossey-Bass, 1973).
2. Karl Mannheim, "American Sociology," in his *Essays on Sociology and Social Psychology* (London: Routledge and Kegan Paul, 1953); Robert K. Merton, *Social Structure and Social Theory,* third edition (New York: Free Press, 1968), pp. 493-509; C. Wright Mills, *The Sociological Imagination* (Oxford University Press, 1959), chap. 3; Claus Mueller, *The Politics of Communication* (Oxford: University Press, 1973); Kurt H. Wolff, "The Sociology of Knowledge and Sociological Theory," in *Symposium on Sociological Theory,* edited by Llewellyn Gross (New York: Harper, 1959). See also *The End of Ideology Debate,* edited by Chaim I. Waxman (New York: Funk and Wagnalls, 1969); *Decline of Ideology?*, edited by Mustafa Reyai (New York: Atherton, 1971).
3. Vernon K. Dibble, "Occupations and Ideology," *American Journal of Sociology,* vol. 68, no. 2, September 1962; Francis X. Sutton et al., *The American Business Creed* (Harvard University Press, 1958).
4. Daniel Bell, "The End of Ideology in the West," in *The End of Ideology*, revised edition (New York: Free Press, 1965); Reinhard Bendix, "The Age of Ideology," in his *Embattled Reason* (Oxford University Press, 1970).

Questioning Science 69

5. Karl Mannheim, *Ideology and Utopia* (New York: Harcourt, Brace, 1946); Edward Shils, "The Concept and Function of Ideology," *International Encyclopedia of the Social Sciences,* vol. 7 (New York: Free Press, 1968); Juergen Habermas, "Technology and Science as 'Ideology,'" in his *Toward a Rational Society* (Boston: Beacon Press, 1970).

6. Ben Halpern, "'Myth' and 'Ideology' in Modern Usage," *History and Theory*, vol. 1, 1961; Nathan Glazer, "The Sociological Uses of Ideology," in *The Uses of Sociology,* edited by Paul F. Lazarsfeld et al. (New York: Free Press, 1968); George Lichtheim, *The Concept of Ideology* (New York: Vintage, 1968), chap. 3.

Among contributors to *Socialist Register,* put out once a year in London by Merlin Press, see for example: Istvan Meszeros, "Ideology and Social Science" (*Socialist Register 1972*); Steven Rose et al., "Science, Racism and Ideology" (*Socialist Register 1973*); Raoul Makarius, "Structuralism— Science or Ideology?" (*Socialist Register 1974*). From *New Left Review* and elsewhere, Robin Blackburn collected similar contributions in a book, *Ideology in Social Science* (New York: Pantheon, 1972).

Marx used the term "ideology" in at least three distinct ways. In his writings, we are told, the term "refers at times to all ideas, sometimes to normative and other ideas which are considered unscientific, and sometimes to such ideas only in so far as they serve the interests of a class" (Bertell Ollman, *Alienation* [Cambridge: University Press, 1971], p. 6). Perhaps the best non-marxist introduction to how Marx treats ideology and false consciousness will be found in John Plamenatz, *Ideology* (New York: Praeger, 1970). A marxist attempt appears in Nigel Harris, *Beliefs in Society* (London: Watts, 1963).

Inbetween marxists and non-marxists falls an essay by Dorothy Smith, "The Ideological Practice of Sociology," *Catalyst* No. 8, Winter 1974. Like Blum (note 1, see above), Smith singles out Marx. Both do so not for his methodology as a whole, but for the dialectic between the knowing subject and the object known; this dialectic our dominant social science (and social order) is held to conceal or distort by reifying it. For Smith, no less than Blum, a critique like that of Marx brings to mind ("recognizes") the deep structure of social science: the critique grounds any concept in the underlying practical activity or historical actuality.

In this light, Marx did not stop at a Scientific unmasking of ideology. Instead, he made much of *Ideologiekritik*, a Dialectical critique of the deep structure of an ideology. On *Ideologiekritik*, see *Ideologie*, second edition, edited by Kurt Lenk (Neuwied: Luchterhand, 1964); Alvin W. Gouldner, *For Sociology* (New York: Basic Books, 1973), chap. 13; Stuart Hall, "Marx's [1875] Notes on Method," *Working Papers on Cultural Studies*, no. 6, 1974; Marlis Krueger and Frieda M. Silvert, *Dissent Denied* (New York: Elsevier, 1975); I. I. Rubin, *Essays on Marx's Theory of Value* (Detroit: Black and Red, 1972); Richard Lichtman, "Marx's Theory of Ideology," *Socialist Revolution*, no. 23 (vol. 5, no. 1), 1975.

Marx stressed the need to lay bare not only a group's distorted self-definition, or false consciousness, but also the rational and hence liberative kernel of any ideology. A grasp of that rational kernel would then help to overcome or transcend the false (alienated) consciousness. All of Marx's lifelong critique of Political Economy, which he saw as the dominant ideology of his time, might well be read as a prime case of just such a mix of Scientific unmasking and Dialectical critique.

7. Alan L. Madian, "The Organization of Ideology, Variations on a Revolutionary Chinese Theme," *British Journal of Sociology*, vol. 18, no. 1, March 1967, and Alan L. Madian, "Ideology and Language," 1968 (unpublished paper).
8. Clifford Geertz, "Ideology as a Cultural System," in his *The Interpretation of Cultures* (New York: Basic Books, 1973).
9. Angus Campbell et al., *The American Voter* (New York: Wiley, 1960); Philip W. Converse, "The Nature of Belief Systems in Mass Publics," in *Ideology and Discontent*, edited by David E. Apter (New York: Free Press, 1964).

10. Kurt Danziger, "Ideology and Utopia in South Africa," *British Journal of Sociology*, vol. 14, no. 1, March 1963.
11. Talcott Parsons, *The Social System* (New York: Free Press, 1961), chap. 8.
12. Joseph Bensman, *Dollars and Sense: Ideology, Ethics, and the Meaning of Work in Profit and Nonprofit Organizations* (New York: Macmillan, 1967); Dibble (note 3); Dorothy Smith, "Theorizing as Ideology," in *Ethnomethodology,* edited by Roy Turner (Baltimore: Penguin, 1974)—this is an abbreviated version of the essay we spoke of in note 6; Anselm L. Strauss, et al., *Professional Scientists, A Study of American Chemists* (Chicago: Aldine, 1962); and Anselm L. Strauss, "The Structure and Ideology of American Nursing," in *The Nursing Profession,* edited by Fred Davis (New York: Wiley, 1966). For a nonideological treatment of an occupation, see George Fischer, "The Changing Work of U.S. Engineers," *The Personality and Labour,* Papers of Symposium 38, XVIII International Congress of Psychology, Moscow, 1966 (Reprint A-454, Bureau of Applied Social Research, Columbia University).
13. Franz Schurmann, *Ideology and Organization in Communist China* (Berkeley: University of California Press, 1966); Victor A. Thompson, *Modern Organization* (New York: Knopf, 1961).
14. William J. Goode, *World Revolution and Family Patterns* (New York: Free Press, 1963).
15. Fowler puts the same stress on the tie of ideology to the sacred: "The modern vogue of the word ideology is a natural result of the decline of religious faith. We have had to find a word, free from the religious associations of faith and creed, for belief in those politico-social systems vaguely indicated by such words as democracy, socialism, communism, and fascism, which excite in their adherents a quasi-religious enthusiasm. Ideology (the science of ideas) lay ready at hand, the more acceptable because it seemed to suggest striving for an ideal. It was therefore pressed into this new service, which has now become its main occupation." See *Fowler's Modern English Usage,* second edition (Oxford:

University Press. 1956), p. 261. One finds a different view of the contemporary link between ideology and the sacred in Thomas Luckmann, *The Invisible Religion* (New York: Macmillan, 1967), especially the last chapter, and in Juergen Habermas, *Strukturwandel der Oeffentlichkeit*, second edition (Neuwied: Luchterhand, 1967). Of late, Robert K. Merton reiterated his view that in a particular time and place it was Puritan religion, and not "other functionally equivalent ideological movements," that served to legitimate the rise of science: 1970 Preface to his *Science, Technology, and Society in Seventeenth-Century England* (New York: Harper and Row, 1970).

16. Thomas S. Kuhn, *The Structure of Scientific Revolutions* (Chicago: University of Chicago Press, 1962); Michael Mulkay, "Some Aspects of Cultural Growth in the Natural Science," *Social Research*, vol. 36, no. 1, Spring 1969.
17. *From Karl Mannheim*, edited by Kurt H. Wolff (Oxford: University Press, 1971).
18. In addition to Blum and McHugh (note 1), also important are the seminal essays in Alfred Schutz, *Collected Papers*, three volumes (Hague: Nijhoff, 1961-1966).
19. A somewhat similar view will be found in Juergen Habermas, *Knowledge and Human Interests* (Boston: Beacon Press, 1971), especially Appendix. See also his *Logik der Sozialwissenschaften* (Frankfurt: Suhrkamp, 1970).
20. *Collected Papers*, vol. II, pp. 122-23 and 129-31.
21. On claims and warrants, see the third essay of Stephen Toulmin's *The Uses of Argument* (Cambridge University Press, 1964).
22. *Knowledge and Belief*, edited by A. Phillips Griffiths, Oxford University Press, 1967, with a bibliographical sketch. As in the Griffiths collection, the term belief is used here not in the sense of a set faith but in a quite opposite sense. The term stands for no more than opinions.
23. In the discussion of common-sense knowledge, the documentary method, trust, and rules, we draw on these works: Peter McHugh, *Defining the Situation* (Indianapolis: Bobbs Mer-

rill, 1968), chap. 1 and also pp. 35-36; Harold Garfinkel, "A Conception of, and Experiments with, 'Trust' as a Condition of Stable Concerted Actions," in *Motivation and Social Interaction,* edited by D. J. Harvey (New York: Ronald Press, 1963); chap. 3 of Garfinkel's *Studies in Ethnomethodology* (Englewood Cliffs, New Jersey: Prentice Hall, 1967); and, from Schutz, on two essays in the first volume of his *Collected Papers:* "Common Sense and Scientific Interpretations of Human Action" and "On Multiple Realities."

24. "The Stranger" appears in the second volume of Schutz, *Collected Papers.*
25. The concept of rules, we should add, constitutes an analytic device and not a literal, empirical characterization. As an analytic device, rules provide a way for the observer to talk about the orderly features of any ongoing activity.
26. Ch. Perelman, *The Idea of Justice and the Problem of Argument* (New York: Humanities Press, 1963), especially pp. 138-41. See also Ch. Perelman and L. Olbrechts-Tyteca, *The New Rhetoric, A Treatise on Argumentation* (South Bend: University of Notre Dame Press, 1971).
27. Marcuse writes of Repressive Tolerance in his contribution to *A Critique of Pure Tolerance,* with Robert Paul Wolff and Barrington Moore, Jr. (Boston: Beacon Press, 1965). George Fischer brings the Soviet case up to date in *Contemporary Sociology,* 1975, no. 3.
28. There are important possible exceptions to this formulation. These have to do with situations in which those who contest the constitutive rules nonetheless use opinion-making forms of argumentation for specific purposes of a tactical sort. They do this either with the people who share their own definition of reality or with potential allies who do not.
29. Shils rests an analysis of worldwide student protests in the 1960s on his past view of ideology, of which we speak in section I. He doubts that the protesters took part in ideological argumentation at all. To him, the student radicals were too nonintellectual, and antiintellectual, to view what they said as ideology (Edward Shils, "Plentitude and Scarcity,"

Encounter, vol. 32, no. 5, May 1969; reprinted in *Selected Papers of Edward Shils,* vol. 1 [Chicago: University of Chicago Press, 1972]). Once more, Shils ties ideology to more or less cohesive and grand thought systems. This leads him, like traditional sociologists of knowledge, to slight all the other argumentation that goes on about what people can treat as real, or fact, or objective knowledge.

30. Bertell Ollman speaks of Reich in chapter 8 of *The Unknown Dimension,* edited by Dick Howard and Karl E. Klare (New York: Basic Books, 1972). Michael Mulkay writes on the Velikovsky case in a *Social Research* piece cited in note 16. Other case studies of possible membership denial can be found in Alan F. Blum, "The Corpus of Knowledge as a Normative Order," in *Theoretical Sociology,* edited by John C. McKinney and Edward A. Tiryakian (New York: Appleton-Century-Crofts, 1969), and in Thomas S. Kuhn, *The Copernican Revolution* (Cambridge, Massachusetts: Harvard University Press, 1966). George Fischer speaks of a current clash on membership in chapter two of this book. In *Against Method* (New York: Humanities Press, 1975), Paul Feyerabend shows how the very place of science in our time, as a fetish and the one established model of learning and thinking, denies membership to all those who would take the ways of science (its method) no more for granted than the rest of everyday practice.

31. We see a clear link between this everyday dialectic, the ubiquitous interplay between people questioning and taking for granted a feature of daily life, and the mix in the work of Marx, of which we speak in note 6. Marx goes back and forth between Scientific unmasking and Dialectical critique. Unmasking rests on a concrete, positive view of social reality; critique treats conceptions of daily life as well as science analytically, as historically specific and hence provisional and problematic. Still at issue, a century after Marx wrote his main work, is whether he gives primacy to a concrete or analytic view of social reality.

TWO
CHOICE IN SOCIAL SCIENCE

Neither a machine nor a dog have or know praxis.
—KAREL KOSIK,
Dialectics of the Concrete

A call has gone out to social science in the United States, to all the fields of knowledge that study human interactions. The call to anthropologists and economists and historians, to political scientists and psychologists and sociologists, is for much more of a choice—and in this way for self rule through a whole new praxis.

The call to question and change comes from left scholars, from radical social scientists. To them, a new praxis at its best means a conscious turn to dealienating, liberation-seeking thought and action. The new praxis must inform everything social scientists, now an elite group, do in their work and all of their lives.

The field of sociology is a case in point. Here we look at this one case.

The call for a new praxis reflects the deep sense of crisis in the field—and in American society—that has arisen in the past decade. Within the field, this sense of crisis accounts for an unprecedented state of self-analysis and attacks on established ways. Today U.S. sociology is torn between its current ways and a new, alternative praxis just now emerging.

What is that praxis? We can tell a lot about the emerging alternative if we first look at the current ways. In their full range, the current ways mean the three schools of thought most active

---

Reprinted (with a few changes) from *The New Social Sciences,* edited by Baidya Nath Varma (Westport, Connecticut: Greenwood Press, 1976) by permission of the publisher.

in our time: the dominant normative school, an interpretative school, and a critical school. But here I shall look at this familiar ground in a changed light. I shall speak of the normative school in terms of a great power sociology that marks established practitioners in both the United States and the Soviet Union. And when I speak of those who now challenge great power sociology within the current ways, I shall do so in terms of their limits. These limits have to do with the positivist or reified side of our interpretative as well as critical schools.

When I turn to the new praxis, I shall single out what seem to me its main building blocks as of now. I shall stress three broad elements of any praxis, or a whole new way of life: existence, creativity, and practice. As such a praxis looms into sight in U.S. sociology, these elements help us sort out a wide range of stray and dissimilar themes.

These elements, or building blocks, make clear what a praxis means. It means far more than just practice, in the sense of problem-solving activity. Any praxis also stands for existence, the sum of subjective, intrapersonal experience. Finally, as the epigraph shows, praxis has to do with something uniquely human: human beings can use conscious joint effort to create social arrangements that suit them best. If that kind of self-determined, consciously shaped praxis is to have a chance in U.S. sociology, above and beyond the three current schools, we will no doubt need to bring to life each of these elements.

Underlying these shifts in sociological inquiry is a shared assumption. In all sorts of ways, the emerging alternative would make people its active subject and relegate the established order (and established science) to the status of human-made objects. Just as Marx, throughout his work, challenged capitalism for making human beings into the object of analysis and policy, and commodities the subject, so the various supporters of a new praxis agree that it must do away with what Horton calls the "fetishism of sociology."[1] The alternative must be dealienating: it must be a praxis that seeks to give people a full and equal role in all things that shape their lives.

The importance of dealienation brings to the fore the transformative method so important to Marx. The transformative method makes problematic all the things alienative ways take for granted. It then looks to the reverse of these things for an unalienated form of life. In our own time, the transformative method leads those moving toward a new praxis in the field to stress modes in drastic opposition to current ways. The attack, we should note, aims at neo-marxists no less than at phenomenologists or at the dominant current school itself. This can be seen in all of the building blocks I link to the emerging alternative:

Existence: Active versus Passive
Creativity: Communal versus Bureaucratic
Practice: Analytic versus Concrete

Together, these transformations sum up a new choice we need in all of social science.

I. GREAT POWER SOCIOLOGY: THE UNITED STATES AND USSR

In important ways, the dominant, established sociologists of the United States are now like those in the Soviet Union. Together with their countries' unique place in the world political balance, the similarities lead me to speak of a single great power sociology.

In the great powers, the main underlying assumptions add up to a strongly normative sociology. In both countries, normative sociology is characterized by its focus on social psychology and on the way the existing social order imposes its rules on individuals and groups. In each case, mainstream sociologists stress interactions guided by established norms. They do this by treating as natural, as a given, the existing social order and everyday life. In other words, the prevailing norms of behavior are taken for granted. Normative sociology then explores how people fit their lives to these norms, or why they fail to do so.

By and large, no American or Soviet practitioner of great power sociology questions either his or her country's main institutions or how people construct social reality in the course of routine face-to-face interactions. Hence they look not at a whole society or all routine interactions, but at certain selected elements. As I have indicated, among these selected elements, one stands out in all of great power sociology: individual and group adjustments to the status quo and the particular values and attitudes that affect such adjustments the most.

Until the 1960s, normative, or great power, sociology was hardly challenged in the United States. But currently, as ample evidence shows, normative sociology is in intellectual disarray and retreat.[2] One cannot find comparably full data on the state of the field in the Soviet Union, but the picture seems clear enough.

If a new Soviet sociology rose and won great gains in the sixties, by now it makes sense to speak of its fall, or at least of a grave slump. In fact, just one side of Soviet work suffered a fall in the early 1970s. The administrative, technocratic, "priestly" side, institutionalized in the sixties, is still alive and well. The last few years wiped out something else: the hope that the other side—"prophetic," critical, liberating—would keep a bit of a toehold as well.[3]

In the United States as well as the Soviet Union, normative sociology assumes that people can tell truth from error solely by means of a natural, "objective" science. It puts complete faith in the duty and ability of scientists, as a secular priesthood, to uncover the truth. Science must draw the line between truth and error not only in its own domain but for advanced industrial society as a whole. Like many others today, mainstream sociologists ascribe to science that all-embracing social task. Nothing else, in this view, can challenge or disprove science, be it personal experience or a creed or art or philosophy. Only as science gives a claim its imprimatur is its standing as truth or knowledge assured.

Normative sociology is strongly positivist. Its logic and procedures, its theorists and practices, rest on the assumption that positive phenomena—things observable through sense experience—constitute reality. Only such phenomena lead to warranted, valid knowledge.

What makes the study of observable phenomena the only valid source of knowledge? Normative sociologists offer several different answers. On the level of ontology, there is a strong belief that a universal structure exists outside of the observer. From this flows a second assumption, that the world functions in terms of lawlike regularities which the scientist can and must discover. The only reliable way of accomplishing that is by following the natural sciences in their mathematics-like logic, precision, and types of measurement.

Each qualified sociologist, in short, refracts his or her own sense experience through the prism of a positivist version of the natural sciences. In this way, he or she contributes to an orderly analysis of an orderly world that sociologists construct. That world is orderly because its procedures are meticulously worked out and recorded; hence the procedures can be subjected to replication, validation, and other disinterested and reliable checks. Positivists speak for nature, as it were, and tell its secrets without bias.

In the United States, these beliefs lead normative sociologists to espouse what they consider pure science, as well as value-free methods of research. Pure science calls for a strict detachment from practical concerns and from commitments that go beyond amelioration of the status quo. Scientists do not address themselves to such "controversial" matters except as technical experts. If they want to do more, they must shed their role as scientists altogether and speak as plain citizens and lay people. American normative sociologists often accuse other scholars of trespassing beyond pure science.

If great power sociologists in the United States equate science with professional neutrality, nothing like that would seem to be the case with their established Soviet colleagues. On the contrary, not only tradition but their current work and style point to a complete denial of science as pure. Soviet sociological writing continues to stress doctrinal commitment and relevance to current policy and public action. Just the style alone could make American normative sociologists see Soviet work in the field as ideology and only their own as science.

The claim of a single great power sociology is clearly in doubt if we fail to account for this sharp contrast.

In Soviet usage, as is well known, science has two very different aspects. In the USSR, as elsewhere, the term refers to optimally rigorous and verifiable methods of seeking knowledge. But at least as important is a second aspect: Soviet usage ties science completely to an officially maintained truth, the state doctrine of marxism-leninism.

Post-Stalin sociology in no way gave up its links to the official aspect of Soviet scholarship. And its style remains much more ideological than scientific, as the West defines the contrast. Although for normative sociologists in the United States science means pure science, for their Soviet colleagues science means what they call concrete research. Concrete research combines the two aspects of scholarship in the USSR. At one and the same time, concrete research fits official doctrine and the universal canons of science. Concrete research aims at piecemeal theorizing about specific portions of social reality with the help of advanced quantitative methods of gathering and analyzing data. Such piecemeal theorizing calls to mind the theories of the middle range that American normative sociologists tend to favor. In each case, the value of middle-range theories depends on how well they can be tested empirically and how well they stand up when tested.

A big gap seems to exist, though, between concrete research and the American notion of middle-range theories. Ideally, the latter rests on empirical data alone. The Soviet recipe for concrete research calls for something else. A general theory of society—the official body of marxist and leninist ideas—serves as the point of departure. Nor need a Soviet type of specialized intermediate theorizing clash with the general theory. For its task is to aid the state to solve practical problems by rigorously reviewing official notions about them.

The gap between prevailing American and Soviet modes of middle-range theorizing brings us back to the broader contrast between established sociology in the two countries. The key realm of theorizing, of just how one generalizes and abstracts observations, suggests that both the specific gap and the broader contrast may be more apparent than real. On closer examination, the gap —and with it the broader contrast—are much smaller than both sides assume.

Whether a normative sociologist sees science as pure or as

concrete research does not actually matter that much if we ask how that sociologist treats all of society and all of everyday life. In either case, the normative sociologist stops short of questioning the established social order as a whole.

When science is viewed as pure science, the canon of strict detachment from controversial practical concerns and commitments leads normative sociologists to avoid or to defuse and trivialize big questions about social reality. For them, middle-range theorizing means just that. Paradoxically, we find precisely the same thing in the seemingly opposite case of science as concrete research.

Like their American colleagues, most Soviet sociologists also manage to skirt the big, controversial questions that face them in their society. True, their definition of social reality assumes that continuous social change is desirable and inevitable on a grand scale, a view alien to American normative sociologists. But this assumption is itself unquestioned and thus absolutized or reified; mainstream sociology in the USSR takes it for granted as part of the official general theory.

With the state controlling the big questions, the Soviet sociologist is thus expected to probe systematically into lesser questions. In this situation, not surprisingly, the dialectical method of Marx —which by its very nature casts doubt on all existing arrangements—fares badly. Avowals to the contrary notwithstanding, the dialectic succumbs to a positivism that assumes stability and hence is deeply conservative.

In the United States, the main work of normative sociology clings to the abstract social-psychological categories and empirical techniques of positivists like Parsons, Merton, and Lazarsfeld. Major Soviet books point to a steady shift in the same direction. This held true in the late sixties for Shubkin on social mobility, Kon on personality, Grushin on public opinion, and Arutiunian on rural social structure. And it holds for the one work of like quality so far in the 1970s, that of Gordon and Klopov on leisure time.

So in one case detachment serves as the political ground for not questioning the status quo, while in the other the reverse—commitment of an official kind—does. This is how, in each national component of the great power school, normative sociologists treat their country's social order and everyday life as givens. In terms of methods of analysis, a ubiquitous positivism has the same effect: normative sociologists tend to ask only how this or that component of an unquestioned social system works, and how it could be made to work more effectively within the status quo. All else, we are told in both countries, lies beyond the realm of the scientific—or of the possible. Most specifically, then, the prevailing work in each great power adds up to a vast process of rationalization that is not only guided by the state but is narrowly instrumental. Here the United States and the Soviet Union converge, in brief, on an administrative sociology.[4]

II. LIMITS OF ACADEMIC CRITICS

Within current ways, both phenomenologists and neo-marxists have been gaining strength in the field over the past decade. Interpretative (or phenomenological) sociology can be said to include ethnomethodology and symbolic interactionism, as well as diverse phenomenological approaches. Neo-marxists make up the other challenger, the critical school of thought.[5]

As we shall see, these challengers share one important limitation. Both turn out to have a strongly positivist or reified side. They treat the underlying assumptions and recipes of their own work as a thing, as a given not to be questioned or relativized. As much as phenomenologists and neo-marxists probe some other human interactions, they stop short when it comes to the grounds for their own.

Most interpretative sociologists, for one thing, choose the priestly faith. They do so in terms of Friedrichs' dichotomy of the logics-in-use of current U.S. sociology. That dichotomy lies between a priestly faith in social order and professional neutrality, and an opposing prophetic faith in social change and professional engagement. In the case of interpretative sociologists, the priestly faith goes back to phenomenology. To tell truth from error, this challenge looks for the meaning or essence of a single thing (or phenomenon), and puts no stress on its external aspects and relations.[6]

More than that, while normative sociology assumes the prior existence of a social structure "out there," interpretative sociology holds that people jointly modify and hence redefine and recreate (or interpret) reality in each and every interaction. Unlike the rest, in other words, the interpretative sociologists deny the need or possibility of a scheme of their own about the uniform patterns of social life. Instead, they assume that such regularities are to be found in how people act in everyday life and in the meaning that people themselves, the actors, assign to what they do.

This perspective leads interpretative sociology to focus on daily life, on the practices and ongoing problem-solving of the everyday world. From the same perspective flows the ontological view that not all truth or knowledge is external, "out there," as positivists tend to assume. In the first place, rather, knowledge is what members of a given collectivity treat as such. This is why phenomenologists stress common-sense knowledge. Here common-sense knowledge refers to the sense that members of a collectivity hold in common. When such common sense takes the form of a set of actors treating something as a truth, then that constitutes common-sense knowledge. Initially, at least, knowledge must be seen as a feature of a particular collectivity and situation. In the end, however, this common-sense knowledge gives way to a higher sort of knowledge, the sociolgists' own. Phenomenologists within the current praxis take that for granted. They assume that the knowledge they generate is objective or universal. It is science agreed upon by another kind of collectivity, that of themselves as scientists, as against the Man on the Street.

Again, like great power sociologists, most phenomenologists fail to question the established social order as a whole. Interpretative sociology says little if anything of larger social arrangements —nations, cities, wars, revolutions, and counterrevolutions. The universe at large, and impersonal larger social units within it, play no active, dynamic part. Nor do "transsituational" phenomena that lie outside a particular situation in everyday life.[7]

By questioning a reified view of routine language and consciousness alone, the phenomenologists of current sociology slight historical and social change. Despite programmatic statements to the contrary, in its work up to now interpretative sociology thus treats much of the social order as unproblematic, as something given in the nature of things. If the positivist detachment (or commitment) of the great power school keeps it from asking the big questions about science (itself) as well as about society, so does the existential detachment of today's phenomenologists.

Neo-marxists, in the current ways of U.S. sociology, stand for antiorthodox marxism. Orthodox (or scientific) marxists stress the inevitable and highly determined; antiorthodox (dialectical or cultural) marxists stress what is possible but only in part determined. Orthodox schools of thought stress the impact of closely linked forces; dialectical schools, the interaction of relatively autonomous forces, or the multiple relations between them. In line with the antiorthodoxy of interwar Europe (Lukacs, Gramsci, the Frankfurt School), critical sociologists speak a lot of the prevailing communication and consciousness that distort our possibilities, the promise of our time and place.

In the same way as a positive science serves the great power school, and the dereification of everyday life serves the phenomenologists in the field, the dialectic method serves the neo-marxists. For critical sociology, the dialectic means most of all unending historical contrast between humanity's potential and actuality. The term stands for a recurring emergence and synthesis of contradictions between humanity's potential in a given time and place—the human potential for self-creativity, self-reflection, and self-emancipation—and how people feel and act.

It is here, the reader will see, that the neo-marxists take issue the most with the positive laws of orthodox marxism—both the earlier, more determinist German orthodoxy of Engels and Kautsky and the later, more voluntarist Russian orthodoxy of Lenin, Trotsky, and Stalin. For the heart of the marxist dialectic lies in measuring the established order against the rationalist and optimistic creed of progress that Marx held high as heir to the Enlightenment. Hence the dialectic denies emphatically the validity of treating any social order as a given. Its recipe takes for granted no macrocosm, either present or future, but the very opposite: the dialectic assumes the continuous and unavoidable transformation of all historically conditioned arrangements. To question that assumption, according to critical sociology, means to uphold a static model of life.

While normative sociology tends to stress the way in which a social system casts people in its mold, critical sociologists hold that man makes himself, that people can and should create their own social arrangements. For this reason, and in line with the dialectic of Hegel and Marx, the neo-marxists give pride of place not to the component parts and their interaction, as functionalists do, but to the totality of social arrangements and the way that the human-made totality shapes all its parts. The totality of social arrangements rests for the neo-marxists not on immutable laws but on the large meaning implied by or immanent in this or that tangible experience. Such a Hegelian reading of Marx's own sociology leads the neo-marxists to stress everyday life almost as much as do interpretative sociologists.

If phenomenologists as a rule treat routine human interaction as problematic only within the status quo, neo-marxists commit themselves to anchoring their critique of everyday life, like each and every human experience, in the ever-changing totality of social arrangements. Like other sociologists, then, neo-marxists look for regularities, for recurrent uniform patterns in the outside world. But for the neo-marxists regularities can be found solely through the study of grand change, most of all the kind of change that ongoing, present-day contradictions lay bare.[8]

In their underlying assumptions and recipes, in sum, the current schools of U.S. sociology differ a great deal. With its priestly faith in a positive science seemingly intact, the great power school of normative sociology questions neither its own country's established order nor routine human interaction. Interpretative sociology by and large questions none of the priestly faith, either in the work of the sociologist or in the established order as a whole. It does treat as problematic the routine interactions of others in everyday life. Critical sociology alone champions the prophetic view of scholarship and challenges, as part and parcel of each other, both the established order and the routines of everyday life. As we shall see all along, though, this school also falls short of a new praxis, of the emerging alternative. What is already clear is that, like the rest of the current ways, the critical school takes its own work for granted. As a rule, a neo-marxist treats as a given some one set of views ascribed to Marx, as either a substantive creed or as a method to which one's work must be true.[9]

In their own modes, then, each of the current challengers fails to address the grounds on which their own work rests, its underlying assumptions and recipes. That leaves the sociologists themselves out of the challenge posed to the dominant, normative school. In turn, that keeps the challenge within the same shared practice, and in this way limits the challenge no end.

III. PASSIVE OBJECT OR ACTIVE SUBJECT

The call for an active grasp of life forms one of the building blocks for a new praxis. To lead an active existence means to be the maker (subject) of one's own life and not the passive object of what others do.

Each individual not only should have but can have a rich, broad understanding of existence, an active grasp of personal and interpersonal life. What marks the human species the most is its will and skill to grasp life. Through thick or thin, and far beyond any one stage such as capitalism or socialism, humanity will keep optimizing its grasp of life. The underlying humanistic view (of progress growing out of all-encompassing rational action and struggle) fits existence once more into a broad social and political philosophy—a broad intellectual context. Of that, the nonsubstantive, instrumental rationality we see in most of current sociology makes it bare, strikingly bare.

Influenced by recently popular schools of thought like existentialism, psychoanalysis, anarchism, as well as neo-marxism, foes of the current ways speak of the highest human potential in the language of liberation: individuals and groups can and must emancipate themselves from social alienation and limited consciousness and move toward full and equal control of their own existence. This view puts much stress on how actively people grasp, or fail to grasp, the contradictions and changes of everyday life—not the least, their own.

Choice in Social Science 87

The focus shifts from how people cope or succeed within an existing order to how they build alternative social arrangements and leave behind those they find oppressive. The recipe applies to the observer as well. If scholars remove themselves from the ongoing conflicts and contradictions, if they partake of the prevailing academic commitment to established modes of living and thinking, such conformity and complicity weaken rather than strengthen their grasp of life and thus their claim to truth. The observer's being engaged, and fighting for basic social change, becomes a virtue and not a vice. In an alternative praxis, it makes no sense for a sociologist to stay passive.

Within current sociology, we find a useful discussion of the active element of a new praxis in the work of Robert W. Friedrichs, *A Sociology of Sociology*, in his dichotomy between priestly and prophetic modes.[10] Now dominant, the priestly mode seeks order and is passive; the prophetic mode is both active and liberating.

In the priestly mode, the sociologist views "his office as but a means by which any given social reality may be revealed to the layman." Like the normative sociologists, the "priests" draw their image of people from the natural sciences, from "a frame of reference that honors ordered efficiency above all." Therefore the priestly sociologist looks for stability—increased stability—in human affairs.

In the prophetic mode, on the other hand, the sociologist is consciously committed to an image of society that transcends any given social reality. To Friedrichs, such a scholar "differs from sociologist as priest not in any temptation to distort the reality of a given situation—he is equally dedicated to honoring the empirical facts." The prophetic sociologist does differ "in his awareness of the value-laden choices and implicit commitments" that any practitioner in the field makes to the future. And in line with this special concern with how human pursuits and the future interact with each other, "prophets" look not for increased stability but for liberating change.

What leads Friedrichs to turn to the prophetic, change-seeking mode? As a means, the priestly faith makes good sense to Friedrichs; what "is common to the sciences is not a product but a means, as the traditional phrase, 'the scientific method,' reminds us." But he echoes many of the recent criticisms of established U.S. sociology by adding that "when a 'method' or 'logic' seeks guidance only from within itself, it projects the very same feature upon its subject matter. The sociology that seeks its bearings internally thus sees man as but *means*" to its own pursuits as a science. Sociology needs the prophetic mode to make and keep clear humanity's goals above and beyond the here and now.

Together with a broad philosophical view of existence, the Friedrichs dichotomy between priestly and prophetic makes clear how a new praxis in the field would differ from current ways. This holds true even in the case of the contending schools of phenomenologists and neo-marxists. For these challengers, too, the stress is on maintaining authoritative and hence unquestioned ways of doing sociology. That fits in well with a passive view of life. Only as each individual gets an active grasp of life can existence itself become active and therefore liberating.

But an active, liberating existence does not stop with a changed grasp of life or a broad philosophical view. As we can see in the case of neo-marxism, a critical, change-minded theory of life or society will not do by itself either. An active existence means more than that. At the very least, it means that the scholar, the academic intellectual, makes all-embracing social change the be-all and end-all of his or her work.

Whether the main scene of that work is the ivory tower or the world beyond matters a lot less than does this active ongoing bond to basic social change. The years one might spend in a library or writing books need not fall outside the pale at all. Scholarship can be as active as anything else, as long as changing the world remains the ground for it and as long as broad group struggles, not accommodation with the status quo, mold one's life. Needless to say, that distinction fits academic followers of Marx as well. If their lives stay within the academy and established modes of scholarship, as is often the case, they too lead a quite passive existence.

All this suggests that for a new praxis the building block of active existence means a good deal more than either activism or a philosophical opposition to the status quo, or the old call to wed theory and practice. Most specifically, a stress on change means a stress on its totality—the totality of shifts in this or that time and place (or history writ large), and on the totality of the struggles that make up these shifts (or politics writ large).

In the current ways of U.S. sociology, neo-marxists, too, of course, put their prime weight on a broad grasp of life, on history and politics writ large. What a new praxis adds is an antipriestly mode; here, living by the authority of someone else, be the authority for or against the status quo, gives way to broad struggles to change (to make active) all of life—not the least one's own life. But this addition to the current ways of neo-marxists can take place only if it goes hand in hand with new modes of creativity and practice.

IV. BUREAUCRACY OR SELF RULE

The creativity that we treat as part of any praxis is a public one. It has to do with the ability of human beings to create, through conscious joint effort, the social arrangements most suitable for their own species. That view of creativity leaves little doubt where current U.S. sociology stands. Almost all its practitioners serve as employees or administrators of vast modern organizations, and before that they are trained at length to serve as such. They tend to see their creative work accordingly—in the main fragmented, standardized, and most of all hierarchic: the conduct, consideration, and acceptance of most scholarly work depends on one's place in our bureaucratic academy and the do's and don'ts that place brings with it. Only in the last few years have more than a few come to treat this bureaucratic kind of creativity as problematic.

Only in the last few years, too, has an alternative view emerged in the field. On and off, in bits and pieces, the view is spreading that working in sociology can and should mean a creativity in which collective and cooperative effort takes the place of individual and competitive striving, and bureaucracy gives way to self rule, to conscious community.

This building block of a new praxis is not embodied in the efforts of practitioners in any of the current schools. Just like other academic professionals, neo-marxists and phenomenologists in the academy are apt to be far from such communal creativity.

Writings that bear on communal creativity point in quite a few directions. In each direction, the call for a new praxis either puts the creative community within the existing academy or makes it a key part of what sociologists would do elsewhere. In short, up to now the emerging alternative leaves a conscious community in or near bureaucracy.

For Gouldner, to begin with, a creative community is very much part of the existing academy. He sees such a community as crucial in terms of the field itself, to enable the field to contribute to its ultimate end of human liberation. In an article that elaborates *The Coming Crisis of Western Sociology*,[11] Gouldner puts the main stress on a new type of work community of reflexive or radical sociologists within the academy. The collective work of such sociologists within this novel form of social organization will sustain and develop a reflective self awareness. "In this sense, what sociology needs today is not so much its first Newton and another Karl Marx, but rather a V.I. Lenin to formulate its organizational requirements."

Along the same lines, but a good deal more specifically, Peter McHugh, Alan F. Blum, and their associates argue that doing sociology is impossible without collaboration at each and every step. Only in the process of collaboration does an ego fill out the deep grammar of his or her creativity with the help of an alter. Collaboration is crucial on a number of planes: within the work of a single author, still more so in the joint work of sociologists, and all along in an unending dialogue between such collaborating authors and their readers. All this rests on the view that no meaningful, deep-going creativity can ever be complete—and that multifaceted collaboration is the closest we come to laying bare our own ways.

In the communal joint work of authors and readers, for instance, "alter, by speaking, by formulating ego's auspices, becomes an ego in his own right." That means that "any formulation of ego by alter can raise the same problem which it solves, namely how *it* is possible. This is where the readers come in." Readers are asked to become collaborators. This, McHugh and Blum say, "is our version of how to read."[12]

Two other authors would replace the bureaucratic with the communal not so much within sociology itself but in the setting of broader movements for social change. These authors are Richard Flacks, who writes of his ties to the New Left and the neomarxists, and Marlene Dixon, who writes of marxism-leninism and more generally of the revolutionary movement. Yet despite this important shift of the community from within to outside the academy, both authors tie to academic sociology (and hence to bureaucracy) much of what sociologists of the left can do for a social movement elsewhere. And like those within the current praxis, both Dixon and Flacks take the work of sociologists such as themselves for granted so far as underlying assumptions and procedures go. As against Blum and McHugh, both dwell not on the process but on the product, not on how sociologists live and do their work but what work they do. Hence, neither seems to care much what type of insights or procedures practitioners in the field draw from it so long as it leads to theoretical or empirical results of substantive value to the larger movement they back. In this least academy-bound direction, then, the call for community pays little heed to the third and last building block of a new praxis: a shift in the sociologist's own practice from an unquestioned "objectivity" to optimal self-awareness of what underlies that practice.

The first of these authors, Flacks, at times comes close to saying that all forms of sociology now lack a purpose of use to humanity and, specifically, to movements of social change. At other times, he speaks of some specialized tasks that sociologists of the left in an academic setting could carry out for like-minded movements here and now. It is only in this limited sense that sociologists as such can become creative in a larger community of emancipatory movements.

How strongly Flacks doubts the value of any sort of professional sociology becomes quite clear: "I cannot help but feel that a genuinely liberative sociology would continuously seek *to enable all the people to do sociology,* to put itself out of business as a specialty, as a profession." More than that, Flacks dwells on the point that the most important sociology of our time is being written not by professional social scientists but by those who are engaged in movements of social change: "Such people," he says, "have understood certain things better than anyone I can think of who works full time as a sociologist or academician."[13]

How, then, does Flacks see the emerging alternative? His scheme, like Gouldner's, would have academic sociologists serve a like-minded movement more as clinicians than as technicians. And Flacks would use all of the tools of U.S. sociology, from opinion surveys to model building, to put forth credible (and now badly missing) theoretical alternatives to the status quo.

Dixon links a new praxis least of all to the usual realms and sites of the field. Instead, she puts most of the praxis within a revolutionary movement. Unique in that avowal within the academy, and yet achetypal in putting it forward when she did and in the way she did it, Dixon saw herself at the turn of the 1970s as above all a member of the revolutionary movement. Thus she is bound to the field, and to academic life, only in part. All the same, to be jointly creative, sociologists need to keep a foot in the academy while they give first place to a revolutionary movement. The praxis she calls marxist is that of the indissoluble unity between theory and practice, between intellectual ideas and political action. It is in this sense, with its full focus on an outside constituency, that her scheme enables a sociologist to move from bureaucracy to community.

Although her views are even less safe to voice in the academy than those of Flacks, Dixon has made two explicit statements, both of which addressed special audiences, on her scheme for a new praxis. Dixon wrote the first statement I quote for (and, in substance, against) the young militants of the Sociology Liberation Movement. She made the second statement as part of her successful appeal against being fired by her department at McGill University in 1971.[14]

To the young militants in the field, Dixon wrote in the late sixties of what she calls the failure of the Sociology Liberation

Movement. In her view, such a radical caucus within an academic profession in the United States today was bound to fail. What made failure inevitable was not this or that flaw of the group itself, but "the irrelevance of bourgeois sociology and the class interests of sociologists."

To the other young radicals in the field, Dixon acknowledged a feeling of ambivalence. "The fundamental ambivalence stems, ultimately, from the question of practice: is it possible to maintain unity of theory and practice within the bourgeois university?" Her final answer is "that the good and valuable people to be found in the university must be pulled *out* of the profession." They must be put "into the production of knowledge which serves the people." They must "accept the vocation of revolutionary intellectual and enter into a life of revolutionary activism."

In her statement to McGill's Department of Sociology, Dixon put forth the same views. Here I shall cite just one point that sheds light on the academy's continuing place in her scheme for a new praxis. For her, a major goal within the university is "a closer and more fruitful integration of the scholarly and activist roles, for it seems clear to me that scholastic analysis has been weakened by its isolation from practical action and practical action weakened by its isolation from theoretical analysis."

While Dixon notes the need for a clarification and extension of a marxist methodology, she states nowhere what kind of theoretical work, and in what ways and spheres, she would do or favor. Yet she makes very clear what kind of academic life her scheme calls for. It must serve both broad theory and broad practice. More than that, academic life must let sociologists (or even ask them to) go back and forth between the two:

> The demands of activism, particularly for those in significant leadership positions, require constant judgement, based on theory and practical knowledge, and those judgements and their consequences are all part of the analytic process. Yet one may never communicate this knowledge in written form ... the activist explicitly recognizes the legitimacy of the oral tradition and the value of collective analysis and decision making.

Activists recognize the need for contemplation and for periodic withdrawal from immediate social action, Dixon goes on. They do a lot "to further theoretical mastery and to systematize and integrate practical knowledge with the existing body of theory." This is the chief reason why marxist activists seek to remain within universities. "Yet the cycles of intense involvement and contemplative withdrawal are not provided for, nor is the importance recognized by mainstream 'empirical' sociology."

As Dixon reminds the sociologist of the left, not one of the great revolutionary theorists of marxism was an academic. In that context, and still more than Flacks, she seems in doubt as to whether it makes sense at all to try to use academic work for basic social change. Within their ambivalence, though, both appear willing to use academic bureaucracy plus any and all tools of the field—not least those of the dominant school—to aid their outside constituencies.

Halfway between these first two shifts from bureaucracy to community stands what is now the main trend among organized groups of radical or socialist sociologists. More and more, they hold that their main contribution to a broader movement is to put in first place the transforming of their own work in the field. In the words of Henry Etzkowitz, "We can not act solely as social and political analysts of the working class in attempting to figure out what are the possibilities for the class to organize itself." Instead, in order to do that, "We have to first introduce socialism into our own lives." While not rejecting jobs in establishments of higher education, Etzkowitz writes, "We have the possibility of achieving this by organizing ourselves into socialist organizations of scholars." This means learning, teaching, and studying as cooperating equals in a freer setting and not just as lone competitors in academic bureaucracies. He dubs such an alternative community the Invisible Socialist University.[15]

Another direction for the creative element of a new praxis also sees the communal in terms of sociologists serving the rest of society. But the community is neither that of like-minded sociologists, as it is for Gouldner or McHugh and Blum, nor that of the movements for social change that Flacks and Dixon have in mind, nor, in between, that of the Invisible Socialist University that

Etzkowitz put forth. Instead, here the community that sociologists can and must join in full is all of society.

To make this point, John O'Neill wrote a book called *Sociology as a Skin Trade*.[16] All those who work with people practice a "skin trade." Priests and doctors work closely with people. So do pickpockets and undertakers. No wonder that working with people is a precarious business. Hence "the skin trades are especially marked with the ambivalent aura of sacredness and profanity."

How this point is related to the creative element of a new praxis becomes clear when O'Neill turns to sociology itself. He would not move the field out of the academy. Yet it should mingle much more, flesh to flesh, with the rest of humanity. For sociology, too, is best thought of as a skin trade. To O'Neill this means that "the rhetoric of scientism in sociology as well as its humanism must be tested against the common-sense relevance of everyday life . . . for all our science the world is still the mystery and passion of being with our fellowmen."

The creative element of a new praxis, in sum, has been seen up to now in terms of a community of like-minded colleagues. These professional sociologists stay within (or close to) the existing academy. But they create jointly, for the sake of their field, or for a sympathetic social movement, or for humanity as a whole. One finds still another call for community, within education as currently established. Paulo Freire takes us back to the dealienating, liberative task of education itself. He speaks of a community of students and teachers. "Education must begin with the solution of the teacher-student contradiction, by reconciling the poles of the contradiction so that both are simultaneously teachers *and* students." Learning and doing becomes human only as all concerned treat each other as members of the same community—equal, active, cooperating.[17]

Whatever shape this building block takes in sociology, a new praxis calls for a far-reaching, full turn from bureaucracy to community. The not quite full turn away from bureaucracy called for by those I cite here rests on a view I myself have come to doubt: I doubt such communities can lead to a rich, joint creativity in or near our highly bureaucratized academy.

V. THINKING CONCRETELY OR ANALYTICALLY

When it comes to their own work, sociologists in the United States as a rule treat it as objective—objectlike, external to themselves. The emerging alternative does the opposite. As a goal, at least, the focus shifts to what practitioners themselves do, as the makers or subjects of their work. Sociology as an object gives way to sociology as the subject.

Most often, the call for a new praxis singles out the need for a new set of problem-solving activities. What we most need within the field, according to this theme, is a reflexive sociology. Speaking of human interests in knowledge, Habermas equates self-reflection with the highest emancipatory interest; self-reflection alone can lead to "analyses that free consciousness from its dependence on hypostatized powers." To Gouldner, the crisis in sociology points, above all, to the need for reflexivity, for a value-committed sociology of sociology. And Colfax sets apart radical sociology from other kinds by arguing that it practices more reflexivity than do the rest.[18]

In the broad, at times vague, terms that so far mark the plea for a reflexive sociology, the best known statement will be found in Alvin W. Gouldner's *The Coming Crisis of Western Sociology;* and in a lengthy later article Gouldner clarifies and extends his views on a new praxis.[19] To him, the crisis of sociology consists of an ever-greater clash. On one side stand the claims and former practices of established sociology. The clash pits functionalism against the growing demands and support of a welfare-warfare state on the one hand, and a rise of dissonance within and around the dominant school on the other.

No new praxis in the field is possible without a reflexive sociology. Students of society must greatly heighten, and ever optimize, their self-awareness of what they actually do in their work. As importantly, they must develop the same deep self-awareness about their lives as a whole and about the world they work and live in. The knowledge they seek as scientists must aim at awareness of what they observe rather than a positivist type of information whose meaning they do not question.

Without a reflexive sociology, the scholar in the field falls prey to the methodological dualism that now prevails. According to Gouldner, "Methodological Dualism focuses on the *differences* between the social scientist and those whom he observes; it tends to ignore their similarities." The development of a reflexive sociology, for Gouldner, requires that "sociologists cease acting as if they thought of subjects and objects, sociologists who study and 'laymen' who are studied, as two distinct breeds of men."

This scheme, the reader should note, does not call for a new content or technique of social analysis. The opposite is the case: "A Reflexive Sociology, then, is not characterized by *what* it studies. It is distinguished neither by the persons and the problems studied nor even by the techniques and instruments used in studying them. It is characterized, rather, by the *relationship* it establishes between being a sociologist and being a person, between the role and the man performing it."

This changed relationship rules out allegiance and service to the "Bismarckian liberalism" of today. Inevitably, the change humanizes and radicalizes a sociologist. Yet in his later article Gouldner makes clear once more that he stays close to the current ways. He casts doubt on marxism as a whole[20] and sees continuing value in the current normative and interpretative schools:

> On the one hand, sociology requires and has ready at hand a developing tradition of hermeneutics, whose function is to engage men's understanding, to ask for and interpret the *meaning* of events. . . . [On the other hand, at times] there is a place for a positivistic study of men as natural objects subject to natural laws. . . . There is an irreducible core where man remains sunk in objectness, where he is, in effect, at one with all the world.

Much more comprehensive and far-reaching than Gouldner or the call for a reflexive sociology, in terms of this building block for a new praxis, has been the work of two former ethnomethodologists. Increasingly critical of the interpretative school from which they themselves came, Alan F. Blum and Peter McHugh view all of the current schools in the field as refusing to treat their own work as problematic. They hold, as I did earlier in this essay, that most phenomenologists are no less guilty of treating what they do as given than are functionalists and neo-marxists. Most phenomenologists, they argue, try to describe in full all that people do in everyday life, yet stop short of showing how it becomes possible for an observer to make this or that claim about what people do. This is why these phenomenologists, like the rest of current ways, take for granted—and hence fail to formulate and demonstrate—how they themselves proceed when they treat something as true or not true.

In all the current schools, therefore, Blum and McHugh find a huge dose of positivism. Each school, they hold, treats some part of what they write of as concrete and not at all analytically. Blum and McHugh claim that a new praxis must do just the reverse. It must be dialectical in the classic sense—like yin and yang, all-embracing, many-sided, going to and fro without end. An essay by McHugh gives some clues to what he means by the key juxtaposition between concrete and analytic.[21]

The insistence on how versus what, or the analytic versus the concrete approach to defining social reality, leads McHugh to rule out the usual separation between theory and method: "There is thus nothing to either theory or method alone, for theory is not distinctive and procedures are without content." Moreover, only by treating theory and methods of research as one can any science, including sociology, set itself apart from the layman's opinions: "Any distinction between sociology and the man on the street can be grounded only if the sociologist's theories-procedures are themselves taken as topics of inquiries." And this is true not only with the topics of inquiries, but also with the main topic of all: "Sociology could be distinctive only by treating itself as the phenomenon for investigation."

Something like what McHugh calls analyzing, his longtime collaborator Blum calls theorizing.[22] Blum sees his kind of analytic theorizing in a most personal, intrasubjective way. His study of Marx helps to bring out what he has in mind. Just how existential, and individualistic, theorizing is for Blum can be seen in his statement that "through theorizing the theorist searches for his self, and his achievement in theorizing is a recovering of this self." If we think of the self as social, as a member, theorizing reveals its whole form of life. Hence Blum argues that "an understanding of theorizing is an understanding of a form of life, and . . . this form of life constitutes a particular method of treating and reconstructing one's biography as a practically conceived corpus of knowledge." In this context, "theorizing is then best described not as a sense-transforming operation but as a self-transforming operation, where what one operates upon is one's knowledge of the society as part of one's history, biography, and form of life."

Turning from theorizing in general to his case study of Karl Marx, Blum puts heavy stress on dialectical themes. He sees Marx as a grand theorist and argues once more that the theoretic character of practice lies in the fact that the theory is essentially the activity of reeducating the soul. Hence, "the failure of mathematical positivist Marxism to understand this is a symptom of its concrete notion of 'revolution' as a change of bodies rather than a movement of the soul."

Applied to Marx, this view of theorizing leads to an interpretation that calls to mind Plato:

> Marx's absolute consisted only, exclusively, in the possibility of his Rational theorist. This theorist was not an actual person, nor a Representation or concept of actual people; rather, it was an ideal to which he stipulated theorizing ought to conform. As an ideal, its Reality consisted in its belonging together with Reason, in the way in which thought "belongs" to Being. The society about which Marx spoke—capitalism—was a corruption of this ideal and in this sense was transitional, i.e. was an image, appearance, reflection, or shadow of the Real.

Together, all these excerpts indicate how, each in his own way, Blum and McHugh see a new praxis in sociology in terms of a subjectlike analysis—and how they come to treat all of the current schools as false in their objectlike concreteness. And they agree that claims to truth—or to what people treat as knowledge or objectivity or science—must rest on an analytic (or dialectical or "theoretical") base and not on a concrete (or positive or "mathematical") one.

How, one might ask, does this view add up to a building block for a new praxis? How does it guide us to problem-solving activity that is both much better than current ways and quite different from them? And how, finally, does the view of Blum and McHugh add to the shared sense of many scholars in the field that self-reflection is the order of the day?

These questions take us back to the way in which this essay treats praxis. If one sees current ways as indeed alienated and alienating, then an alternative must show for practice, as for existence and creativity, how a field can move from alienation to liberation, from the fetishism of sociology to activity that makes optimally equal, active, and cooperating human beings the measure of all things.

In this context, the views of Blum and McHugh offer some important answers to the questions raised. On the level of its problem-solving activity, they suggest, current sociology is profoundly alienative because it leads its practitioners to do their work without making clear to themselves or to others the grounds for what it is they are doing, the form of life which their work expresses. We can hope for no decrease in self-estrangement without asking the kind of tough questions—procedural as well as existential—that some consciousness-raising radicals have tried to ask of late outside of academic life, notably among feminists and gay activists.[23]

Although they do not say so, McHugh and Blum's insistence on close questioning of the self ties an alternative practice in the field to the kind of heightened consciousness that looms large today among this country's younger "cultural" radicals. This link—and the crucial shift, for instance, from product to process—Blum and McHugh adumbrate more tangibly and forcefully (if quite technically) than did either the plea for a reflexive sociology or the countless attacks on current ways. We have here, in other words, not only a call to sociologists to question all they themselves do, but also a fairly clear hint of how to practice what critics preach.

At the start of this essay, I spoke of two shifts that sum up the emerging alternative in U.S. sociology. In the first shift, some practitioners in the field have moved from object to subject. In the second shift, some have moved from a seldom questioned academic bureaucracy to new, communal ways in or near that bureaucracy. In closing, we need to consider where these shifts point in terms of the still disjointed alternative I have brought together here.

Just as the past decade went far to negate the status quo within U.S. sociology, we must now move beyond that negation. To the liberative, dealienating shift from object to subject we need to add the reverse. We need to find new ways to face up to the thinglike, dehumanized side of our life. If we fail to do that, we run the grave risk that subjectivism and antipositivism will make us mindless (and speechless) when it comes to all that lies beyond firsthand, face-to-face interactions.

By the same token, the lack of a full break with the academy as now set up brings with it a problem, a big problem. For our academy serves to choke off the alternative praxis if and when we bring it to life not in parts but as a whole. And the professionalism of current ways makes a cult of academic routines and privilege. As Marlene Dixon's resignation from her job at McGill in the midseventies helped to show,[24] this professionalism denies meaningful membership to those who break with most of the current ways, whose form of life leaves little room for either passive existence, bureaucratized scholarship, or mechanical, unquestioned positivism.

The problem is clear from how quick the ax is to fall when academics move from piecemeal to more complete departures from current ways. Most people lose academic jobs when they turn to the mix inherent in the new praxis: a mix of a change-minded intellectual alternative (like the paradigm of Marx) with continuing activism not only outside the academy, but also right on campus.[25] At least for now, self rule may not break the stranglehold of bureaucracy until a good deal more of the praxis, of a self-determined form of life, lies altogether outside the academy.

Heeding object as well as subject, leaving the academy more and more—as we move beyond the past decade's negation of the status quo, we honor the negation, the alternative, as an ongoing achievement. When we look at that achievement, we go back to its underlying form of life: we ground the new praxis in inverting the current ways, in consciously transforming our existence from passive to active, our creativity from bureaucratic to communal, and our practice from concrete to analytic. Going back to the grounds of our achievement means to speak of our possibilities. To think of our achievement lets us see our possibilities.

ACKNOWLEDGMENT

My thanks to Stewart Albert, David Anderson, Alan F. Blum, Roslyn Wallach Bologh, Judith Clavir, Wesley A. Fisher, Paul W. Massing, Helen Margaret McClure, and Peter McHugh.

NOTES

1. John Horton writes of fetishism in the field in "The Fetishism of Sociology," in *Radical Sociology*, edited by J. David Colfax and John L. Roach (New York: Basic Books, 1971). See also Horton's "The Dehumanization of Alienation and Anomie," *British Journal of Sociology* 15 (December 1964), and his "Combatting Empiricism," *Insurgent Sociologist*, vol. 3, no. 1 (Fall 1972).
2. Alvin W. Gouldner, *The Coming Crisis of Western Sociology* (New York: Basic Books, 1970); Robert W. Friedrichs, *A Sociology of Sociology* (New York: Free Press, 1970). Within the dominant school, perhaps the most comprehensive (and the most sanguine) view of the current state of the field is to be found in a 100-page monograph by Paul F. Lazarsfeld entitled "Sociology," chapter 1 in UNESCO, *Main Trends of Research in the Social and Human Sciences*, Part 1 (Paris: Mouton, 1970). See also a set of new journals that speak for critics of the dominant school: *Berkeley Journal of Sociology* (University of California), *Human Factor* (Columbia University), *Insurgent Sociologist* (University of Oregon), *Telos* (Washington University), *Theory and Society* (Amsterdam, The Netherlands), and *Catalyst* (Trent University, Ont.).

3. Elizabeth Ann Weinberg, *The Development of Sociology in the Soviet Union* (Boston: Routledge and Kegan Paul, 1974); George Fischer, "The Development of Sociology in the Soviet Union," in *Contemporary Sociology,* no. 3 (1975).
4. Comparisons of Soviet and U.S. sociology can be found in Norman Birnbaum, *Toward a Critical Sociology* (Oxford University Press, 1971), as well as in chapter 12 of Gouldner, *The Coming Crisis,* and chapter 11 of Friedrichs, *A Sociology.*
5. Two other genres do not back the dominant school and yet stand closer to it than to any other one school. One of the genres is summed up well by a recent collection, and by its title and subtitle: *Muckraking Sociology: Research as Social Criticism,* edited by Gary T. Marx (New York: Dutton, 1972). The same link to the mainstream of the field holds for some basic rather than ad hoc research and criticism. Major examples of this second genre can be found in John C. Leggett, *Class, Race, and Labor* (Oxford: University Press, 1968), and Richard F. Hamilton, *Class and Politics in the United States* (New York: Wiley, 1972). In each work, the author rests his whole case on survey data from opinion polls, a cornerstone of normative sociology. A survey-based work of my own—*The Soviet System and Modern Society* (New York: Atherton, 1968)—also fits into this genre. For both of these genres, unorthodox political views go hand in hand with the same research methods and underlying assumptions that I sketch here for the normative school.
6. The main statements of ethnomethodology are Harold Garfinkel, *Studies in Ethnomethodology* (Englewood Cliffs, N.J.: Prentice-Hall, 1967), and two works by Aaron Cicourel, *Method and Measurement in Sociology* (New York: Free Press, 1964), and *Cognitive Sociology* (New York: Free Press, 1974). On ethnomethodology, see also chapter 1 of Peter McHugh et al., *On the Beginning of Social Inquiry* (Boston: Routledge and Kegan Paul, 1974); and Paul Attewell, "Ethnomethodology Since Garfinkel," *Theory and Society* vol. 1, no. 2 (Summer 1974).

On symbolic interactionism, see Herbert Blumer, *Symbolic Interactionism* (Englewood Cliffs, N.J.: Prentice-Hall, 1969); *Catalyst*, no. 7 (Winter 1973); "Comments" in *American Sociological Review* 39, no. 3 (June 1974); and the works of Howard S. Becker, John R. Seeley, and Tamotsu Shibutani. Important among individual advocates of phenomenological sociology are two prolific figures, Peter Berger and Erving Goffman, as well as Alfred Schutz, the seminal figure in that school.

Among recent introductions to interpretative sociology are Peter Berger and Thomas Luckmann, *The Social Construction of Reality* (New York: Doubleday, 1966); *Understanding Everyday Life*, edited by Jack D. Douglas (Chicago: Aldine, 1970); Stanford M. Lyman and Marvin B. Scott, *A Sociology of the Absurd* (New York: Appleton-Century-Crofts, 1970); and Maurice Roche, *Phenomenology, Language and the Social Sciences* (Boston: Routledge and Kegan Paul, 1973). An overview of Schutz appears in the second of these volumes. See also Schutz's own *Collected Papers*, vols. 1-3 (The Hague: Nijhoff, 1961-1966).

7. A prolific phenomenologist illustrates the one-sideness in a volume he edited on "social problems in a technological society." Global in scope, his introduction draws on well-known recent views and commentaries outside of interpretative sociology. But the author shows no special insight deriving from that school or from its recipe of common-sense knowledge. See *Freedom and Tyranny*, edited by Jack D. Douglas (New York: Knopf, 1970). The same is true of other books written or edited by Douglas: *The Relevance of Sociology* (New York: Appleton-Century-Crofts, 1970); *American Social Order* (New York: Free Press, 1971); *Crime and Justice in American Society* (Indianapolis: Bobbs-Merrill, 1971); and *Defining America's Social Problems* (Englewood Cliffs, N.J.: Prentice-Hall, 1974). In his contribution to *Understanding Everyday Life*, Douglas makes a programmatic plea for analyzing "transsituational" phenomena, but none of his work offers a case of transsituational analysis.

8. Herbert Marcuse, *Reason and Revolution* (1941; republished 1964 by Beacon Press); same, *Soviet Marxism* (1958; republished in 1961 by Random House); Shlomo Avineri, *The Social and Political Thought of Karl Marx* (Cambridge: University Press, 1968); George Lichtheim, *From Marx to Hegel* (New York: Seabury Press, 1971); Bertell Ollman, *Alienation* (Cambridge: University Press, 1971); *The Unknown Dimension*, edited by Dick Howard and Karl E. Klare (New York: Basic Books, 1972); Raymond Williams, "Base and Superstructure in Marxist Cultural Theory," *New Left Review*, no. 82 (November-December 1973); comments in *Telos*, no. 22 (Winter 1974-75), on Martin Nicolaus, Foreword to *Grundrisse*, by Karl Marx (New York: Random House, 1974); Richard T. Bernstein, *Praxis and Action* (Philadelphia: University of Pennsylvania Press, 1971); and Martin Jay, *The Dialectical Imagination* (Boston: Little, Brown, 1973).

Among the leading neo-marxist writers in U.S. sociology are Stanley Aronowitz, *False Promises* (New York: McGraw-Hill, 1973), and *Food, Shelter, and the American Dream* (New York: Seabury Press, 1974); Norman Birnbaum, *The Crisis of Industrial Society* (Oxford University Press, 1969), and *Toward a Critical Sociology;* Bruce Brown, *Marx, Freud, and the Critique of Everyday Life* (New York: Monthly Review Press, 1973); and Trent Schroyer, *The Critique of Domination* (New York: Braziller, 1973).

On the much-discussed critique of everyday life, most of the recent work (except for that of feminists) seems to come from like-minded European sociologists. Examples can be found in Henri Lefebvre, *Everyday Life in the Modern World* (New York: Harper and Row, 1971); Guy Debord, *Society of the Spectacle*, special issue of *Radical America* vol. 4, no. 5 (1970); and Agnes Heller, *Alltag und Geschichte* (Neuwied: Luchterhand, 1970), chaps. 2, 3, and 5.

9. An influential British follower of Marx, E. P. Thompson, speaks against treating as a given any one set of his views or analytical procedures. Thompson rejects both doctrine

and method in favor of a more open way to view Marx and his corpus of knowledge: tradition. By that he means a very wide tradition (or whole way of thinking) that Marx gave rise to. See *Socialist Register 1973,* edited by Ralph Milliband and John Saville (London: Merlin, 1974), pp. 18-27. As an example of what Thompson rejects, I would cite the subtle and yet unquestioning dispute of Bertell Ollman and Isaac D. Balbus on the method of Marx, in *Politics and Society* vol. 3, no. 4 (Summer 1973).
10. All quotations from Friedrichs are from chapter 12 of *A Sociology of Sociology.* Throughout this essay, italics in quotations appeared in the original.
11. Gouldner, "The Politics of the Mind," *Social Policy* vol. 2, no. 6 (March-April 1972), reprinted in Gouldner, *For Sociology* (New York: Basic Books, 1973), chap. 4.
12. McHugh et al., *On the Beginning of Social Inquiry,* chap. 1.
13. Richard Flacks, "Notes on the 'Crisis in Sociology,'" *Social Policy* vol. 2, no. 6 (March-April 1972). Flacks says more about some of the same points in his article "Towards a Socialist Sociology," *Insurgent Sociologist* vol. 2, no. 2 (Spring 1972). See also Flacks, *Youth and Social Change* (Chicago: Markham, 1971); and his "Strategies for Radical Social Change," *Social Policy* vol. 1, no. 6 (March-April 1971). While Flacks points to key figures of the left outside the academy as perhaps the best sociologists of our time, among all those I cite here only Nicolaus (see no. 8) rests his scholarly work on such nonacademic figures.
14. Marlene Dixon, "The Failure of the Sociology Liberation Movement (Revised)," *Human Factor* vol. 10, no. 2 (Spring 1971); same, "Academic Roles and Function," *Insurgent Sociologist* vol. 2, no. 2 (Spring 1972). See three other articles by the same author: "On Women's Liberation," in *Radical Sociology,* edited by Colfax and Roach; "Why Women's Liberation?" in *Female Liberation,* edited by Roberta Sapler (New York: Knopf, 1972); and "Public Ideology and the Class Composition of Women's Liberation," *Berkeley Journal of Sociology* vol. 16 (1971-72).

Probably closer to Dixon than anyone else, at least in their opposition to cultural Marxism and their espousal of a positivism close to orthodox Marxism, are Albert Szymanski, "Toward a Radical Sociology," in *Radical Sociology,* edited by Colfax and Roach, and Tamar Pitch, "The Roots of Radical Sociology," in *Insurgent Sociologist* vol. 1, no. 4 (Summer 1974).

15. Henry Etzkowitz, in *Invisible Socialist University* (Newsletter of East Coast Conference of Socialist Sociologists) vol. 1, no. 1 (May 10, 1974). The same year Etzkowitz published a collection entitled *Is America Possible?* (St. Paul, Minnesota: West, 1974).
16. John O'Neill, *Sociology as a Skin Trade* (New York: Harper and Row, 1972), chap. 1.
17. Paulo Freire, *Pedagogy of the Oppressed* (New York: Seabury Press, 1970), chap. 2.
18. Jürgen Habermas, *Knowledge and Human Interests* (Boston: Beacon Press, 1971), p. 313; Gouldner, *The Coming Crisis,* chap. 13; Colfax, in *Radical Sociology,* edited by Colfax and Roach, p. 87.
19. *The Coming Crisis*, chap. 13; "The Politics of the Mind," *Social Policy.*
20. In the *Social Policy* article quoted here ("The Politics of the Mind"), Gouldner lumps together orthodox marxism and antiorthodox neo-marxism, and makes short shrift of both. Elsewhere, he takes a much closer and more favorable look at the subject ("The Metaphoricality of Marxism and the Context-Freeing Grammar of Socialism," *Theory and Society* vol. 1, no. 4 [Winter 1974]; as well as the whole last part of *For Sociology*). Still, Gouldner's goal is to bring new life to sociology; to him demystifying Marx is but a step toward that goal and not a way to build an alternative to sociology. (Gouldner called his book *For Sociology*, he tells us, by contrast with *For Marx.*)
21. Peter McHugh, "On the Failure of Positivism," in *Understanding Everyday Life,* edited by Douglas. The main application of this view is to be found in Peter McHugh et al.,

On the Beginning of Social Inquiry. See Introduction and chapter one of this book.

22. Alan F. Blum's general statements appear in his "Theorizing," in *Understanding Everyday Life,* edited by Douglas. The other quotations come from "Reading Marx," *Sociological Inquiry* (February 1973). See also the author's earlier paper, "The Corpus of Knowledge as a Normative Order," in *Theoretical Sociology,* edited by John C. McKinney and Edward A. Tiryakian (New York: Appleton-Century-Crofts, 1970); his "Positive Thinking," *Theory and Society* vol. 1, no. 3 (Fall 1974); and his new book, *Theorizing* (New York: Humanities Press, 1974). John O'Neill shares Blum's view in *Making Sense Together* (New York: Harper and Row, 1974); there he speaks of a Wild sociology and its Commonplace method.

23. 25 to 6 Baking and Trucking Society, *Great Gay in the Morning* (Washington, New Jersey: Times Change Press, and New York: Monthly Review Press, 1972); Marge Piercy, *Small Changes* (New York: Doubleday, 1973).

24. Dixon, Statement on resignation from McGill University, *Insurgent Sociologist* vol. 5, no. 2 (Winter 1975).

25. J. David Colfax, "Repression and Academic Radicalism," *New Politics* vol. 10, no. 3 (Spring 1973); Peter Stein, "Institutional Repression in Higher Education," *Insurgent Sociologist* vol. 3, no. 4 (Summer 1973); "Radical Economists Under Fire," business section, *New York Times,* February 2, 1975. If moves within the academy to set up an alternative praxis stress accommodation rather than all-out dissent, this need not save the academics from the ax. Worse yet, such attempts may keep up the appearance of change but fail to save the most far-reaching alternatives to current ways. By now this turns out to be true of *each* of the six attempts I traced in *Urban Higher Education in the United States* (New York: Central Office, City University of New York, 1974), see also Introduction and chapter three of this book.

THREE
REFORM OF URBAN COLLEGES

When we look at higher learning in urban America, two things stand out: a swift rise in enrollment, followed by a wave of educational reform. Urban colleges saw the start of a more basic kind of reform only in the wake of first a boom in enrollment and then an educational reform of a limited and highly official kind.

At metropolitan public colleges, in short, enrollment more than doubled in the 1960s. This urban college boom meant a far freer access to higher education for those who could not have gone to college before. But the boom stopped short in terms of open-door, free-access, universal higher education. Since much less than half of the college-age group got a four-year college degree at the time (or do now), nothing like universal attendance marked the boom.

Freer access gave a chance to seven out of ten new high school graduates to get at least a try in college (Warren W. Willingham, *Free-Access Higher Education* [New York: College Entrance Examination Board, 1970], chap. 1, tab. 1). But it did so within three strict limits. First, a lot of people found college no more than a revolving door, which pushed them out soon after it let them in. Second, contrary to the common view, whites more often than not make up the students brought to college by the boom. As a third limit, the boom did not mean a chance at any and all schools; by and large, it meant just a chance at the local two-year community colleges. For most urban students, then, the boom meant a revolving door or at best a new form of tracking, or Differential Access.

Reprinted by permission from George Fischer, *Urban Higher Education in the United States,* New York: Central Office, City University of New York, 1974, Conclusion (with data from chapter one). The Introduction to this book speaks of the study for CUNY and the few changes made here.

TWO MODELS OF DIFFERENTIAL ACCESS*
California State System of Higher Education and City University of New York

	Approximate share of enrollment
High rung (selective)	
California: leading university	20%
City University: four-year schools that stress preprofessional training	40%
Middle rung (less selective)	
California: four-year or five-year schools	25%
City University: four year schools that stress training in human services (and transfer programs of some two-year schools)	35%
Low rung (nonselective)	
California: two-year schools	50%
City University: Two-year schools that stress clerical and vocational training	25%

A second big change, the top-down innovations made at the fringe of learning, touched most colleges in the country at the turn of the seventies. As I spell it out in *Urban Higher Education in the United States,* this official college reform gave both new and old types of students a good deal more choice when it came to the time and place and pace of their formal schooling.

Three groups did the most to plan and urge the reform.

---

*A.J. Jaffe and Walter Adams, "Two Models of Open Enrollment," in *Universal Higher Education* (Washington, D.C.: American Council on Education, 1971); Ellen Kay Trimberger, "Open Admissions," *Insurgent Sociologist,* Fall 1973; and CUNY Enrollment Report for Spring 1972. The California enrollment is for 1968.

Reform of Urban Colleges 111

A Task Force on Higher Education was chaired by Frank Newman, at the time an executive of Stanford University close to leading Republicans in California. The group grew out of a suggestion from President Nixon's first Secretary of Health, Education, and Welfare; that task force put out its first report through the Government Printing Office. Clark Kerr set up the Carnegie Commission on Higher Education, by far the most prominent and prolific of these groups, soon after he lost his job as president of the University of California. The smaller Commission on Non-Traditional Study has been led by Samuel B. Gould—once the head of Antioch College and then of the State University of New York.[1]

When we move from these shock troops of the reform to the big guns that back them, we find ourselves at the core of the country's educational establishment.

The Ford Foundation, the largest private philanthropy of all, backed the Newman task force (and in part *Change* Magazine and the University Without Walls). The Carnegie Corporation, with Ford and Rockefeller one of the Big Three of private philanthropy, gave funds for the work of both the Commission on Non-Traditional Study and the Carnegie Commission on Higher Education, the latter leading to dozens of research and policy publications.

Two of the main gatekeepers of higher education in the United States—the Educational Testing Service and the College Entrance Examination Board—set up the Commission on Non-Traditional Study. The U.S. Office of Education helped to fund the official reform, and, of late, two new government agencies joined the cause: the National Institute of Education and its twin, the Fund for the Improvement of Post-Secondary Education. Key national organizations of the educational establishment joined as well: American Council on Education, Association of Junior and Community Colleges, Council of Graduate Schools in the United States, Federation of Regional Accrediting Commissions of Higher Education.

While the resulting changes made by urban schools either during or since the sixties barely touched the core of learning, we find some notable exceptions. What stands out is not only the sheer growth of urban higher education but the shifts at the very core of learning that a few metropolitan public colleges did make in the wake of the boom and official reform. For the higher learnin urban America, these shifts point to a revolution—but a quiet revolution with no rage or gore, and an unfinished one . . .

Here I sum up all of the aspects of this new move toward change. Although it can be found in all sorts of schools, here I speak only of what took place in cities with more than a million people, and in publicly backed undergraduate schools (most of them launched in the last few years) that gave wide access to new as well as to old student populations. And I speak of the quiet revolution as we find it so far in a metropolitan public college as a whole, where the move from a single mode of learning to a second one can be found throughout the school's learning process.

Needless to say, the unfinished quiet revolution does not take place in a void. This birth of something new comes to us in the midst of a time of troubles. The trouble is rooted most of all in the main contradiction of our social order—the contradiction between technical overdevelopment and political or social underdevelopment. The contradition leads to an ever faster pace of economic change on the one hand, and ever more social strife and malaise on the other. The way Americans live—especially in the cities—lays bare a host of clashes over what people could do, and need to do, to make life better in this time and place. Right now we see a growth in people'e sense of this gulf, between what is happening today and all the things that could be (and ought to be) different. But it is too soon to speak of anything like a new awakening.

Our set ways of acting and of thinking—our institutions and our consciousness—give way to change slowly. We can see this well in the realm of urban higher education where the more basic shifts in ways to learn meet with strong doubts or fierce opposition. Here the pressures for change are tied to the main areas of trouble and struggle in our time: a fair share, the quality of life, our environment, as well as self-actualization and self rule. The faculty backlash in metropolitan public colleges can be seen as a good example of that opposition.

Because of the contradictions of the social order itself, those in charge can put to good use both the old mode of higher learning and a new one. Thus the system turns out either the student as robot[2] or the student as adult. Robots learn to conform to the dominant ways by means of docility; adults learn to use individual choice and initiative as they move through life.

No matter what stand they might take, one finds in all key groups—students, parents, alumni, college staff, the educational establishment and philanthropies, as well as big and small people outside of academe—little grasp of the new choice that urban schools with a changed core have brought forth. This is understandable since the shifts are recent, and those who made them have yet to speak out loud and clear. And all the current commissions and reports on higher education fail to give their due to metropolitan public colleges or to the quiet revolution launched there.

We can see this lack of recognition in three new books with case studies of innovating schools. *Five Experimental Colleges,* edited by Gary B. MacDonald (New York: Harper & Row, 1973) includes no urban schools at all. Two other books do deal with urban schools in part, but none of the urban schools does more than what the official college reform calls for: Lawrence Hall et al., *New Colleges for New Students* (San Francisco: Jossey-Bass, 1974) includes chapters on LaGuardia Community College of the City University of New York and Third College of the University of California at San Diego, while Harold L. Hodgkinson, *Institutions in Transition* (New York: McGraw-Hill for Carnegie Commission on Higher Education, 1973) includes case studies on the State University of New York at Buffalo and Chicago State University. Likewise, the two books of the Carnegie Commission that deal with urban higher education, as such, hardly acknowledge the growth of a second mode of learning in some metropolitan public colleges: *The Campus and the City,* a report by the Commission (New York: McGraw-Hill, 1972); George Nash, *The University and the City* (New York: McGraw-Hill, 1973). Of the eight case studies in this last book, not one deals with the urban schools I single out, or with any schools like them.[3]

With my larger work, I try to close the gap. Here, before I sum up the quiet revolution at its halfway point, to date, I discuss the main doubts voiced about higher education in America. And then, in closing, I turn to what we should do (or should not do) to round out a basic reform of urban schools.

I. TOO MUCH CHANGE? OR TOO LITTLE?

In the wake of the boom of the 1960s the problem of what to do with vast new student populations, and how to do it, continually came to the fore in urban higher education. While the primary and secondary schools of our big cities brought forth a whole movement for basic change on the plane of action as well as criticism and protest, no such movement will be found in the higher learning of urban America. Until now, most answers called for shifts at the fringe of learning (as put forth by the official college reform), and for holding fast to the old core of standardized learning of specialized and set content.

There are, of course, a handful of metropolitan public colleges that have taken action like the ones I single out here. Yet little has been seen or heard of them. They owe little if anything to any strong push from educational critics and reformers as a group—or, for that matter, from established educators, leaders, foundations or government agencies. No national goal or scheme or movement influenced them or their sponsors to back a quiet revolution. Not much took place even on the familiar organizational plane of national or regional conferences, consortiums, and research projects. Instead, change at the core of urban higher learning happened through local impetus and took different forms at each of the colleges I cite. And the local lead came from—and stayed with—not dissenting radicals but liberals—prudent established liberals.

True, one does find more change when we turn to Open Admissions, the move to make initial access to higher education more or less universal in the United States. The fact stands out, though, that thought and action on Open Admissions stop short of change at the core of learning. Like the official reform as a whole, Open Admissions still means, in the main, a novel delivery system to the academic status quo. The strong attachment that institutions have to the old school ways has ruled out a push for a changed core. Insofar as critics or established groups called for change in urban higher education, the result took the form of single, limited types of action like instituting programs such as Open Admissions or basic academic skills or more ethnic studies and staffing. And few people considered the key position that metropolitan public colleges hold in the growth of access and the deep implications of that fact.

When some changes at the core did take place, it spurred at least some discourse on the matter. One theme marks all of this discourse. It is a conservative one that raises the question: has too much change taken place? But all too few have pressed the opposite question: has there been too little change? To be sure, Too Much and Too Little are gross measures, and on their own will not do. Yet they bring out the conservative, negative thrust of past discourse, and the largely defensive response of those who asked for change. Too Much Change stands out as the main battle cry; Too Little Change comes back as a weak echo.

What are the doubts raised by those who fear change at the core of learning? Here are the doubts heard most often, and how I would answer them in terms of this work.

Do urban schools with a changed core deprive their students of things that well-off students get?

This key question rests on two views: that elite students gain from elite colleges the academic learning that the old school ways stand for, and that most urban schools now give their students more or less the same fare. The question is based on the view, too, that what top students at selective institutions learn is what most urban students both want and need. These views are important factors in the fight for change at the core of urban schooling. But each of these views is open to grave doubts.

In and out of the classroom, for one, many elite schools give their students at least as many broad as narrow skills; students arrive at school with some sense of mastery already, and it is that active sense, and not passive mimicry, that the best of the selective institutions build up. The bulk of urban schools fail to do just that. No more than narrow skills make up their fare, and that means most urban schools are not at all like elite schools in what they offer. And we cannot be sure these days that narrowly traditional content and the traditional student-faculty relations are what helps any student, elite or urban, to do well in the job market.

True, most employers still prefer to hire graduates willing and able to play the game by all the established rules. Hence they prize the student as robot. Yet more and more employers now want what the student as adult gains from learning broad skills—self-confidence and self-understanding, generalized judgment and analytic ways, a sense of mastery in thought and action—at least as much as they do the academic or vocational specialization. The same, our Detroit case shows, is true of professional and graduate schools. Thus to question the moves toward change at the core makes little sense, since those who raise these questions are basing their views on shaky ground.

Only when a second mode of learning, with quality as well as breadth, gets a real chance can all concerned test if this fear of change is sound. In other words, here the problem turns out to be not too much change, but too little: we will not know what urban students need the most, and like the best, as long as so few of them have more than one choice.

Does learning broad skills come down to rap sessions? Or, would you trust a person with broad skills rather than narrowly traditional ones to do heart surgery or build a bridge?

As soon as traditional content and student-faculty relationships give way to something more open, fluid, and varied, the sense of rigor and clear authority gives way to what looks like drift, chaos, and goofing off. Hence the favorite canard—that a changed core of learning means nothing more than rap sessions, or no end of aimless and useless talk. Up to a point, that canard goes back to the great need, once a school gives up the old ways, to let students and faculty find new ways by means of unstructured, open-ended dialogue of all sorts. If no search takes place, the same old school ways are bound to fill the void.

As urban schools looked for a changed core in the past few years, they found it hard—as hard as the experimenting elite schools had found it—to know just where and how to draw the line, to put a halt to a free search by means of dialogue-type "rap sessions." Those programs that did not draw a line tended to fail, since most people do need some set frame for a hard task like advanced formal schooling. The urban schools I sketch here do draw a line, and "rap sessions" do not rule the learning process in any of them. Yet in all of them an open, often seemingly loose flow of student-faculty discourse plays a key role. The traditional school ways fail to make good use of free talk. The student as robot was not allowed to talk freely; the new breed, the student as adult, does and should.

In the most harsh attack to date on Open Admissions at the City University of New York (Martin Mayer in *Commentary*, February 1973), the author claims a relationship between non-traditional schooling and professional incompetence. And he ends his piece with the point that few people would trust a badly schooled physician to do heart surgery or a badly trained engineer to build a bridge. True, very true. But what does that prove? In a time and place full of ethically slipshod doctors and engineers, for whom private gain means a lot more than the human hearts and grand bridges they work on, the link between traditional schooling and professional competence is moot at best.

More and more, questions are being raised about a lack of humaneness in the professions today. This condition has come about while narrowly traditional learning made up the dominant mode. Here, too, we won't know which type of learning can solve that problem and serve urban students and the rest of us best as long as most metropolitan public colleges back too little change, and not too much. Once we give students more than just one mode of learning, then let the best schooling win, be it with or without "rap sessions."

If an innovating school does something well on a small scale, would it work for a large school?

The problem of size is a very real one, and I say more on it later. The administrators who run the oldest of the innovating urban colleges, discussed in my larger work—Monteith College of Wayne State University—believe that they can make the highly analytic and cerebral General Education scheme work well for a fair sample of urban students because of the small size of the school as a whole and of key learning groups. Most other schools, too, find that their students gain a lot from learning on a small scale. For these reasons, among others, urban schools with a changed core focus most of the time on small size, be it of classrooms or student body or institutions as a whole.

In the wake of a swift rise in enrollment, coupled with a trend of no-growth right now, all urban schools feel hard pressed to take in as many students as they possibly can. Small scale gets lost in the shuffle, of course. In that light, how much can innovations on a small scale aid the problem of the large urban school? Up to a point, a good deal. If the need is clear, large schools can turn to small learning groups and the like. What the large institution loses are the benefits of the immediacy and human interconnection that a small institution makes for. Here the way out may well be nothing less than a full-fledged shift from large to small scale for whole institutions. Once more, we need to take a close look at the terms under which small institutions may work as well—not just educationally but administratively and fiscally—as the large ones are supposed to work. As long as we continue to take large scale for granted, we will never find out if we are wrong.

If urban higher education turns from narrow to broad skills, would the cost per student go up or down?

Since only one of the schools I write of comes close to the full range of broad skills—the Manhattan branch of SUNY's Empire State College—no answer is at hand. In that case, the cost would seem to be no more, but also no less, than that of traditional undergraduate instruction.

Beyond this question lies an important element in the whole clash of Too Much Change versus Too Little. A good deal of the official backing for nontraditional education flows from the hope that it would bring down the cost for each student and would save money that way. In this sense, those who fear Too Much Change might well be in the right. As a way to save funds, a turn from narrow to broad skills is not at all a sound bet. That holds true in terms of learning, since to base educational policy most of all on money makes sense only for a profit-seeking venture. And in fiscal terms, too, as I have said, the little we know suggests that big savings are not apt to come from a turn to broad skills.

True, a shift away from full staffing and campus facilities does save a great deal of funds, and the External Degree plus a minicampus (the Empire State scheme) need less funds for full-time faculty and quarters than do traditional schools. On the other hand, urban schools with a changed core have a great need for funds for things traditional schools may hardly do at all.

For example, a full range of broad skills calls for a lot of tutorial and counseling services, a close assessment of programs and students that goes on all the time, plus a far flung staff of community faculty and nonacademic experts with whom relationships must be kept up at some cost. To all this we must add a novel and difficult mastering of city life, so that students can prove that learning of advanced and high quality can take place in the community as its main site, in place of the campus. When moved from theory to practice, schools will find that costs match those of campus-based learning. Too Much Change is a risk here, in short, only if it grows out of a false hope that a turn to broad skills will cut down costs per student.[4]

How soon does a new mode of learning come to be set in its ways? Or, how long can we make the urge to innovate last?

Content aside, Americans tend to look on innovation as a Good Thing. In the case of urban higher education, though, people who like innovation want to feel sure that a program set up to probe and push change will go on in the same vein for a long time to come. Hence this question. For if a school goes to the trouble and cost to change a good deal, but then soon gets set in its ways, why should a parent body or institution bother?

The answer to whether change can go on and on without let-up seems to be no. The people who lead a school toward change are working for tangible goals. Once goals are met, or a school is stopped from reaching the goals from the outside, an urban school with a new core is not much more apt to keep changing than is a school ruled by the old ways. In that case, why change at all? Because change by nature tends to be incremental. If in our time the thrust of urban higher education shifts from narrow to broad skills, that itself will be a big gain. Once some such gain takes place, then new grounds and most likely new people will come to the fore to push for a new round of change.

In our case in Chicago, a strong attempt has been made to build change into everything the school does; it is constantly changing to fit in with things to come and has all sorts of self-destruct mechanisms for existing arrangements. These moves might make a school that much more willing and able to keep on changing. Yet Governors State University stands out as an exception. As a rule, we can probably ask no more than that a school with a changed core see through to the end the working out of that new core of learning. That in itself is no mean task.

When the times comes for another new mode of learning, it will call for new people and new schemes to fit that time and place.

Just what are the goals of urban schools that now change the core of learning?

No one has given a single answer to this question, and none may exist. Each in its own way, and with its own mix of schemes, the most innovative urban schools have tried in the last few years to come to grips with a wide range of changes: new student populations, a changed job market, deep shifts in the mood and needs and struggles of America in general and key urban groups in particular. In the midst of all these shifts, the schools changed, too.

Reform of Urban Colleges 121

Each of them sought to find ways to serve the urban mission, to do its share to save the life of the city. As publicly backed institutions in our metropolis, none of them aimed at all-out change of education or society as a whole. Instead, they speak of a changed core of learning in terms of a move from set, long-established learning content and relationship to much more varied and nonacademic ones.

If any one goal is evident, it would seem to be the goal of full human growth—a full growth both in the world of work and in life as a whole. The urban schools with a changed core take the view that the old ways of learning stunt and hobble that full growth, that the quiet revolution must in truth change what students learn from mimicry to mastery. A century apart, two critics spoke to this question, one of them a well-established educator in our own time, the other a great rebel against the status quo. Despite the gulf in place and time, the critics stress the same things. The new critic speaks for creativity, depth, and subtlety, and against the "conforming plodder" that traditional school ways reward. The old critic speaks of the fully developed individual as the wave of the future, and sets him off from "a mere fragment of a man" that the status quo breeds.

The new critic:

> Just as a broader spectrum of students was gaining access to higher education, the measures of selection and evaluation were becoming increasingly focused on narrow concepts of academic ability.
>
> The continuing focus on current measures rewards the conforming plodder at the expense of creativity, depth, and subtlety.
>
> Even worse, current testing practices often fail to measure those very characteristics traditionally considered central in the process of a liberal education: the ability to think critically, to organize in order to accomplish a task, to tolerate ambiguity and differing points of view, to master the process of learning—all those characteristics which insure the useful-

ness of the student's education in life beyond the academy (Frank Newman, et al., *National Policy and Higher Education, The Second Report of a Special Task Force to the Secretary of Health, Education, and Welfare* [Cambridge: MIT Press, 1973], chap. 1).

The old critic:

> [Modern Industry] imposes the necessity of recognizing, as a fundamental law of production, variations of work, consequently fitness of the labourer for varied work, consequently the greatest possible development of his varied aptitudes. It become a question of life and death for society to adopt the mode of production to the normal functioning of this law.
>
> Modern Industry, indeed, compels society, under penalty of death, to replace the detail-worker of today, crippled by life-long repetition of one and the same trivial operation, and thus reduced to a mere fragment of a man, by the fully developed individual, fit for a variety of labours, ready to face any change of production, and to whom the different functions he performs are but so many modes of giving free scope to his own natural and acquired powers (Karl Marx, *Capital*, vol. I, chap. 15, Sec. 9 [New York: International Publishers, 1967]).

What would you put in place of the old school ways—of academic merit for faculty and academic merit for students and then jobs?

A number of people in and out of academe say they share the views of the two critics I quote. But many of them fear Too Much Change, all the same, when the scene shifts from theory to practice. Not only do the old school ways seem to be the sole mode of higher learning that people know, but, as yet, those who change the core have not spelled out what a second mode of learning puts in place of a single mode. At least in rough form, though, the urban schools with a changed core show what could take the place of academic professionalism and academic merit.

Let me bring up once more the charge of antiintellectualism, a charge that the foes of change in urban schools aim these days at those who back change. From all that has been said here, it should be clear that the charge makes sense only if things intellectual, or the life of the mind, are tied hand and foot to narrow academic specialization and pre-Ph.D. norms for undergraduate schooling. If that link remains, then all critics of academic professionalism might indeed be guilty of antiintellectualism. But if such a link makes no sense at all, then the charge fails. More than that, the same charge might well be aimed at the old school ways that still shape and rule most of urban higher education. For by following these traditional ways we exclude broad mental skills and the private skills that go with them. In this way we make much of academe sterile and hence deeply alien to the life of the mind, to thought as a whole. What most promotes antiintellectualism in urban schools right now is not too much change but too little.

College faculty who revere academic professionalism cling to just one field of specialization and research within it. All else, not least their work with students and their schools and communities, must take a back seat. More than that, academic professionalism emphasizes not scholarship of clear worth and use but any and all things that point to a teacher's bond to his or her field. That bond is what counts, no matter how trivial or spurious things, such as doing chores for a professional organization, might be in terms of real scholarship.

In this light, it should not be that hard to spell out—and reward—an alternative type of teaching. With this alternative, faculty see all of their college work as equally important, and give first place to the needs of students in and out of the classroom. Scholarship and service to college and community gain reward if and when they fit well what teachers do with students, and the quality of all this work gets more weight than (as is too often true now) sheer quantity.

The same answer holds for academic merit when it comes to students and then jobs. Here, too, a stress on narrowly specialized fields of academic work makes no sense at all. Even if students are later involved in just these fields, no "fully developed individual" can come out of a program that puts first and last a single academic field or a mix of narrow specialties. As long as that view holds, arid and hence trivial scholasticism will crowd out the kind of breadth in thought and action that people need for all aspects of their lives. And such a meager view of merit either puts down most students or makes them act like the conforming plodder that Frank Newman and the HEW task force warn of.

Insofar as the goals and means of a changed core of learning make sense, the higher learning in urban America has seen not too much change, but far too little. And as long as we change too little, most urban schools will bring forth the drudge—the mere fragment of a man—and not the fully developed individual who could help to master life in the city and the world of work. Step by step, and each in its own way, the most innovative urban schools show that right now we need to fear too little change a lot more than too much change.

II. WHAT'S NEW SO FAR?

What is new so far at the core of urban learning?

Few things are all new, and much that we call new is not new at all. Change tends to take the form of waves and spurts and cycles. At each turn, we take to be new what did not stand out at the last turn or two. In these terms, much of what has seemed new in higher education over the last five or ten years turns out to be no more than reinventing the wheel. This should be kept in mind when reading about the shifts of which I speak here. Also, one should link up educational reform schemes that John Dewey and Robert Hutchins made known in the 1920s and '30s.

Yet this very link with the past helps to bring out one thing that seems in truth new in the quiet revolution. If a generation or two ago the reform schemes of Dewey and Hutchins clashed as much with each other as they did with the status quo, I see the recent shifts as part of a single choice in lieu of our status quo. That the varied first steps of innovative urban schools add up to a single choice is itself new. Now it seems possible to fuse the skills Dewey urged—problem-solving, experiential, participatory, open-ended—with the highly structured and cerebral learning of Hutchins. Now, as never before, urban higher education holds out a chance to fuse what I call broad private skills with broad mental skill—or Dewey with Hutchins!

One more thing is important when we look for the new in urban higher education. Change at the core now comes in a most novel setting. While the near ubiquitous revolving door makes it much too soon to speak of free or open access to college, for the first time in history a fair sample of average urban students can claim wide if not free access. This in turn means that what urban schools manage to do well for the huge new mass of students is new.

The main point of *Urban Higher Education in the United States* is that the novel setting of wide access, with all the new student populations it adds, leaves urban higher education little choice but to change the core of learning. Urban schools fail to do well by their students as long as they cling to the old ways. Such traditional learning of traditional skills fails students on a host of planes, from occupational to broadly human and social.

For all students in our time, but for unevenly prepared urban students most of all, traditional (standardized) learning of traditional (specialized and long-established) skills makes little sense. The campus upheavals made that clear. The huge turnover rate in urban schools makes that clear. Everything we know about the job market points the same way.

The core of learning bears on two things and just those two things: the teacher-student relations that make up the learning process, and the content of what students learn. In these terms, the official college reform fails to touch the core. Its much-praised innovations are no more than shifts at the fringe of learning. These innovations do a good deal to fit all sorts of students into the established core; the reform schemes, in short, turn out to lend diversity and flexibility to the delivery systems but not to what people learn (the established rules of the game) and through what human relationships they learn (the student as robot). On content and student-faculty relationships, the official college reform leaves the old school ways intact.

It is within this context that urban schools with a changed core are unique. For they do the most to meet new times, new needs, and changed student populations. While the innovative urban schools I describe do draw on the official college reform, they are unique because they do not stop with those innovations. They go on from change at the fringe to change at the core of learning. In the terms I used here, they stress new content or new student-faculty relationships, or both. That leads these urban schools to turn from traditional learning and narrow skills to nontraditional learning and broad skills. "Traditional" here means no more than the old school ways, of course, and nontraditional means change at the core and not (as the term tends to be used) any or all shifts at the fringe.

In terms of broad private skills that make for an active and not a passive self, no scheme matters more than *self-directed learning*. And all sorts of schemes, like competency and External Degree, flow from self-directed learning. Such learning puts the brunt of designing, implementing, and at times even assessing a student's college work on the student. Though the faculty members who work with the student play quite a role, they give up most of the parental role, *in loco parentis,* that marks the old school ways. If done well, self-directed learning serves as a key step in the move from passive to active modes of life. Little that people had done up to that time gives them the same scope to think and plan out a chunk of their lives, and then to stick to their own plan through thick and thin, or change it on grounds that relate to a student's own work and life, and not from ideas set down by others. The main case I sketch of self-directed learning is Minnesota Metropolitan State College in the Twin Cities.

As part of self-directed learning, students show what they know through *competency*, rather than by standard tests. The goal is not to pass one or more tests but to show by a tailor-made mix of means that the skills to be demonstrated have in fact been mastered. The proof can take the form of independent research projects and creative work, participation in group projects on or off campus, formal or informal evaluation by experts other than faculty, on the job training, as well as classroom or national tests. In each case, competency-based learning consists of a clear goal for what is to be learned, and a suitable means to show how a student has met that goal. In line with self-directed learning, the competency scheme as a rule leaves it up to a student to pick the means by which to show what he or she has learned. *Chronicle of Higher Education* (March 18, 1974) tells of the spread of this scheme, and I speak of it in terms of the College of Public and Community Service, University of Massachusetts in Boston, Governors State University in Chicago, Minnesota Metropolitan State College, in the Twin Cities, and Empire State College in Manhattan.

Adult or continuing education is not a bit new in higher learning. What makes the External Degree movement of our time new is that it does more than teach traditional content in a traditional way to different kinds of students (adults) in a different place (off campus) at a different time (evenings or weekends). Adult and continuing programs did that in the past, and quite a few still do just that. The External Degree makes a change at the core of learning since it rests on self-directed learning and competency, and hence on a novel relationship between student and faculty. More than that, the urban school that gives first place to an External Degree has no campus at all (as in our Twin Cities case), or just a minicampus with no full staff, library, laboratories, or buildings of its own (Empire State College).

Through the years, most schools, through *off-campus learning,* let students earn some of their course credit by individual or group projects away from the site of the college. Off-campus learning is a pet scheme of the official college reform. What sets all that off from urban schools with a changed core is that most of these now treat off-campus learning at least on a par with learning on campus (our Boston case) and at times as the main fare (Twin Cities). In each case, too, the underlying assumption shifts. What students learn off campus no longer needs to be closely related to traditional skills, be they academic or vocational, as long as a student can demonstrate an agreed upon gain in competence. That can lead to college credit for esoteric learning at one end, and at the other end for narrowly applied skills that formerly found no place in the curriculum. For urban schools with a changed core, the prime test stands: does such learning help a student gain the college-level competency she or he seeks? If yes, the new mode lets anything go. Once more, of the schools I sketch, Minnesota Metropolitan does the most in this area.

In terms of *general education for students*, few of the most innovative urban schools emphasize broad mental skills, skills that go beyond established disciplines to build up analytic minds (questioning "facts") as against concrete minds (taking facts for granted). Both Livingston College of Rutgers University and Empire State do stress such skills. But our main case is Monteith College at Wayne University, which makes the old and troubled General Education scheme work for a fair sample of average urban students. Here regular disciplines give way to superdisciplines such as natural science, and a set core curriculum takes the place of self-directed learning. General Education seems to work in this case due to a seasoned faculty, the small size of the school and its learning groups, and a stress on a never ending student-faculty dialog on large intellectual themes.

How do these innovating urban schools deal with the fact that most urban students feel a strong need to come out of college with a job skill? How do the schools match this need to their own stress on broad skills, which may not be specifically job oriented? Most of all, the answer lies with *double majors*. These schools do not ask students to drop their cares about a job. Quite the opposite. Several of them make it simple for students to learn narrow vocational skills at the same time that they gain broad skills.

What I call double majors means that students are free to concentrate, if they so choose, in a career program as well as a program that singles out this or that change at the core of learning. In short, they major in both fields at the same time. Our New Brunswick case makes it easy for students to sign up for a career program at some other part of Rutgers University. Monteith College does the same. Most of its students work on an academic or vocational program in the rest of Wayne State University at the same time that they go through the large core curriculum of Monteith.

In Boston, the College of Public and Community Service gives training on the job plus a double major. Students there choose how to combine some one liberal arts cluster with a vocational curriculum, and these in turn with job training under college auspices. In this way, a double major and job training form a single whole. The learning experience offers a good deal of emphasis on broad private skills, some emphasis on broad mental skills, and a good deal of job training. Thus job skills do not lose out in the shuffle. On the contrary, a highly innovating urban school makes the job part and parcel of a changed core of learning.

In terms of *size or scale*, the most innovating urban schools point to some clear patterns. As background, let me cite two reports of the Carnegie Commission: *New Students and New Places* (1971) and *The More Effective Use of Resources* (1972). These reports state that for liberal arts colleges (those that stress no major career program or just one such program, like teaching), economies of scale plus the scope of curriculum point to a size of no less than 1,000 and no more than 2,500 full-time students or their equivalents. The next larger school is the comprehensive college, which seeks a wide range of undergraduate career programs as well as humanities, science, and social science. Here the Carnegie Commission holds that a full-time enrollment between five and ten thousand students makes the best sense.

If we use this scale, four of the six innovating schools I sketch plan to keep the size of a liberal arts college: Boston, Detroit, Manhattan, and Twin Cities. The others—Chicago and New Brunswick—plan to grow to the size recommended for a comprehensive college. These last, the reader should note, come the closest in my list to a comprehensive set of standard fields of concentration. The rest put self-directed learning in place of standard majors (Manhattan and Twin Cities), or mix a single scheme with double majors elsewhere in the parent institution (Detroit), or, as in the case of Boston, link a small range of career fields to a liberal arts major within the same school. In short, small size goes with some nontraditional scheme that comes close to the range of subjects we find in a liberal arts college but not with what we find in a comprehensive college.

All of the cluster colleges, I might add, stick to small scale except for the one with faculty and programs for Ph.D. candidates (New Brunswick). One of the two freestanding, separate institutions (Twin Cities) plans to stay small, while the other (Chicago) opts for a larger scale. This last, though, calls for cluster colleges of its own that fit the scale of liberal arts.

In light of all I have said, large size would not seem to support a quiet revolution in urban schools. In the preface to *Institutions in Transition,* Harold Hodgkinson sums up why. Larger schools have a more diverse student body, he writes, but also "a more research-oriented faculty, less institutional loyalty, more transients in the student body, poorer communication, and more student protest."

The established sociologist Peter Blau comes to the same conclusion. Although he argues all through his book that "large academic institutions tend to be less bureaucratic than small institutions," he ends up with an opposite view. His conclusion calls to mind Veblen's book on academe: "As increasing numbers of students go to college, the danger of bureaucratization grows. . . ." This is so "since bureaucratic procedures, though not inevitable in large institutions, are the easiest and cheapest to give a semblance of higher education to huge numbers" (*The Organization of Academic Work* [New York: Wiley, 1973], chap. 10). And the academic vice-president of Empire State College adds: "The basic point is that an institution should be large enough so that each student frequently must confront and operate within a variety of significant settings, but not so large that he becomes superfluous and disappears in the huddle" (Arthur W. Chickering, *Education and Identity* [San Francisco: Jossey-Bass, 1969], chap. 9).

But no longer is the sole choice that of whether an institution should be large or small. Lately, quite autonomous subunits have spread—cluster colleges at universities, schools at colleges—that share the good things of both. Such subunits can stay small and at the same time give their students the choice that comes with large size. Most of the double majors I cite call for some such larger parent institution like Wayne State University. For the sake of all concerned, such a halfway house may work best, at least for now. Although the old school ways still set the tone for most urban universities, programs with a changed core may serve students well if they can feel free to move back and forth between several units of the same parent institution. If such programs stand on their own or, at the other extreme, lack autonomy from the parent institution, students will be denied the choice—not least the choice of double majors—that a subunit such as the cluster college gives them.

Cutting across all other themes of urban higher education in our time, *racial pluralism* helps answer the need to do well by those students who bring to college the least—economically, educationally, and all the other ways that are associated with poverty and poor schooling. In this age, many such students are not white. They are black or brown or red or yellow. Up to a point, many of the official college reform voices—and the Open Admissions program pioneered by the City University of New York (1970-75)[5]—speak to just this need. Yet Open Admissions, like the official reform schemes, tends to take the old school ways for granted as the core of learning. Insofar as these old school ways make little or no sense for most students these days, they make even less sense for meeting the need of poor students. This need is not just for remedial schooling or financial aid or personal and academic counseling, but for a whole new way to relate to an alien, long hostile world of advanced learning for whites, and most of all well-off whites.

Here the most change by far will be found in our New Brunswick case. More than that, for Livingston College racial pluralism turns out to serve as the prime way to gain broad mental skills. In theory and in large part in practice, racial pluralism means nothing less than a fair racial mix of students, faculty, and staff. And top stress on the needs of new student populations, most of whom come from the Other America of poverty. And, most actively educational of all, an unceasing open struggle in the course of joint, shared governance of the college. In a still racist society, a shift of such sweep leads to no end of strain and strife. For urban schools with a changed core, though, racial pluralism stands out as one of the most important, and novel, schemes.

Few colleges these days turn back either miscellaneously schooled adults or young students whose goals and mode of life make them heirs of the counter culture of the sixties. These two groups make up *the new breed of students*. Just now, adult students make up the main source of growth for all of higher education, and one hears much talk of them. Yet the old school ways ask this new breed of students, who share a wish and need to mold their own learning, to stick to set, tight modes. This holds true despite all the fringe shifts of the official reform. When they have a choice, such students now turn their backs on the old school ways and pick metropolitan public colleges that offer self-directed learning, the External Degree, and the like. What makes this new is thus not so much the type of student but that the changed core of learning shows a close relationship to the wants of these students. This can be seen in all the schools that stress broad private skills: Governors State University, College of Public and Community Service, Minnesota Metropolitan, and Empire State.

In the end, we come to a scheme that is spoken of often in the official college reform—*credit for life experience*. Hence to give students credit toward their degree for work they have done before, or for nonacademic experiences other than a job, is not new. All the same, the most innovative urban schools are also the ones that are most active in this realm. They do the most in terms of how much credit they grant, and also in terms of the care and consistency with which they do so. These schools gain the lead, and may keep it, since they are not hobbled by a bond to the core of old school ways as is the official reform. They can make prior experience part and parcel of a curriculum, while the stress on narrow skills rules that out. The same schools sketched above serve as a case in point.

In this type of summation I can give only the high points of the story. For the rest, the reader must go to my larger study. What is new to date in the second mode of learning is both the large shifts and the schemes that now help urban schools meet the needs of students. And they do so not for selected students but for a fair sample of average ones, and not for elite jobs but for all the new professional jobs on the middle level.

III. A GAP IN BROAD SKILLS: SELF RULE

Sooner or later, urban schools with a changed core must turn far more to a third kind of broad skill than they have up to now. That third broad skill lies in the realm of the civic, the communal, the political.

If in the 1950s some people feared creeping socialism, now many people fear creeping fascism. However, they do not talk about it much. Such a stark view seems alarmist, extreme, unsound. It finds little room on the agenda of public discourse, be it lowbrow or highbrow, in the academy or in the mass media. At the same time, many people believe that traditional liberties are losing ground and that we nowhere find new modes of self rule.

Specifically, the swift pace of change in our time, and the vast complexity of organized modern life, leads to a grave clash between the age-old goal of self rule, on the one hand, and the strength and claims of dominant groups on the other. In the face of that clash, our past ways of public life seem feeble indeed. Individuals and local face-to-face groups cope little if at all with the massed strength of super organizations. This holds for private as well as public power, and elected as well as appointed officials. Given the scale of public life, most people in our time feel a sense of powerlessness, of estrangement from both their surroundings and themselves. Hence they lack the faith or the skills that could make self rule work in our day and age.

As long as more and more people see public life this way, the chance is all too real that the United States will turn before long to some "liberal" form of a totalitarian state, such as Friendly Fascism.[6] To stem this tide, new ways must be found to act in the public realm. Most of all, we need to focus not on hierarchic relationships based on domination and subordination, but on cooperative ones based on equality and joint, shared effort. Yet in all parts of our society, be it work or school or home life, we learn just the reverse. In each area hierarchy stands out; cooperative relationships strike people as weak, strange, even utopian.

Public skills raise big problems. For one, civic learning has to do with the distinct role of urban higher education. That role, to repeat, should be to give broad skills of quality to people in big cities who seek a college degree for a middle-level job. That means a much broader sense of mastery of work and life than metropolitan public colleges have given the average urban student until now. In terms of the public realm, such mastery calls for the same kind of faith that elite schools show—that the commonweal and body politic are their oyster; that their students can and will play a key role. For urban students, be their aim professional work or a job in management or teaching in college, a hierarchical structure is apt to reign supreme. The average urban dweller will gain a sense of mastery in college solely if he or she can act in groups that rest on cooperation and equality as against hierarchy and domination by someone else.

In a time and place far from grass-root democracy or community control, such a view may make little sense for the average urban student. Yet without such a view, and hence without a prime stress on civic learning, urban students can hardly gain a sense of mastery in realms other than the public. Life is made of one piece and if, in a key realm like the public, urban higher education does little to make people feel and act like anything but drudges, then how can we hope for more in things mental or private?

This problem points to a still larger one. We live in a time when shifts in the class structure and all that goes with it leave little of the bourgeoisie, the ample middle class of well-off businessmen and self-employed professionals who did so much to shape Western life in the eighteenth and nineteenth centuries. We cannot quite say, of course, that the bourgeoisie is dead or that the social order it wrought is gone. The late capitalism of our own time bears many of the signs of the early capitalism of the classic bourgeoisie. Yet a change marks the social order and the people who run it. Now technical learning is indeed the main tool; much of the time, the people who have such technical learning are prized the most. That is what the meritocracy[7] school of thought and others tell us. At the same time, most people share the view that technicians cannot, on their own, run either a smooth or a free society. People with much broader skills, in my terms, must play a large role.

But how do we bring back to life, and spread to one and all, the truly civic learning that marked the classic burghers of old? That is a huge problem, and the official college reform speaks to that problem no more than does the meritocracy school of thought. What launched the civic learning of the old burghers was the view that all of life was in truth their oyster, and the whole public realm very much their concern. That led to a lifetime of close involvement, in theory as well as practice, in civic discourse, arrangements, decisions. Whether the issue at hand dealt with a tax or schools or the world at large, the university-taught bourgeoisie did not doubt that it had the moral and applied skills, the high culture and the profane, to step in, to take a very active part in running things.[8]

With centralization and fragmentation, and the specialization they bring, few people treat public life in that way. For urban higher education, then, a mastery of public skills means not just to match what elite schools give the elect of our own time, but to go beyond that. With both history and class standing arrayed against them, urban schools face no mean task. We should add, too, the wounds left by the 1960s and by the social and academic strife that swirled in and out of schools at the time. The sheltered higher education of the United States had no taste to deal with such strife. To make part of the learning core anything at all like that *Sturm und Drang* is bound to chill the hearts of most academics.

Tied to all this is the creed of political neutrality. Once an academic institution moves past technical learning of this public realm, learning that is duly detached in tone and space, the risk seems huge that political neutrality must give way to entanglement in the political battles and passions of the day, and hence political interference in academic work. That way, most academics hold, lies utter disaster. In the words of the Carnegie Commission,

"The academic world has fought for centuries to free itself from political domination and to uphold the supremacy of the mind" (Carnegie Commission on Higher Education, *Reform on Campus* [New York: McGraw-Hill, 1972], chap. 4).

On all these counts, the specter of "politization" looms large right now. Modern higher learning is, of course, part and parcel of the dominant modes of power. As such, and quite inevitably, all that colleges and universities do is political through and through. Hence the claim of political neutrality makes sense on just two grounds: that the higher learning in America is not run by the state in a crude or harsh way; and that groups and schools of thought outside the political mainstream will not be found in or near the academic corridors of power. True enough. Beyond those grounds, though, the claim of political neutrality cannot hold. All the same, academics and those in charge go on to claim that higher learning is in truth politically neutral and must dread politization most of all.

In the face of that claim, can urban higher education make public skills part of the core of learning? And can that be done short of any more politization than marks our schools now?

The answer depends on where we draw the line. If specialized learning of a narrow kind remains the sole mode, then the answer must be no. If, on the other hand, learning broader than the old school ways comes to serve as a second mode, then urban schools could well give great emphasis to public skills. Some of the schools I sketch give us ample clues on how urban higher education can add broad public skills to a changed core of learning.

At Governors State University, the initial goal of futurism (adapting all the time to a lot of change) let students play a strong role in how the whole school is run—governance, curriculum, staffing, plant, planning. The more that students take part in academic self rule, the more will hierarchical relationships give way to cooperative ones. At Minnesota Metropolitan State College, students get little or no say in what the school does, but are helped instead to make their own community the place where they learn public skills. The reason for the shift of scene is the view that adult students are not apt to make a school the focus of group action. A more basic reason is that public skills are best gained not in a place one leaves soon, but where one works or lives. Either way, these schools put public skills high on their list of things to learn.

The same is true of our New Brunswick case. Students learn public skills most of all by the shared governance on which racial pluralism stands or falls at Livingston College. Since racial pluralism means in that case a rare mix of black and brown students, staff, and faculty with whites, shared governance leads to no end of dialogue, struggle, and confrontation. Most of the struggle takes place outside the classroom, and students learn from each other that way. But the themes and strains of a key social conflict like racism spill over into the classroom, of course.

In all this, the public skills students learn in college must start and end with praxis, in the large classic sense. Praxis means far more than practice or problem-solving activity. Praxis also stands for existence, the sum of subjective, intrapersonal experience. Finally, praxis has to do with something uniquely human: only human beings can use conscious joint effort to create social arrangements, such as self rule, that suit them best. When we speak of praxis, in short, we mean all the things that go, day by day, to make up a self-determined, consciously shaped way of life. It is that mix of practice, experience, and joint creative effort that a few urban schools already give their students. By means of praxis, and only in this way, do students get a rich dose of public skills, sustained and cohesive; none of the old schools ways match that.

Like private skills, public ones are viewed in academe as beyond the pale, as something that has no place in advanced formal education (but for small bits of community service or field work). Urban schools with a changed core show that this need not be true at all. The higher learning in urban America can gain depth and quality if we make the praxis of broad public skills a key part of the student's fare.

That change seems called for, too, by the great need to find ways of self rule that suit our own times. In the face of that great need, and a trend to Friendly Fascism, it would be the height of folly to make no room in advanced schooling for whole new ways to tackle that side of life, be the new ways in school or a place of work or where people live—or be it a new praxis in the realm of politics as such.

Urban higher education will be unable to play a role of its own as long as there is a gap when it comes to learning cooperative and not hierarchical relations in public life. For as long as that gap lasts, things will be done for people and not by them. People will go on to be mere objects of what takes place and not full-fledged subjects. At base this is why the quiet revolution will be incomplete without broad public skills.

IV. LIBERALS STOP HALFWAY

In the age-old tug of war between human flowering and submissiveness, between equality and repression, the urban schools with a changed core have done quite a bit of late. Yet the shifts that took place do not add up to a full new choice at the core of learning. We can now see that plainly. Rounding out what had been launched, and building it up into a full second mode of learning along with the dominant one, is what the liberal reformers failed to do. In that sense, they stopped halfway.

Specifically, three main shifts failed to take place at the core of urban learning. Only when they do will this quiet revolution come to an end of some kind.

The first shift lacking is the fusion of all the broad skills into the added mode of learning. The second is the capability to serve a wide range of students. The third is the build-up of safeguards for that second mode. In reforming urban colleges, the liberals stopped short of all these shifts.

Fuse All the Broad Skills

Of the most innovative urban schools I sketch, only one shows strength in more than just one of the broad skills. Our Manhattan case does that with its mix of private and mental skills. The other schools show strength either in broad private skills (like Minnesota Metropolitan, Governors State, and the College of Public and Community Service in Boston) or in broad mental skills alone (Monteith and Livingston). And none put full stress on public skills, though some come close to that sphere.

Each broad skill on its own fails to give students a whole choice along with the old school ways. If students are to gain a sense of mastery, they very much need both an active self (not a passive one) and an analytic mind (not a concrete or fact-bound one). And they need the cooperative as against hierarchic relations I just spoke of.

In the 1920s and thirties the educational reform schemes of Dewey and Hutchins seemed to stand far apart from each other. We still tend to draw a line between the self and the mind, things personal and intellectual. Yet the gains of psychoanalysis, on the one hand, and the counter culture, on the other, blur that line, so that more people are now open to the idea that it makes little or no sense.

By and large, the old school ways do stick to a sharp line between private and mental skills (and public ones too), and tie the academic task to mental skills alone. To make a prime goal of personal growth, of a change from passive to active self, is viewed as off limits—as beneath and outside the job of higher education. Some urban schools with a changed core turn their backs on this view, and make much of personal growth as part and parcel of true advanced learning in our time. Yet these same schools have not found a way to fuse private skills with broad and hence non-traditional mental skills of quality. The same goes all the more for public skills.

The Manhattan branch of Empire State College shows that at least two of these skills can be fused. In this case, an urban school brings together key schemes that aid personal growth—most of all self-directed and competency-based learning—with a strong intellectual thrust with the aid of what I call triple tutors: a small staff of tutors who give each tutee individual help on personal growth and nonacademic studies, as well as tailor-made intellectual projects of high quality.

When to this mix we add junior faculty tutors and part-time community plus the city as a whole, the adult tutees and triple tutors one sees in our Manhattan case serve as a most promising model for fusing mental and private skills. And three other innovating schools show that public skills can be fused with the rest if we do not let current fears and foes block the way.

Serve a Wide Range of Students

No urban school should turn to a whole new mode of learning without including a fair sample or cross section of students. Schools with a changed core, in particular, must serve a wide range of students. As can be seen in the case of the oldest and most cerebral of the innovating urban schools I sketch—Monteith College in Detroit—change at the core may quickly lead people to the view that a metropolitan public college chose to single out just one type of student.

Our Detroit case makes clear that the quiet revolution must serve each and every type of student, the academically bright or average as well as those below average. Otherwise, a very real risk exists that a school with a changed core will turn out to be an elite program for just the intellectually (or politically) aroused or academically skilled students, or a remedial program for the least involved—or just the students in between. A choice of one kind of student population leads to a ghetto of one kind or another. No change from narrow skills to broad is apt to last while any such ghetto exists, be it gilded or not.

The Detroit case points to one way to avoid that outcome. Monteith College sets no admissions requirements other than those of its parent institution. More than that, it takes students on the basis of first come first served. Also crucial is the stress on job concerns; without such a stress, many a student fears to change from known, traditional schooling to nontraditional and unknown. No less crucial is the racial pluralism in which our New Brunswick school pioneered.

Above and beyond these specific steps, serving a full range

of students has to do with one big, overall change right now. That change is of course wide access to higher learning in general, and Open Admissions in particular. Up to our own time, the system of higher education as a rule picked as students those who met its own needs and tastes. All others were kept out—or quickly pushed out through the revolving door. Now wide access and, most of all, Open Admissions, or truly free access, brings to metropolitan public colleges a lot of students with weak academic skills.

The few schools that turned in full to Open Admissions, notably the City University of New York, treat it as a new delivery system for the old school ways. In other words, students who lack academic skills must gain these first; then they are put into the same traditional content as all other students. That means they learn their basic skills through remedial, compensatory, or "developmental" programs that stand off on their own, apart from regular students, staff, or college work. And once these students make it through such segregated programs, they must do the regular college work by the old rules of the game, with narrow skills at the core of learning.

Up to now, the most innovative urban schools have done little to make students with weak academic skills part of their changed core, their changed content and student-faculty relations. So far Open Admissions students tend to learn basic skills in the same kind of segregated remedial programs that marks the bulk of urban schools. Not surprisingly, urban schools with a changed core run the same risk of becoming Two Nations, with a body of regular students and one of "deprived" or "underprepared" students. As long as these Two Nations exist, as they do now, the possibility of a core of broad skills is limited.

How to end the Two Nations is now the theme of many an academic study and dispute and experimental program, not least in and around the City University of New York. It seems clear that much of the current trouble goes back to the standardized, rigidly quantified ways of testing basic skills. Change-minded urban faculty point to very different tests and standards. These weigh the skills and gains of Open Admissions students in terms of overall growth of understanding and ease in standard communication and computation. Just as all people learn things at their own pace, so overall growth might take much more time for some students than for others. And while some skills, highly specific and technical, might best be gained in separate courses or tutorials, much of this growth takes place with the full mix of students one finds in regular course work alone.[9]

Yet effective learning is possible only insofar as faculty, students, and all of us share a larger view of what college-level competence means. As long as we equate competence with nothing but narrow basic skills, we are bound to put down otherwise able and promising students who need more time and a new mode to make up for earlier gaps in their schooling. And regular faculty, most of all in innovative urban schools, must be willing and able to tackle gaps in the basic skills of their students as part of their own work with them from day to day. Instead, all too often even antitraditional faculty look down on this task and take it for granted that not they but some separate staff and program will do all of it. Or they let such gaps ride, in the false hope that they help students that way. Both views lead straight to the Two Nations among urban students, and are bound to remain prominent as long as we fail to put first the needs of a wide range of students.

As we change, Open Admissions will have to transcend its limited remedial help. A veteran fighter for this change, Mina Shaughnessy of the City University of New York, holds that the change is on foot already now (1973 essay, expanded in Shaughnessy, *Errors and Expectations, A Guide for the Teacher of Basic Writing* [New York: Oxford University Press, 1977]). The change will bear fruit only if schools serve a fair sample, a cross section, of all urban students.

Build up Safeguards

Born of doubts and struggles on and off campus, the recent shifts at the core of learning meant a high rate of illness if not death for new schemes and programs. In view of the time of troubles we live in, and the novelty of recent change at the core, the high death rate among the most innovative schemes and programs should not cause surprise. Now, however, we can stand back and take stock.

The past few years laid bare some trouble spots, things we can guard against more clearly than did liberal reformers after the urban college boom. They failed in a key task—to build up safeguards. The safeguards will not save shifts at the core of learning from either illness or death. But they can do quite a bit to cut down the death rate among new schemes and programs. If nothing else, they will make us keep in mind the pitfalls of the past few years.

Little of worth has come out on this dark side of change in urban higher education. If we look past urban schools, a report of the Carnegie Commission, *Reform on Campus* (New York: McGraw-Hill, 1972, p. 21) holds that "experimental colleges have had less of an impact than the merits of their own programs might have warranted; so often they have either ceased to operate altogether or have gradually turned toward conformity with standard practice, or have had a narrow appeal outside their own boundaries." In *The Cluster College* (by Jerry G. Gaff et al. [San Francisco: Jossey-Bass, 1970], chap. 5), the senior author tells of how a highly innovative subunit saw the rest of the college as its foe, and how a Manichean split ensued between the Children of Light and the Children of Darkness. This new program found it hard to keep up the initial mood of enthusiasm and optimism; its staff fought more and more on problems of curriculum, too—most of all when new approaches were not working well.

In *Academic Transformation* (New York: McGraw-Hill for Carnegie Commission on Higher Education, 1973, p. 446), David Riesman points to a college that "conducts simultaneously experiments in race relations, curricular structure, and participatory governance—a melange so overwhelming that it will be impossible if there are failures to attribute them to any single source." Riesman calls to mind what I write here of shared governance at Livingston College of Rutgers University, too, when he notes (with little enthusiasm) that at some innovating schools "undergraduates appear to have in effect a second major . . . in political science as they involve themselves in struggles over governance with faculty, administrators, trustees, and each other." All these comments ring true. But if they blame anyone, it is a new program and not the setting, the powers that be—or a lack of safeguards.

To learn from the pitfalls of the last few years means to build up safeguards—and these following safeguards most of all.

CHANGED REWARD SYSTEM FOR FACULTY

A changed core in the urban schools of our time calls for much stress on the faculty's work with students, be it in or out of classroom and on or off campus. The faculty of new ventures must feel safe, too, if now and then it steps on the toes of the less venturesome as it plumbs the depths of the unknown. A new faculty, in short, should feel free to act like Young Turks. Right now such a focus receives little consideration even in most innovating schools when it comes to appointments, promotions, and most of all permanent appointments with tenure. Professionalism in a loose sense ranks first, of course, and then institutional service and accommodation (*read*: no Young Turks, no stepping on toes).

For urban schools with a changed core, the present reward system is nothing less than a calamity. Time and again it makes teachers turn their mind and time away from their students and educational change to the things that will give them a fair share of advancement.

That may not happen right away; in the flush of starting or joining a new venture, most faculty members make light of the effect of the reward system upon them. At some point, though, the faculty of new ventures are apt to cave in one way or the other. They switch their own priorities to fit those of the old reward system. Or, as so many others do, they at least mouth its rhetoric and hustle and bustle, and fear to step on toes. Or they just drop out of teaching, and schools thus lose teachers willing and able to seek some big change in educational ends or means.

As long as new ventures fall under a reward system that makes no sense for their faculty, such ventures are bound to fail. This holds true even if a school provides each and every other safeguard.

STRONG MANDATE

The most innovating urban schools all bear out the great need to start educational change on a sound basis. That is not to say that one can hope—or even should try—to spell out all that is to be tried and done, or to settle only for schemes that seem sure not to fail. Shifts and problems and regressions are apt to mark all such probes of things unknown. To leave no room, or too little of it, for all the ups and downs and the doubts and gray areas of probing the unknown means that a probe is not in fact a probe at all. Any systematic educational change must leave lots of leeway for trial and error, for unanticipated consequences bad as well as good.

At the same time, though, each shift needs a strong mandate from the start, even though a weak one could get by the powers that be more easily. The mandate needs to be broad but candid and concrete, with goals spelled out and priorities ranked. Perhaps the most important factor is that the mandate must be clear to all concerned. A lack of such mutual understanding either hobbles a change altogether or leads to bad blood later on, when the powers that be charge innovators with having gone past their bounds. As things stand now, the most feeble old program lasts just because we have come to take it for granted, while really new schemes all face trouble due to their very novelty. Only a strong mandate can end this anomaly.

CLOSE EVALUATION

By the same token, close and continual evaluation from the start could help not just a school with a changed core itself but its ability, and that of its sponsors, to tell one and all in full just what is going on. All too often new programs lack just such an evaluation, and pay a heavy price for that lack—educationally no less than operationally. In the words of Harold Hodgkinson of the Berkeley Center for Research and Development in Higher Education, "Right now there are almost no experimental colleges in the United States—that is, a college which deliberately keeps data on what it is doing to people and evaluates its program as a result of that data. . . ." And: "There are very few experimental or experimenting colleges that year by year move their programs to a higher level of sophistication or impact on the basis of what they're doing thus far."

No economic venture would last long if it paid as little attention to the research and development of new products as does urban higher education. And none would dream of doing so—or of doing away with a costly new product that is flawed until doing a good deal of work first to get rid of these flaws. Yet little or no R & D, plus quick loss of backing when a new venture runs into trouble, is just the way quite a few sponsors react in higher education.

Little close evaluation can make sense in only one case: when an institution of higher learning finds itself in the midst of so much deep strain and strife that it would rather not know (or tell) what takes place in this or that subunit. In that case, though, the institution builds up no safeguards for change at all. On the contrary, avoiding close evaluation means in effect that a parent institution programs a new venture to fail. This happens all too often.

Ample Time

Finally, a strong mandate and close evaluation point to one more need. Urban schools that change the core of learning gain a lot by an ample time frame. From the start, it should be agreed that a new program can count on an adequate length of time—at least four or five years—in which to carry out its mandate and to evaluate and modify its scheme. A time frame might call for a full-scale official assessment at the halfway point. If such an assessment showed that a probe failed in too many ways to live up to its mandate, then at that point it could be terminated (or

Reform of Urban Colleges

a change imposed from the outside). If an overall assessment showed a good or at least fair correlation between mandate and outcome, then the probe could count on its full time frame (and full funding) with no ifs or buts.

In the years just past, the liberal reforms after the urban college boom showed all too few of these safeguards. In the future, urban higher education can change with less trouble insofar as it learns the lessons of the recent past. These lessons point most of all to the need for a changed reward system for faculty, a strong mandate, close evaluation, and an ample time frame. Such safeguards will help still more if linked to what I stressed at each step: the need to help students combine their job concerns with learning broad skills. Highly innovating urban schools show that the last can be done well by means of double majors (one of the fields of concentration in broad skills and the other in a career program) and of autonomous subunits such as cluster colleges (the subunits stress broad skills while their parent institutions offer a large choice of career programs).

In the end, how much hope does the future hold out for completing the quiet revolution in urban schools? Most important, no doubt, is which way schools in this country move in the years to come. Just as reaction serves to block change, so struggle breeds change. We are apt to see the college scene change a lot when strife and strain grow still more in the schools and in the country as a whole. As people in and out of school wage fights for more change of this or that kind, a second mode of learning will seem less far off or far out.

With or without the growth of a "liberal" form of totalitarianism, or Friendly Fascism, the social order itself might turn to basic educational change to ease strife and strain, and to boost legitimation as well as accumulation. Should that happen, we may see one more case of the American genius for cooptation, for incorporating into the social order things and people who had stood outside and against it.

More generally, for example, those in charge of business and government might, at least for a while, get the underclass and actively disaffected parts of the middle and working classes (the

McGovern coalition of 1972) to join them as junior partners in a vast new Social Industrial Complex. A bigger and better welfare state would then take first place in lieu of the warfare state, our Military Industrial Complex (James O'Connor, *The Fiscal Crisis of the State* [New York: St. Martin's Press, 1973], chap. 9). In that context, the powers that be could do the same with change at the core of urban higher learning. Whatever happens, the struggles that lie ahead will move urban schools to more change, just as the social and economic upheavals of the 1960s led to the official reform at the fringe and half of a quiet revolution at the core.

With all the growing contradictions of our social order, equal opportunity still stands out as the main promise of America. We put equal opportunity first in the old sense of a fair chance—an individual's fair chance, at the start of the race, to move up in the world. Or we put it first in the new and larger sense of a fair share—a fair share, all through life, for each class or race or sex. In either sense, this promise will be a false one as long as urban schools treat the great mass of students in line with what they bring to college. That leads to tracking, pure and simple. For it cuts the choice down to a single path: the high road for those well off economically and in terms of narrowly academic merit, the low road for all the rest.

As we know from grade and high schools, tracking gives a lot of people no fair chance or share when it comes to changing their lives by means of formal schooling. In general, more schooling seems to have a limited effect on reducing inequality: "No manipulation of the educational variables is likely to have more than a moderate effect on either inequality of educational opportunity or inequality of social opportunity" (Raymond Boudon, *Education, Opportunity, and Social Inequality* [New York: Wiley, 1974], chap. 10. A like view will be found in a much discussed work *Inequality* by Christopher Jencks and others [New York: Basic Books, 1972]).

Within these limits, a turn to broad skills does just the reverse of tracking. A sense of mastery of the private, public, and mental sides of life can win for students more of a fair deal, be it as individuals or as members of a class or race or sex.

In its second half as in the first, the quiet revolution means most of all more of the broad skills that a fully developed city dweller, and a free urban people, need in our time and place. Only with more broad skills for middle jobs can the higher learning in urban America claim a role of its own in city life, now the crucible of our promised land. If no such change takes place, then metropolitan public colleges will go on to turn out the conforming plodder and mere fragment of a man, a drudge who lacks the wish or the skills for self-actualization and self rule. A clash of trends marks the higher learning in urban America, as it does the rest of our lives. One way lies something like Friendly Fascism, the other—all the things that still make this a land of promise.

ACKNOWLEDGMENT

My thanks to the eighty-seven faculty members and administrators who in 1973 shared with me thoughts and facts on what self rule meant at the core of urban higher learning (I list them at the start of *Urban Higher Education in the United States*); to students and faculty of the Integrated Studies Program (1970-75) of what is now City University's College of Staten Island, with whom I first tried out this way to self rule; and to the central staff of CUNY who gave me two years of time and aid to do my larger study. And my continuing gratitude, individually, to Scott Anderson, Allen B. Ballard, William M. Birenbaum, Frederick Burkhardt, Vera S. Dunham, Isabella Halsted, Timothy S. Healy, Audrey King, Steven Leberstein, J. Joseph Meng, Geoffrey Q. Ralls, Mina Shaughnessy, John Summerskill, and Harold Taylor. And collectively to Alligerville, where my children, Sara and Mark, and my good neighbors made it a pleasure to write.

NOTES

1. Each of these groups put out a report that tells us the most in one place about its own role and views: Frank Newman et al., *Report on Higher Education* (Washington, D.C.:

Government Printing Office for U. S. Department of Health, Education, and Welfare, 1971); Carnegie Commission on Higher Education, *Priorities for Action* (New York: McGraw-Hill, 1973); Commission on Non-Traditional Study, *Diversity by Design,* edited by Samuel B. Gould (San Francisco: Jossey-Bass, 1973).

2. At the height of the struggles in the sixties, Jerry Farber spoke of such students in a famed piece: *The Student as Nigger* (New York: Pocket Books, 1970), pp. 90-100.
3. Next to the spate of books on shifts at the fringe of learning, all too few books deal with change at the core and with a whole second mode of learning. Some of these books are: Paolo Freire, *Pedagogy of the Oppressed* (New York: Seabury Press, 1970); Judson Jerome, *Culture Out of Anarchy* (New York: Seabury Press, 1970); Eleanor Burke Leacock, *Teaching and Learning in City Schools* (New York: Basic Books, 1969); Arthur Pearl, *The Atrocity of Education* (New York: Dutton, 1972); Michael Rossman, *On Education and Social Change* (New York: Random House, 1972); and two books by Harold Taylor: *Students Without Teachers* (New York: McGraw-Hill, 1969), and *How To Change Colleges* (New York: Holt, Rinehart and Winston, 1972). Yet these books, too, do not single out the few urban colleges that helped to launch a quiet revolution.
4. A leading authority on college finance bears out this view on the strength of detailed calculations on a key innovation: Harold R. Bowen, "Financing the External Degree," Appendix C of *Diversity by Design,* edited by Samuel B. Gould (San Francisco: Jossey-Bass, 1973).
5. Allen B. Ballard speaks of the roots of Open Admissions in *The Education of Black Folk* (New York: Harper & Row, 1973). Stanley Aronowitz shows in *False Promises* how little such a program could mean to those whom it brought to a community college (New York: McGraw-Hill, 1973), chap. 2, sec. 3. Two forthcoming books, by Frieda Silvert and Marlis Krueger and by David Lavin, deal with Open Admissions as well.

6. Bertram M. Gross, *Social Policy*, November-December 1970; Stanley Aronowitz, *Food, Shelter and the American Dream* (New York: Seabury Press 1974), chaps. 4 and 5; Michael E. Brown, "Fascism as a Social Problem," unpublished, 1974 (Department of Sociology, Queens College, City University of New York).
7. The term means no more than the rule of merit, of course. That kind of meritocracy makes much more sense for urban higher education and free people than does the divine, aristocratic, and plutocratic means which let some people get to the top (or stay there) and the rest stay back on unfair grounds. According to the rule of merit, all people should get what they earn, what they show they deserve. In a complex society like ours, such merit must perforce be weighed and then rewarded in far from personal, individualized ways. This, too, makes sense. Yet the current school of thought that puts prime stress on meritocracy does not stop at this point. It fights hard to define merit as that which is achieved through the old school ways, through the credentials that people earn in a single mode of advanced formal learning.

   Those who speak for meritocracy in this limited sense rank among the top social commentators in the country. They include Daniel Patrick Moynihan, Robert Nisbet, Milton Friedman, Talcott Parsons, Irving Kristol, Nathan Glazier, and Edward Banfield.

   Few fight as hard for The Best and The Brightest as does Daniel Bell, a Harvard sociologist. In a closing section of *The Coming of Post-Industrial Society* (New York: Basic Books, 1973), he dwells at some length on the theme of meritocracy. There Bell talks not only in terms of education; he sees a university-based meritocracy as the key to all that lies ahead.
8. Norman Birnbaum makes this point in chapter 9 of *Content and Context,* edited by Carl Kaysen (New York: McGraw-Hill for Carnegie Commission on Higher Education, 1973). So does Juergen Habermas, at length, in *Strukturwandel der Oeffentlichkeit* (Neuwied: Luchterhand, 1968). Birnbaum

goes on to set off liberal education, which he associates with the old bourgeoisie, from the technocratic schooling of our own time.

9. The much debated Coleman Report held, of course, that just such an optimal classroom mix of students in terms of social class did more to help the poor who were educationally weak as well (in the sense of cognitive skills) than anything else that schools could do (James S. Coleman et al., *Equality of Educational Opportunity* [Washington, D.C.: Government Printing Office for Office of Education, 1966]).

FOUR
AGAINST ALL BOSSES

The pieces in the present chapter first appeared in different issues of Against the Grain, *a left New York newspaper for self rule, in 1976-1978.*

The first piece, a general statement on the paper, I wrote together with the rest of the collective that publishes it. On the Skokie controversy (the fifth section of this chapter), I joined eighteen other radicals in signing the first of four letters reprinted here. All other pieces come from my own pen.

I. ANTIAUTHORITARIAN AND ANTICAPITALIST

We are a small group of New Yorkers. Most of us work in various trades, social services, and offices, A few of us study or can't find jobs. We put out this paper as a team, a collective, on our own time and with no paid staff.

Like you, we hate to see our town wrecked these days. Crowded, noisy subways. Boring unhealthy jobs. High rents and prices. Hospitals that don't heal. Schools that don't teach.

In our own city and all through the world, others decide everything for working people: our bosses, politicians, union leaders, the press and TV. We do the work. We raise children and pay taxes. But we control nothing.

Against the Grain backs and reports on actions where groups of working people try to fight for their own rights, in small ways or big. And we care just as much for the individual, for how individuals think and feel from day to day.

SMALL STRUGGLES, small victories matter, a lot. Working people learn and gain from them. But are they enough?

Even if tenants win a rent strike, the landlord still owns the building and gets the profits. Even if the union rank and file kicks out the old guard, chances are the rank and file become the new bureaucrats. Even if trains and buses get better, the fare goes up. Even if the community "wins control" over schools and day care, they still face government-controlled budgets and Con Ed utility bills. Even if we try to raise our children in non-racist, non-sexist, cooperative ways, too often they learn the opposites from TV, schools, movies.

Causes of these problems stare us in the face. To really improve things, we have to reorganize all of society. It's not enough to fight City Hall. Sooner or later, we need to do away with it.

OUR VISION, simply put, is of a future where we working people run our lives ourselves. Where we take over our workplaces and make the decisions about what products we need and how to go about producing them. Where we take over our communities and run our own hospitals, schools, day care centers, utilities. Where our communities and workplaces cooperate, and coordinate what they do, through a web of federations responsible to them.

Our vision is antiauthoritarian and LIBERTARIAN—a community of free people, without bosses of any kind. And our vision is anticapitalist and SOCIALIST—a community of equals, without the rich living off the rest of us.

The struggle for the future goes on right now, every day. *Against the Grain* wants to report all that working people in New York do to take charge of their own lives, without counting on "leaders" to tell them what they can or should do.

We urge OUR READERS to share with us and other readers your agreements and disagreements with our ideas, what you're doing, how we can help. In turn, we need you to help us in any way you can: suggestions, articles, donations, artwork, distributing the paper. Come and work with us—for a better today and tomorrow!

II. NEW YORK: WHOSE CRISIS?

New York's crisis of the past year, the greatest ever, hit working people but not the rich and the powerful. Up to now, though, workers have fought back only sporadically or indirectly. And many don't know just what is going on—and worse yet, what they can do about it.

Least of all do working people know that the city crisis is part and parcel of a world crisis. More than anything else, New York suffers because of a global threat to those who rule the United States.

In the last few years, a clash came to a head. In a nutshell, this clash links New York's crisis to the world as a whole.

On the one hand, our rich spread their hold on the world by a new means, their vast multinational conglomerates. These act as super-corporations on a world scale. On the other hand, the United States lost some of its economic and military empire due to resistance everywhere. Resistance from capitalists in Europe and Japan. From the communist bloc of the Soviet Union. From Vietnam, Angola, Panama, and much of the Third World. This tug between gains and losses, plus troubles at home, plunged American capitalists into a wholly new kind of crisis.

The Rich Come First

Now as never before, the wealth and power of our rich rests no more so at home than they do all through the world. To save their top place in the world, they hope—for the first time in history—to turn their backs on most of the production, and most of the work force, of their own country. What our capitalists plan is to give up the highly paid labor and rundown traditional manufacturing of the United States as their main source of more wealth. Instead, they would keep up profits through cheaper and more specialized labor, plants, resources, and production elsewhere— either abroad or in our own Sun Belt (Florida through Southern California).

Those of us whom this plan leaves behind would have to do with a lot less pay, goods, and services. And we would work a lot more for them. In the city as well as the world crisis, then, our capitalists ask the rest of us to bail them out and not ourselves.

And note this: unless we block the move to downgrade most of the American economy in favor of more profits elsewhere, we would in fact help the rich get richer while we get poorer.

The novelty of this crisis makes one thing clear. As against earlier slumps, this time the switch from "affluence" to scarcity may well be for good. After two centuries of capitalist growth and popular faith, the American Way of Life no longer delivers the Goods. For working people all this means that they face an assault on their standard of living and rights, much more fierce and lasting than ever in our history. This goes for New York most of all.

Why did our rich and powerful single out this city for a special assault?

And why didn't working people fight back more? What holds back all-out resistance so far?

Let's start with the basic facts. New York stands out because it adds up to the largest job market in the country. It serves as the corporate headquarters as well. And it has the largest share of unionized wage and salary earners, and of vocal poor. As a result of this last fact, New York had built up the nation's least inadequate municipal services.

Unemployment: 24 Percent and Rising!

While national unemployment figures stand at 8 percent, New York's are no less than 12 percent. Still worse, the Urban League tells us that such official figures should be doubled to give the real story. This means that one out of four workers here is out of a job. The worst off are those Last Hired, First Fired: teenagers, women, Blacks, Hispanics, and so on. Their unemployment rates exceed that of the work force as a whole by two or three times.

When our rich try to move the rest of us from "affluence" to scarcity, they could ask for no better starting point or scapegoat than the Big Apple. If they beat down working people here, what a lesson for the whole country!

Accordingly, last year saw a $1-billion cut in essential city services. Twenty-five thousand employees lost their jobs then, and more did since. Now, once again, one hears talk of cutting $1 billion more from the municipal budget and more jobs as well.

For each job cut in the public sector, moreover, loss of business leads the private sector to fire one worker too.

Once the world crisis hit most of our big cities, the rich of New York used it well for their own gains. Mayor Beame admitted that the city's crisis was "created by the sudden embargo on the part of the banks." The banks blamed their refusal to lend more funds to the city on its deficit financing and other practices. But even Beame could point out that "the Bond Council, representing the banks, knew all these things."

For years, banks and real estate interests had reaped huge gains from municipal loans and city-aided land speculation. Now with the crisis as an excuse, big business could gain still more. It could squeeze more profits out of the city.

Take, for example, the scare play last fall about New York's default. It was the big banks—think of the Rockefeller clan—who profited most from the subsequent "bail out" by the Federal Government. Not only did they secure their past and new investments in city bonds (paying them off eats up just about one-third of all city taxes). The big banks got back a record interest of 9 percent or more—almost tax free, to boot. Meanwhile, the rest of us pay more and more taxes as our own real income shrinks.

The city crisis leaves no doubt who gets most of our public welfare. It's the rich for sure, and not the poor!

To keep raising this welfare for the rich, public power in the last few months passed from city government to business. Not only in backrooms but up front, officially, bankers and other tycoons now run New York. They do so through the mayor's Municipal Assistance Corporation (Big Mac), the governor's Emergency Financial Control Board, and a deputy mayor for management who serves for $1 a year on leave from a top corporation job.

In light of all this new misery, why don't the city's working people fight back more?

When you ask workers these days, they give different reasons. First, people feel confused. Sure, they know in rough terms what's going on. And they don't like it. But leaders of business, government, and labor flood people with conflicting, misleading messages.

Huge new cuts are announced, then denied, then modified

and wrapped in silence for a while. Finally the cuts go into effect when people have lost their sense of what goes on. Each cut brings new scare stories, numbers games, and cover-ups.

Today many working people look back with envy to the 1960s. In those years a lot of New Yorkers fought long and hard for good causes like civil rights, peace in Vietnam, community control, rent strikes, child care, the old and sick. Circumstances then gradually made fighting citizens out of plain people. Why, workers themselves ask now, hasn't the city crisis brought forth the same kind of involvement yet?

Divide and Rule

Many people tell you, in so many words or indirectly, that they are the victims of Divide and Rule. By means of this method, ruling groups hope to stay on top by pitting one nationality, race, sex, or age group against another. It's worked well in the past, and it rides high again in New York now. Despite all the shock and misery people share in the city crisis, they still forget the old battle cry: "United we stand, divided we fall!"

People speak of their own intimidation, too. Those with jobs knuckle under to tighter work schedules. Instead of organizing, the unemployed hope to get a job if they make no trouble. And though one seldom hears it said out loud, many workers fear that this time around repression will be unprecedentedly harsh once those in charge try to crush popular resistance as Nixon & Co. tried to do.

Finally, when people explain why so few have fought back so far, they point to a lack of leadership. In the past, they say, powerful unions, liberal Democrats, and radical groups helped to make New York special. All of them are still around, yet in this crisis not one of them has done much to help working people.

Needed: New Directions for Struggle

The facts bear out what people say. We see the lack of any new directions or struggles in the public employees union led here by Gotbaum, in Shanker's union of teachers, in large unions in the building and needle trades. We see it in usually vocal liberals like Bella Abzug, Herman Badillo, and Paul O'Dwyer. On the left, we see the lack of big new moves both among social democrats (Michael Harrington's Democratic Socialist Organizing Committee) and among leninists (the Communist Party and a handful of less known "vanguards").

The liberals and our unions still urge us to trust the system and their ability to get a piece of the pie for working people. And the old left still calls on us to fight for that same piece of pie— or to let them lead us to the good life. With the new kind of world and city crisis, though, the old pie may well be gone for good.

To stay on top in the world, American capitalists now need to keep for themselves all they loot at home and abroad. Either working people go along with that and bail out the rich and powerful. Or they fight back to save and extend their hard-won gains of the past. To do that, they cannot put hopes in outside leaders, be they procapitalist or anticapitalist. As workers of all sorts, they can only help themselves, count on themselves, fight for themselves.

III. LESSONS OF CITY UNIVERSITY

The struggles around CUNY (the City University of New York) reached their peak at a great rally June 9, 1976. Seven thousand students and staff of every kind marched on City Hall and circled it for hours.

The rally helped to end a dramatic two-week closing of CUNY. The rally brought out, too, a deep gulf between the demands put forth by the established organizations of students and faculty and those of a rank-and-file coalition that came into being, and moved into the forefront of the struggles, just at that point.

Rank and File Versus Union

On their own, the dormant University Student Senate and the Shanker-affiliated Professional Staff Congress of CUNY asked for no more than the status quo. The picket signs they printed up for the June 9 rally urged the reopening of the university but touched on none of the cuts made so far. The picket signs read: 1. Re-open CUNY, 2. Pay teachers, 3. No mergers.

The just-born Mobilization Committee of activist members of the faculty union pressed much broader demands. Together, the six demands of the Mobilization Committee tell the story of all that CUNY already lost in the past year of global, national, and local squeeze play by Big Business and Big Government. These six demands tell us what working people need to win back as a minimum if the university they pay for is to serve them at least as well as it did since they won open admissions in 1970.

Through the Mobilization Committee, the rank and file called for nothing less than:

1. No tuition at CUNY or State University
2. Restore open admissions
3. No closing, no mergers, no firings at CUNY
4. Full funding for all CUNY schools and programs
5. Full pay for faculty and staff
6. Restore cuts in social services for New Yorkers

These demands rightly stress the essential minimum—adequate funding and equal treatment of different groups and schools that make up CUNY. Beyond the essential minimum lie some lessons that all of us would do well to learn from CUNY.

Workplace Democracy

The killing first of open admissions and then of free tuition, plus the sudden if temporary closing of the whole university, made clear just how little active, meaningful participation the people who work there had in running the place. That lack of workplace democracy stands out as the first lesson of CUNY.

Like other public services that working people pay for, the events showed, the City University runs not like a democracy but like a corporation. A huge bureaucracy and top-down hierarchy along business lines weigh much more than do the voice or needs of students, faculty, and other staff. Appointments, funds, and even basic educational policies flow not from below, from those who learn or teach or work there, but from above, from the powers that be in and out of the university.

Much of the senior teaching faculty view themselves far above CUNY students and other staff. They act like an autonomous and privileged elite and not as working people and fellow employees of a large business-like bureaucracy. In the end, though, elitism helps faculty not at all. For their fate, too, lies with bodies over which they have no say. Any illusion or pretense to the contrary should have gone up in smoke by now.

Community Control

A second lesson flows from the first. If CUNY lacks workplace democracy, it lacks community control as well. It lacks community control both in the formal sense of the 1960s—grass-root elections of governing bodies—and in a broad sense, of ongoing active intervention from below.

This spring CUNY did in the main only what our rich and powerful wished. Events left no doubt that New York City as a community, or the neighborhoods around each campus, played a role only as uninvited guests. The unions, whether the Professional Staff Congress or Gotbaum's District 37 of public employees, worked hand in hand with the powers that be. They turned only little and late for support or action by their own members, by the city's working people. Thus while CUNY like our other public services found themselves crushed from above, neither established unions nor our elected representatives lifted a finger to make anything but an empty phrase of community control.

We see just one exception to this lack of community control. A tough fight saved the bilingual Hostos Community College in the South Bronx. The neighborhood united with students and staff, and with a few local politicians, to wage the fight.

Education Without Bosses

A third and last lesson of CUNY goes to the heart of its mission, to teach working people well.

Before and after its closing in June, the City University gave no sign of trying any mode of learning other than a single choice —either a professionalism aimed at favored students and local elite jobs, or a low-grade vocationalism for most lower income and minority students. Either choice means learning by rote, conformity, authority from on high. Whether CUNY tracks students into middling or lesser jobs, they make it only if they play a narrowly scholastic game, and a bureaucratic game to boot.

Yet alternative modes of schooling can help urban college students a lot. In the early 1970s, half a dozen public colleges outside CUNY showed that a cross section of big-city students gained academically when their curriculum and relations with teachers cut out much of the usual stress on intellectual and administrative goose-stepping. These urban colleges of quality showed that education without bosses helped both students and teachers insofar as it made them into free and equal partners. Yet CUNY pays no heed.

As long as our rich get away with it, they will now keep cutting public services that help working people but not profits. As a "luxury"—a rare door to a better life—the City University of New York gets hit even more than other public services. While that double threat hangs over its head, we can look to CUNY being cut more and more and more. Its time of trouble has just begun.

In this time of trouble, the new Mobilization Committee (now part of the Professional Staff Congress) seeks a broad unity to win full funding and equal treatment for the workers of all sorts, students and staff, who make up CUNY. Beyond that essential goal lie goals we must seek as well, to save a public service from losing touch with everyday felt needs. High among these further goals stand workplace democracy, community control, and relating to each other as equals. That would seem to be the big lessons CUNY taught the spring of 1976.

IV. SECOND THOUGHTS ON MAO'S DEATH

A lot of liberals as well as radicals mourned the death of Mao. They saw him as a great man. Perhaps the greatest man of our time.

I myself mourn much more for China's unique "Cultural Revolution" of the late 1960s. This leads me to call for some second thoughts on Mao's death.

True, Mao launched the very Cultural Revolution that I mourn for. But then he helped to kill off the best of it quite some time before he died.

That, in brief, is what calls for second thoughts.

What we think of as the Cultural Revolution in fact took the form of two very different upheavals. One was an official revolution from above, the other a popular one from below. It's not too much to call both of them unique. Yet Mao's role in the two differed no less than did the two revolutions themselves.

Alone among Communist rulers all through the world, Mao did more than launch an official move toward more self rule from below. Tito went that far in Yugoslavia, too. Yet Mao went much further than did Tito: for a while he let the mass of people seize and keep up that self rule more or less on their own.

What followed for a couple of years, at the end of the sixties, stands out as a great popular, antiauthoritarian upheaval. As such it ranks with the main revolutions from below in all parts of the world. In terms of the West, it ranks with the Paris Commune, Russia in 1917, Spain in 1936, France in 1968.

The first, official part of the Cultural Revolution took place within strict limits: the limits of continuing organizational and doctrinal control from above, most of all by Mao himself.

Within these limits, the official revolution sought a grand shift. It sought to put in first place popular participation and a good deal more equality between classes, between physical and mental work, between town and country.

In marxist terms, China chose not to go the Soviet route. The USSR stressed swift accumulation of capital, at all costs. In China truly socialist relations of production would weigh more than such accumulation.

Or, in terms that we might use now, self-management by workers comes out on top. That kind of decentralized, self-governing socialism would keep a public employer (the state) from trying to squeeze just as much surplus value (profits) out of workers as a private employer does under straight capitalism.

Unlike Stalin, Mao thus held back from forcing and exploiting workers like a capitalist. In turn, this meant no quick economic growth; China's choice ruled out an all-out push for industrial and military might.

In lieu of what Stalin did, "Red" (the Mao brand of socialist politics) was to keep a tight reign over "Expert." Here Experts stood for all the bureaucrats and managers and professionals who make up any state that treats economic gain and military might as its end-all and be-all. With Red politics in command, Experts would at the most play second fiddle.

But then this grand shift from above gave way. It gave way to still more grand shifts from below.

Here and there, all through China, people on the spot took charge of their own lives. They took charge of factories and farms. Of communities and institutions. Even of party and army units.

At this point, in other words, a popular revolution took the place of an official one. And all too soon Mao joined the rest of China's rulers to make short shrift of the later, democratic part of the Cultural Revolution.

In this light, I take the post-Mao drive against the so-called Gang of Four, who with Mao served as the official backers of the Cultural Revolution, to mean LESS than meets the eye. To me, it means no more than the last nail in the coffin of a top-down mix, of the official part of the Cultural Revolution.

With Mao died his attempt to fuse local self rule—truly socialist relations of people—with the Democratic Centralism that Lenin built up in Russia. With Democratic Centralism, a top group pays heed to the rest of us but stays in full charge all the same.

Like Lenin, and like Tito as well, Mao showed little use for those who backed popular, antiofficial struggles and upheavals: the Ultra Left. Like Lenin and Tito, Mao held the Ultra Left to be bad—Petty Bourgeois, Utopian, Adventurist. In no case, to Communist rulers, could the Ultra Left be good—Proletarian, Scientific, Realistic.

In each case, committed socialists and revolutionaries made up the Ultra Left. Yet they saw only full democracy—full equality and self rule from below—as democratic or socialist. In short, the Ultra Left stands for free, libertarian socialism.

Mao no less than Lenin and Tito worked with libertarian socialists only in a pinch. Be they in a Communist party or out of it, each as a rule fought them tooth and nail.

The popular, Ultra Left part of the Cultural Revolution, then, did not die with Mao. We can see that from two documents that reached us from China's Ultra Left. The first document goes back to 1968, the second to 1974.

In the form of excerpts, the first document—"Whither China?"—comes to us from an Ultra Left body set up late in 1968: the Hunan Provincial Proletarian Revolutionary Great Alliance Committee.

In short, by the end of that tumultuous year, this body in Hunan Province took on a leading role both in the practice and the theory of what Mao as well as the Ultra Left at the time called The People's Commune of China. Modeled in so many words on the Paris Commune of 1871, the People's Commune of China changed form a great deal in the course of 1968.

In the words of "Whither China?," that year saw no less than two distinct revolutions. The January Revolution saw the mass of people push aside the rule of entrenched party and government officials. Next month came a counter move, in which Mao took part. He called for a Three-In-One reorganization: the authorities and the army would share power with the grass-root rebels called Ultra Left.

Then came the August Revolution. Now the Three-In-One counter move gave way to a new struggle. This time the mass of people aimed at arming themselves. In this way they neutralized for a while the armed forces, which had gained the most from the Three-In-One counter move.

Thus, the August Revolution struck out against the armed branch of the status quo, just as the January Revolution had done against the civilian branch. This "accomplished the fact of turning the whole nation into soldiers for the first time in socialist countries."

Still, as "Whither China?" says more than once, the year of

1968 brought out people's lack of political experience, too. Old and new ways got mixed up with each other; the confusion of the two made way for self rule slowly and unevenly.

The August Revolution, too, met its defeat at the hands of a status quo backed by Mao as well as by all-out foes of the whole Cultural Revolution. Next month Mao took back his own slogan of Arm the Left. He closed down, too, the Shanghai Commune that led the way in the August Revolution.

The 1968 upheavals of January and August did not end the clash of the official Cultural Revolution with the popular one. "Whither China?" hints at the struggles that marked 1969 and 1970.

These struggles aimed at nothing less than the removal from power of all ruling groups. That's what the document has in mind when it says: "In the new society of the Paris Commune type this class will be overthrown." With self rule as its goal, the 1968 document ends with, "The China of tomorrow will be the world of the 'Commune.'"

The second Ultra Left document comes to us from a group of young Chinese libertarian socialists in exile, called the 70s Front. Many in this group left the mainland not long ago.

In words that ring all too true now, the libertarian socialists of the 70s Front mourned the Cultural Revolution at least two years back. I would like to quote from a 70s Front statement of that time, "Our Position." The statement came out in English in a Hong Kong monthly, *Minus Eight*, issue of June-July 1976.

In terms of second thoughts on Mao's death, the main point of that statement was that "the Great Cultural Revolution, beginning with top-to-bottom pseudo revolution, was transformed into a bottom-to-top genuine revolution."

The mass of people on their own, the statement went on, "organized and took control." And: "They discovered that even without the bureaucrats and supreme directives, their factories could maintain and even increase production." More than that, people "found that their lives were fuller than ever before, the gap between people closed."

As the Chinese libertarian socialists saw it, the Cultural

Revolution brought to the fore a spontaneous mass movement. This movement from below, they held, stood "diametrically opposed to the religious socialism of Mao Tse-tung; the authority of the 'pope' lost its glamor."

In divorcing Mao altogether from the Cultural Revolution in its democratic stage, they clash with the conventional wisdom of both our liberals and radicals. Still, for the antiauthoritarian socialists close to the scene, self rule from below died years before Mao died.

"The fear-stricken bureaucrats shed their masks, revealing their ferocious features . . ." Once more, the bureaucrats "mobilized the state apparatus to lord it over the people." And "then the military fired its guns." In this way, an Ultra Left "revolutionary generation became a generation ground underfoot."

A couple of years back, too, members of the 70s Front wrote prophetically, as if they had in mind what takes place right now. Their words shed light both on the Gang of Four and on the cowed mass of their compatriots: "Over 20 years of authoritarian control had forged an authoritarian character in a great majority of the people."

Hence, they stressed, "even within the ranks of the Ultra Left, not a few of the anti-bureaucrat fighters still subconsciously fashioned themselves after their rulers."

Here the libertarian socialists from China come back to a key point for all of us.

In no part of the world, we need to keep in sight, can people run their own lives till they (we) by and by wipe out the age-old gulf between the ruled and those who rule them. No wonder that China's grass-root revolutionaries lost ground by 1970. True to their own land and our whole age, they too could not shed the main traits of those who had ruled them.

This point brings us right back to second thoughts on Mao's death.

In our lives, and our minds, human history still grows much too much out the deeds of a few great men. We feel this way whether they be men who lead and rule, or men who touch and mold our souls, or both. With a lot of help from those on top, we still tend to see life and change in terms of patriarchs, of male authority figures.

As long as we think and act that way, though, how can we ever come to run our own lives? How can we possibly fuse a faith in authority figures with self rule? For how long, and how well, can we mix a deep trust in what great men do for and to us with the equality and liberty and community that people build by and by on their own?

On second thought, then, let us mourn less for one more great man. Let us mourn for a great democratic revolution. Let us learn from its highs and its lows. And let us stand in awe and love, not of a great man but of a whole people who for a couple of years fought so hard to take charge of all they do.

As the free socialist exiles from China put it, "The revolution died. Long live the revolution!"

V. SKOKIE: FOR NAZI RIGHTS

Right of Nazis to Demonstrate

Members of the Nazi Party wish to hold public demonstrations on the streets of Skokie, Illinois. The American Civil Liberties Union, in adherence with the First Amendment, has been supporting their right to hold these demonstrations. As a result of the ACLU's position a substantial number of people have decided to resign from the organization.

We feel compassion for, and solidarity with, those who experienced the Holocaust and whose relatives and friends were its victims. Nevertheless, we believe the opposition to the ACLU stand on this issue plainly reflects the increasing tendency of many people to advocate authoritarian interference with expressions of ideas and attitudes they consider evil. As radicals and libertarians it is our duty to combat the growing spread of mind-control ideology.

We hold the view that in our society pervasive manipulation of feeling and experience renders one's degree of freedom highly circumscribed. Nonetheless we wish to preserve whatever measure of freedom still exists and foster the ideal of liberty as essential to our vision of the new society. We therefore join the American Civil Liberties Union in its support of the Nazi Party's right to hold public demonstrations.

(Signed) Gwenda Blair, Mark Blumberg, Bruce Brown, George Fischer, Lancelot Fletcher, Dick Goldensohn, Mimi Hart, Marilyn Kaggen, Elliot Linzer, Staughton Lynd, David McReynolds, Margaret Mercer, Louise Rader, Igal Roodenko, Robert Roth, Arnold Sacher, Peter Sanders, Jo Tavener, Pete Wilson

Why I Signed "Pro-Nazi" Letter

In its last issue, *Against the Grain* ran an open letter by nineteen left people. The letter backed the currently disputed right of American Nazis to demonstrate in Skokie, a heavily Jewish suburb of Chicago.

As the one member of the *Against the Grain* collective to add my name to that "pro-Nazi" letter, I would like to say just a few words here on why I did so.

Most of all, I feel strongly that freedom means little if we don't treat it as indivisible, absolute, sacred. I don't see how you can slice up the freedom to write, speak, march. And to see and hear. How can freedom grow if you (or the state) give or deny basic human rights in bits and pieces?

Also, the open letter rightly speaks of "the increasing tendency of many people to advocate authoritarian interference with expression of ideas and attitudes they consider evil." As in the Skokie case, alas, this charge fits quite a few anarchists and socialists, too.

Lastly, if a whole way of life makes people ripe for fascism—be it brown, red, or red white and blue—just shutting up fascists seems to me like shutting the barn door after the horse got out. So I doubt that keeping Nazis from marching would have saved my fellow Jews from the Holocaust. And it won't, I fear, save us from 1984.

Much less negatively, people can use the freedom we do have to move on from state to community. From an inhuman "representative" monster to a web of free associations in neighborhood as well as workplace, of consumers as well as producers. To save us from 1984 or one more Holocaust, that kind of change might well make all the difference.

(Signed) George Fischer
New York City

A Postscript

Here is a postscript, involving Leo Tolstoy, to my letter in the last *Against the Grain*. There I said why I signed the Open Letter by left people backing the currently disputed right of American Nazis to demonstrate in Skokie, a heavily Jewish suburb of Chicago.

In my letter, I stressed that all too many people on the left now seem willing and able, in the words of the Open Letter, "to advocate authoritarian interference with expression of ideas and attitudes they consider evil." Yet such people draw a sharp line between repressiveness like their own and repressiveness that comes from their foes.

Like me, it seems, the great Russian writer saw little difference between repression from the left and the right.

According to Theodore Roszak (*The Making of a Counter Culture* [New York: Doubleday, 1969], p. 296), Tolstoy made this comment on the issue:

". . . when asked if he did not see a difference between reactionary repression and revolutionary repression, [Tolstoy] replied that there was, of course, a difference: 'the difference between cat shit and dog shit.' "

(Signed) George Fischer
New York City

Fascism of the Left?

Yes, as my friend Stew Albert charged in last issue's letter page, I do equate repression from the left (Our repression) to repression from the right (Their repression). No, contrary to what he charged, I do not look to the state to defend the Nazis and thus make it possible for them to march in a place like Skokie, the Jewish suburb of Chicago that touched off a debate.

As I said at the end of the first of my two letters on the debate (*Against the Grain,* December 1977-January 1978), to me the way out lies with moving altogether from state to community, from our representative democracy to direct or participatory democracy. Such a grand change would not stop conflicts or dilemmas. Yet it would presumably cut down a lot the possibility and inclination of people to solve them by means of repression or the harassment of one group (like the Jews) by another (like the Nazis) that Stew rightly dwells on.

Right now my quarrel, and I think that of the other people on the libertarian left who signed the Open Letter backing the right of Nazis to march in Skokie (*Against the Grain,* October-November 1977), is not on the state intervening but on something else altogether. The quarrel has to do with all too many people on the left being willing to deny basic human rights to their foes.

That way lies authoritarianism. And quite conceivably a fascism of the left, as we see it in Russia and quite a few communist countries and leninist parties and sects. That was the main issue raised.

I agree with Stew Albert that we face a very specific problem, and have yet to deal with it well. I'd like to make just three brief points on that.

First, I don't think the trouble here lies with being, as Stew puts it, "much too abstract and mystifying." True, we might abstract badly: we might single out wrong aspects of a broader picture. Or we might generalize about it in a wrong way. But surely that's no reason to put down trying to analyze and generalize.

By the same token, to debate how liberty or freedom or basic human rights apply to Skokie need not mystify the Skokie problem at all. For the debate as a whole did NOT treat liberty as absolute and sacred—as something other than human-made and hence always changeable and to be questioned. My own stand did treat liberty as absolute and a given. If that mystifies our specific current problem, I plead guilty.

But Stew did not address my stand on that. Instead, he seemed to use "abstract" and "mystified" to put down all of this debate on liberty versus repression.

On the Skokie scene itself, secondly, I had hoped to see lots and lots of people go into the streets to meet the Nazis face on and show them in this way—not from the top down but from the ground up—how others feel about them and their harassment. And I planned to be there myself. That's the way, and not repression either by the state or by foes, that we might best fight any such foes.

My last specific point has to do with trouble I myself have with the Skokie debate. As to many others, to me the main repression now comes not from the far right but from our System itself. It comes not from a small fringe but from a Friendly Fascism—an authoritarianism with a long leash—that we find more and more at the core of our whole way of life. Those on top and in charge threaten the basic human rights people did win through the years much more than do the fifty Nazis who wished to march through Skokie and harass my fellow Jews there for their own gain.

This last point, though, brings us right back to the kind of broad issue that Stew Albert calls too abstract and mystified. How we fight any foes makes all the difference. If the ends or means—that's one and the same—point to new repression in place of the old, then I don't think it's worth fighting for. Even if it has not done so well enough, the Skokie debate spoke to just that issue. To that I say Right On, Amen.

(Signed) George Fischer
New York City

VI. NEIGHBORHOOD POPULISM

On a snowy and sleety Friday-the-Thirteenth weekend in January, up to two hundred people met for two days in Newark.

Neighborhood activists came. People tied into the neighborhood movement, a currently growing network. People from the

City and Connecticut and Boston. And from Jersey and Philadelphia and Washington.

They spoke of all sorts of themes and fights of the day. And they did so in a way I had heard and read of: a new mix, a new hybrid. On that Friday the Thirteenth, I met the new hybrid for the first time face to face.

We spent the two days in and out of People's Center, the heart of a community development project in the West Ward of Newark's inner city. The project, now ten years old, covers just twelve blocks. Called Tri-City Citizens Union for Progress, the project was launched by clergy and civil rights activists in the wake of the Newark riots. It grew to a large "show place" of a neighborhood trying by itself to revive a rundown area.

With forty paid employees, and activities in buildings spread throughout the area, Tri-City's programs come close to what the neighborhood movement seems to emphasize right now. These programs run a wide gamut:

* Rehabilitation of hundreds of housing units, most of them in abandoned buildings
* Conversion of rehabilitated units into a housing cooperative for local residents, most of them with low incomes
* Housing maintenance program
* Neighborhood employment and training
* Bicultural child care program
* Women and children's preventive health program
* Neighborhood aid and information center
* Youth activities
* Energy conservation
* Technical assistance to smaller community-based programs
* Coalition-building and advocacy to put neighborhoods on the public agenda

The Tri-City group added this last item only in the last couple of years, according to the group's director, Rebecca Andrade. Only then, she told the conference, was the neighborhood movement big enough to give coalition-building among such local groups a chance.

A new organization in Washington, the National Association of Neighborhoods (NAN), encouraged Tri-City to start moving toward alliances with others like them. The project in West Newark then joined NAN. In turn, NAN served as the main sponsor of the Newark meeting.

Along with Andrade, the Executive Director of NAN, Milton Kotler, set the tone for the meeting.

Back in 1969, Kotler put out a book that was a clarion call for this whole movement of the midseventies: *Neighborhood Government*, with a telling subtitle: *The Local Foundations of Political Life* (a Bobbs Merrill paperback). Kotler also served as the founder and guiding spirit of the National Association of Neighborhoods.

Coming out of the struggles of the sixties, Andrade, a local black, and Kotler, a white professional, now speak in terms of self-determination and self-development. The same double theme came from a typical symbol of the third part of this new neighborhood movement, the white working class "ethnics." Father Joseph Kakalek, the first head of NAN's board, now serves as president of the Philadelphia Council of Neighborhood Organizations.

In a workshop on neighborhood governance, New Yorkers heard with envy of the autonomy Congress granted of late to the District of Columbia. For the change included a referendum-backed provision for an elected Advisory Neighborhood Commission.

Continuing local organizing plus court litigation, commission member Charles Richardson said, force Washington officials and politicians to pay ever more heed to the body. The Advisory Neighborhood Commission stands in direct contrast to New York's appointive new community boards whose huge and gerrymandered districts bear little if at all on how people who live in them see their own neighborhoods. The Commission does this through regular meetings and hearings, through mandated review of official plans related to a neighborhood, and through district boundary lines drawn to fit actual neighborhoods closely.

Legislation, though billed as the focus for the Newark meeting, took a second seat to other goals, broad as well as specific. True, legislation often came up as one of the key means. And NAN's Kotler, in an opening address, urged peace between neighborhoods and government in place of confrontation. That sort of confrontation, he said, both sides had by now mastered well, in the spirit of Chicago's organizer Alinsky and Mayor Daley.

Among top goals, none stood out more than housing. That came out at the end, for instance, in two hours of brainstorming by a dozen people from the city.

New Yorkers who took part differed widely. From several Brooklynites active in the National Congress of Neighborhood Women, including its president, Laura Polla Scanlon, to Ruth Messinger, an Upper Westside militant just elected to the City Council. And from Gerald Taylor, director of Neighbors of Greenpoint and Williamsburg, to Michael Bobker of the People's Development Corporation in the South Bronx.

Veterans of battles with real estate, the media, politicians, and bureaucrats, these New York activists spoke with much knowledge and anger of all the ways the powers that be keep housing from working people in the city.

How landlords and bureaucracies eat up, or tie up, large funds that might spell some hope and renewal for neighborhoods now starved for just such help. How local people could and in bits already do take community development into their own hands. How big shifts in official rules and laws may help working people stay where they live if their neighborhoods revive and attract the well off.

Up to a point, all I saw at the Newark meeting fit what I thought to find. Beyond that point, it didn't a bit.

I saw the often-mentioned new mix of race and class. Black and Hispanic activists, whites (mainly Catholics) in traditional working-class jobs and of recent immigrant stock, white and black professionals: well-off activists, lawyers and other advocates for the less well off, likeminded experts in and out of government.

I saw the expected mix of goals from the sixties and seventies. Then process: community control. People's active participation in running their own lives and neighborhoods. Now product: self-reliance based on decentralization. Local economic development and social services. Alternate, small-scale technology.

Ideologically, in terms of world view, the Newark get-together bore out a new populism.

This new populism starts and ends with the local base, with localism. With people's own neighborhoods. And, though not brought out at this meeting, with their workplaces as well. As in the old populism, to be sure, the people as a whole oppose a minority of entrenched interests. But now, at the core, stands self rule from the ground up.

New to me, next to a quiet, down to earth faith and warmth, was the main view on tactics. What means do neighborhoods use from day to day now to reach their goals?

Here, one part of the new mix still puts stress on organizing people to confront their foes on key goals. The other tactic tries to win more and more acceptance and interaction with politicians and government agencies whose funds and help neighborhoods need. Hence Kotler's call for peace between neighborhood groups and the government.

NAN's leader meant peace, I fear, with the likes of Lindsay, Beame, and Koch. The likes of "Life is unfair" Carter, HEW secretary Califano, HUD secretary Harris. Of New York's main scourges in Congress, the liberal senators Proxmire and Brooke. Of our own bipartisan liberal team in the Senate, a Javits wed to Wall Street and a Moynihan who does a lot more for the Pentagon than all he claims to do for plain people in the city.

With such a call for peace, it makes sense that I heard no one speak of more basic trouble and change in the face of the rot that marks so much of our system and daily life. Nor did I hear anyone wonder out loud how those now on top may absorb ("co-opt") the new populism—how they might make self-determination and self-development one more commodity they market for their own gain. Just as, eight or ten years back, they absorbed and marketed the community base of the War on Poverty . . .

In short, what I saw, faults and all, looks like an honest to goodness movement of working people.

In Newark I saw a movement bringing together diverse neighborhoods and needs. A movement alive and growing. With real gains in slow, bad times. And yet with some hopes and ways, too, that raise doubts in one's mind.

Most of all, it seems fair to ask one question in this, as in each case. When the rest of us deal with the folks on top, how long can we hold our peace and still change what we feel needs change?

ACKNOWLEDGMENT

My thanks to the rest of the *Against the Grain* collective, a team of equals who taught me a lot of the ups and downs of self rule: Colette Amoda, Ezra Birnbaum, Tom Boshell, E. Buonatesta, Richard Giordano, Mary Howe, G. Merovich, and Renee Shanker. And my thanks, too, to Roy Herrera and Carol Lopate, who shared this and other encounters.

FIVE
SELF RULE OR 1984

Two prospects mark our form of life—late capitalism. One is 1984, the most total rule by a state that seems to us possible. The other prospect, the "spectre" both Bakunin and Marx saw in their time, is communism. But now this second prospect takes the shape not of en route struggles between labor and capital, but of the end goal of communism: modern people themselves producing conscious community.

I. THE IDEA OF SELF RULE

That possibility stands for a community consciously chosen, consciously self-governing, consciously free. A modern community that forms the active core of a complex and varied world. A new form of life in which people produce and reproduce not only a freely chosen community but a culture and means of subsistence that make that form of life plausible in the first place.

This second prospect, a grand finale to many a grand dream, means free individuals running their own lives through free associations. The prospect means direct, participatory democracy in place of indirect, representative democracy. It means not a *better* state, but statelessness: a worldwide web of small and big coordinating bodies run by face-to-face communities from the ground up—as against our helter skelter of huge states, ever more repressive at home and expansionary abroad, that run our lives and globe from the top down.

Presented as a paper at the annual meetings of American Sociological Association, New York, September 1, 1976. Published for the first time in this book, in considerably revised and expanded form.

Self Rule or 1984

In broad terms, self rule stands for this prospect we face next to 1984.

Right now, the prospect of 1984 strikes most people as far more possible and immediate than that of self rule. All trends seem to point to less self rule, and not to more of it. Here I want to make a case for the opposite, for self rule as a real possibility in our own time and place.

This is not to say that I see 1984 as less plausible. Quite the reverse. Just because most of us now view the prospect of self rule as much more unlikely than that of 1984, I move the prime contender to the side here and push the underdog to the fore. Not empirically but analytically, I hope to make sense of how the underdog might come out on top.

On this analytic plane,[1] just how to ground the possibility or prospect of self rule seems to me far from clear at this point in time: much more needs to be thought through, spelled out, debated back and forth. For now, I would like to argue for our prospect of self rule in terms of the changed historical specifics of late capitalism as against the high capitalism of a century back.

I start by assuming two main opposing tendencies within capitalism. The rest of this chapter brings out these opposing tendencies: *social separation from above* versus *social unity from below*.

In our time, *separation from above* means here fragmentation throughout people's lives in the form of hierarchy, institutionalized domination, structured inequality, endless divisions of labor. Conversely, *unity from below* means both sporadic and varied struggles in all spheres with things as they are, and a mode just as crucial: the whole range of much less intentional or explicit bonds and interactions by which people integrate their daily lives in spite of that separation from above.

Three Conceptions

Under late capitalism, we might think of unity from below as vertical and not in the main as horizontal. That conception puts in doubt two notions widespread in our time. One notion views integration among most people as more or less passive; this notion would seldom let us see those who are ruled cross the line that sets them off from those who rule them. The other notion sees a clash between top and bottom in terms of two unified wholes.

In a word, I assume here all kinds of social forces struggling from the ground up, against no less diverse forces pressing from the top down.

By contrast, the other conceptions of our form of life treat it quite differently.

Mainstream sociology speaks of Order. It grounds this conception in taking the status quo for granted. It then celebrates the system's seeming ability to keep up a twofold separation of most people, in the sense of vertical domination as well as horizontal fragmentation.

That ability of the few to manipulate the many from the top down, in short, mainstream sociology treats as Order.

A third and last conception, of Critique, comes from Dialectical neo-marxists (as against orthodox Scientific marxists). Here the stress falls on one kind of separation only: capital and labor split and clash along a horizontal axis, top versus bottom.

Hence the conception presupposes that within these two wholes most people are not in fact separated. It sees each side unified in itself (unconsciously) even if not for itself (consciously). That means a struggle takes place between two separated unities. This struggle is seen to produce, through change and strife, the end of separation.

To do sociology as Critique, then, means to lay bare internally the dialectical process—the mutual interaction of opposing tendencies—by which people produce the separation between capital and labor in the first place, and by which it will end as well.

To sum up, these conceptions can be seen in two quite different ways. One is in terms of form of struggle, the other as ways of knowing.

Each conception, for one, sees struggle in its own way. If Order stands for no struggle at all, and Critique for struggle between two unities, Self Rule presupposes a myriad of disparate struggles between groups at the bottom and at the top.

Secondly, each conception does the same in terms of ways of knowing:

1. Mainstream sociology views our form of life from the top down, and the rest of us the way the people on top do.
2. Critical sociology views our form of life from a midpoint; it dwells on the separation and struggles between top and bottom.
3. My own conception, that of self rule, looks at our form of life from the ground up. Here the focus lies on vertical change and struggle: top-down separation versus unity against those on top.

Only this last conception might let us see the possibility of self rule in our own time and place.[2]

II. MARX PLUS BAKUNIN: RIGHT GRASP, WRONG WAY

... I am your disciple and proud to be one.
—BAKUNIN TO MARX, 1868

All I know is that I am not a Marxist.
—MARX, 1882

The idea of community self rule as an heir to capitalism comes to us most of all from two witnesses of its high noon. I have in mind Karl Marx (1818-1883) as well as Michael Bakunin (1814-1876): Marx put stress on the idea of self rule by conscious community just as much as did Bakunin.

Marx of course looked for struggle against separation and not just within it. He too looked for a transcendence of capitalism and not just critique. In turn, critique assumed—as does self rule —that in producing and reproducing their whole existence people will create not just new ways of meeting material needs but a new kind of person and a whole new culture.

At the high point of capitalism, though, Marx saw conscious community as no more than a far off goal. And he felt sure no one—neither he himself nor his "utopian" fellow prophets of revolution—could tell much of a form of life yet to come. No one, he held, grasps the sociological and historical grounds for a form of life till it takes full shape, till Becoming yields to Being.

Hence Marx said little of self rule. Like Bakunin and other anarchists, though, he took self rule for granted as what full communism would be like—and as the next, postcapitalist stage of history.

The Unfinished Symphony

Nor did Marx show just how capitalism would produce its own gravedigger and heir. How would it turn alienated labor into a proletariat eager and able to end capitalism and build conscious community? That transformation plays no great part in his internal and retrospective analysis of capital. This holds for all of his main critiques of political economy, all of the many drafts and fragments that make up the Unfinished Symphony of this work.

The transformation of alienated labor into conscious proletariat stands as a given, as a *deus ex machina,* a magical device, that Marx felt sure capitalism would produce. His faith flowed from the same dynamic that helped him conceptualize the process of capitalism—the process by which people in the capitalist form of life produced the separation between labor and capital in the first place.

Everywhere Marx looked, he saw the same. He saw the same rationality and yet fetishism of commodities. The same idealization of progress and freedom while people were being turned into things. The same free labor and yet crass inequality. The same booms and slumps. Time and again he stressed capitalism's unique, revolutionary need to grow and build and change. And a need to draw people into the social order and school them formally. All this, he thought, would step by step produce a conscious proletariat out of animalized, separated labor. And do so not just in the realm of material production, but in circulation, distribution, consumption as well, and in culture (or consciousness) as well as in material life (or political economy).

Today, in the light of late capitalism, Marx's deep faith in this transformation no longer makes sense.

Most of the steps that Marx assumed would make up the transformation turned out to do just the reverse. They did so by making labor that much more part of a capitalist form of life. We can see that with the spread first of labor's economic struggles and organizations and then of political ones. The same goes for the spread of science and technology, of schooling and better living.

As late capitalism reproduces itself with ever fuller absorption and domination of labor, the shifts serve to deepen social alienation, passivity, conformity. And people's ubiquitous divisions in terms of income, skills, race, and sex. And, up to a point, the legitimacy of the established order.

How did Marx fail in this prophecy of capitalism's transforming alienated labor into a conscious proletariat when his critique of capitalism as a whole form of life still stands up so well? In dribs and drabs, his great foe Bakunin gave us some clues.

Critique of Critique

Most importantly, Bakunin saw that capitalism meant a vast growth of state authority on top of all the dynamism and contradictions and miseries that Marx laid bare. Though lacking Marx's theoretical force, Bakunin still saw much better than did Marx that conscious community could not flow out of more hierarchy, more and more authority from above.

Secondly, Bakunin was one of the first to see science as a foe no less than a friend of social unity, of conscious community. If Marx as the last great figure of the Enlightenment put much of his faith in the healing power of science, Bakunin drew a sharp line between science as a new authority, or a superstition, and science as the means to Reason, to a rational life. Up to a point, Bakunin treated as problematic the same men and means of science that Marx took so much for granted. And Bakunin termed formal schooling just as much capital as Marx did commodities.

Tied to Bakunin's dread of authority from above was his struggle against organizational and doctrinal authority among those who fought the status quo. While Bakunin preached against authority, to be sure, he like Marx turned out (once his works came to light posthumously) to practice authoritarianism in his own revolutionary politics. All the same, his fierce pleas give us a clue how the grand labor unions and parties that capitalism spawned by the turn of the century moved labor as much away from as toward conscious community. For in each of these groups, authority from above and the divisions of labor presupposed in such outside authority loom as large as they do in capitalism as a whole.

As one more clue, Bakunin did not share Marx's faith that progress lay with the economically and organizationally most advanced part of labor. As Marx charged more than once, Bakunin saw much hope in working people at the fringe of capitalism— *Lumpenproletariat* (or, in our terms, underclass), peasants, déclassé (or underemployed) intellectuals, and university students. As I will spell out later, some such spread from purely a manual or industrial proletariat to a wide range of working people makes a good deal of sense in our own time. Not only for the Third World but for the West.

Finally, Bakunin warned against the unstated, mystified role Marx gave to revolutionary intellectuals—to bring to life a conscious proletariat and then lead it. It is true that most of the time Marx stressed that the working class should (and would) free itself. At the same time, though, he put much stress on theoretical consciousness. This the proletariat would draw from revolutionary intellectuals or from self-educated, intellectualized workers. And Marx made clear that faith in a conscious proletariat grew as much out of the key role of revolutionary intellectuals as it did out of labor.

In sum, Bakunin hinted how Marx failed to see what late capitalism subsequently produced as a form of life. As Bakunin hinted, late capitalism presupposes multiple authority, or more than any one decisive hierarchy: big government and big science, big labor no less than big business. It coopts labor much more fully, culturally as well as economically, then did high capitalism. And the revolutions of our century bear out Bakunin's sense that some intellectuals on the one hand and, on the other, class elements outside a narrowly defined proletariat of manual factory workers act much more as its foes than Marx would have granted.

Thus Bakunin left us some shrewd clues on how Marx's view of the proletariat, as the agent of grand social change, might not hold up. For the rest, though, Bakunin could speak in good faith when he told Marx he was a marxist. He shared more than Marx's critique of political economy. He shared with Marx two traits alien to my own conception of self rule: elitism and millenarianism.

Millenarian Elitism

We just saw that in their practice both Marx and Bakunin did not leave it up to working people to free themselves. On the contrary, both had such a struggle led by a vanguard of revolutionary intellectuals, people more schooled and committed to grand change then were run-of-the-mill people. And even in their theorizing we can glimpse how these grand proponents of community self rule side here in part not with social unity from below, but with separation from above.

For Bakunin no less than Marx, revolution called for a sharp division of labor between a counter-elite of revolutionary intellectuals and the rest of us. Such division of labor meant, of course, just the kind of social alienation that Marx showed in capitalism. And it meant elitism, which makes no sense in terms of community.

Millenarianism flows from elitism. In fact, we can speak of a millenarian elitism.

In our age of science, of secular Rationality, Marx and Bakunin would not use a word of the church like millennium. Both felt sure, though, that through a great social change history would unfold a Rational society (communism) in place of the non-Rational society we know (capitalism).

To seek a great change means to put your faith in people, groups, and struggles that go far beyond the ordinary. Average people and events do not lead to a millennium, to a nirvana of Rationality. That does call for the elect, for quite special guides—an elite. Just such millenarianism will be found in the way that the ardently Scientific Marx no less than the unabashedly Romantic Bakunin saw humanity getting from capitalism to conscious community. But if an elite of revolutionary intellectuals rules out equality for plain mortals, so does a millenarian view of social change.

Here a present-day conception of self rule parts ways with Marx and Bakunin. The new conception does owe to Marx the critique of capitalism. Through his reading of capitalism Marx showed social unity and separation to be opposing tendencies of our age. To Bakunin, our conception owes a critique of Marx. In dribs and drabs, that critique helps to set off late from high capitalism. And all of us owe them, of course, the first clear glimpse of self rule as a possibility, a conceivable alternative to capitailsm.[3]

Neither Marx nor Bakunin, then, can a new conception of self rule take for granted—or slight.

In general, I think we need to draw on marxism and anarchism and at the same time move beyond both. At their best, I credit the first with a still unmatched critique of our own form of life and the second with linking well the ends and means of self rule. But neither marxism nor anarchism does both. And each fails to make room for the kind of changed needs and struggles that I take up in the rest of this chapter and in the next one.

III. BEYOND SCARCITY, BEYOND INDUSTRIALISM

The specter Bakunin as well as Marx stressed flowed from their own time: the swift growth and spread of high capitalism of the brand new realm of industrialized production of more and more profitable goods by the many and their private ownership by a few.

Postindustrial Society

It makes good sense to equate this high point of capitalism with industrialism. By that we mean a society focused on the mechanized mass production of goods. Late capitalism, on the other hand, one finds equated more and more with a postindustrial kind of society—a society no longer giving its main concerns and priorities to the "mere" growth of material production.

True, people define the much used term "postindustrial" quite differently right now. Here are a few key examples:

1. Postindustrialism might mean just the end of a state of mind, the end of people's preoccupation with material production. Production, private ownership, and the status quo go on just the same. But the emphasis now shifts from material growth to the growth of knowledge and from social strife to guidance by experts.

2. We must make our peace with scarcity; we must treat as given bigness and inequality as well as state capitalism or state socialism. Within the established social order, we can seek to stop material growth or industrialism altogether. Thus defined, as no growth or stable state, postindustrialism could save both our natural environment and our human prospect.

3. We can treat not the whole of humanity but just the established social order—a highly centralized monopoly capitalism, where all but a few owners and executives have next to no say in shaping their lives—as the cause of ubiquitous social and ecological harm under industrialism. To bring humanity and nature into harmony, in this last definition, capitalism gives way to autonomous and humanized ways such as "eco-communities" and "tools for conviviality." In turn, this would make it possible to end personal and social repression. Born of age-old material scarcity and of costly gigantic technologies, these now lead us to view social control from above as unavoidable.[4]

Of these highly distinct definitions of "postindustrial," only the last one fits the case made here for self rule in our own time. For the last definition alone provides for both an end to the established social order and its replacement by self rule. For self rule to have a chance in our time, we must end in full our focus on industrialism.

Step by step, currently growing localized modes of social organization and technology make such a historic change plausible and intelligible for us. And they make an end to industrialism not a luddite or romantic return to a lost past, but a possibility of modern, complex integration of a host of face-to-face communities on a regional and world scale.

An End to Scarcity?

But the change from high to late capitalism does not stop with a drop in the role of industry. A second new term now speaks of "post-scarcity."

In all of civilization—of our more populous and more hierarchical forms of life that, in my conception, precede conscious community—scarcity held reign. Most recently the struggle for survival seemed a given of capitalism at its height, the competitive capitalism of the past century that Marx and Bakunin grasped and fought. With late capitalism, by the middle of our own century, the age-old fact and dread of a life of scarcity in meeting basic needs starts to give way to a possibility of ending it, a unique first glimpse of a life without dire scarcity.

This first glimpse doesn't mean we've actually seen a world without poverty, without the fear of starvation and suffering. They are all around us. But we rightly sense that the resources do exist now to guarantee survival for everyone, if only we used them for that purpose in place of war, waste, and extremes of consumerism. In the United States, both the heady "affluence" of the 1950s and the sixties' stormy rise in expectations had much to do with just such a first large sight of what a possible alternative, a life beyond dire scarcity, might be like.

Here, we must be clear, both scarcity and a possible end to it flow not only from organization and technical gains, but from historically specific definitions of reality. In this sense, to glimpse a possible end to scarcity means in part to conceive for the first time an end to late capitalism's ubiquitous, obsessive flood of ever new and ever more commodities. To consume this flood of goods, we must continually be persuaded that we still don't have enough to survive. The result, of course, is a dread of eternal, irremediable scarcity. I come back to this "need" to consume in the third section of chapter six.

This glimpse of a possible end to scarcity, in turn, makes for whole new grounds for seeing self rule as a real possibility for our own time and place.

Where age-old scarcity made a push for growth and gains through centralization and bigness the grounds of our form of life, a possible end to scarcity shifts the grounds to quite a changed plane. As never before, we can now treat as plausible, as intelligible, a form of life in which constant growth of production and domination gives way to the opposite: a slowed pace and smaller scale of life. Such a scale, I stress again near the end of this chapter, in truth makes for self rule. Only then could free individuals find it not only desirable but possible to run their own lives through face-to-face communities.

Together, these ongoing shifts beyond industrialism and scarcity add up to no less great a change in the prospect of self rule. Where in the midnineteenth century the possibility for self rule took in the main the form of either reformism within the status quo or the millenarian elitism of revolutionaries like Marx and Bakunin, now new grounds for self rule loom large. These grounds take us back—and forward—to the end goal of the 1848 Manifesto: community as the core of a new form of life.

IV. FROM NATURAL TO CONSCIOUS COMMUNITY: BEYOND CIVILIZATION, TOO?

If self rule as I conceive of it leaves little or no room at the core for either scarcity or industrialism, then what does community call for? What makes for conscious community, the social form of self rule conceivable in our own time and place?

Here people tend to answer with either all-out optimism or all-out pessimism.

The full optimist sees our complex society, our civilization as a whole, give way to a no less complex society but minus the current rot and loss of faith or hope. The full pessimist feels sure our ways took root much too well for anything but more of the same, or at best bits of change.

As I pose our choice—self rule or 1984—neither all-out pessimism nor all-out optimism makes sense.

Willy nilly, we must probe, weigh, and choose all those parts of the here and now that don't mix at all with self rule and community. These we must set off from those parts that do mix well with self rule and community. And set off, too, from parts of civilization that, in a changed setting, at least need not keep us wed to the here and now—or 1984.

Perhaps the three main critics of our age—Rousseau, Marx, and Freud—can be read to deal with this task by means of a line drawn between community and civilization.[5] Each in his own way, they see the community of old yielding to civilization. Rousseau harked back to that old community. Freud tried hard to make his peace with civilization. And we saw that, with Bakunin, Marx stands out as the prophet of a new community that would take the place of the civilization we know, just as surely as that civilization took the place of a past community.

Short of the millenarian elitism that steered Marx and Bakunin to wrong ways to self rule, how does a threefold scheme—of old community, civilization, new community[6]—help us sort out what we need to shed beyond scarcity and a preoccupaion with modern material growth?

Here a few definitions seem in place. With some help from critical anthropology, this is how I see the three parts of the scheme I want to use.[7]

An old or *natural community* stands for a small, face-to-face group of people who in times gone by lived more or less on their own and by set ways they treated from birth as their own and hence as a given.

A new or *conscious community* means a small, face-to-face group of people who, now or in years to come, choose of their own free will to make and run in common a life of their own; they do so in a complex and dynamic world they deal with in a host of ways.

By contrast, *civilization* stands for a mass of people who gain in goods, mobility, and individuality at the cost of a life based first and last on face-to-face ties—and on ways people took on at birth from a little changed past (natural community) or choose on their own (conscious community).

In the light of all this, how much of our civilization is apt to mix—or fail to mix—with a world of self rule, of conscious community?

No Patriarchy, State, Empire, or Capitalism

At least by and by, as I see it, patriarchy and capitalism and our huge state must go if self rule is to have a chance. Plus all forms of empire, of external or internal rule by one people over another.

This list is not a random one, I should stress. From points Marx made and Engels filled out in the 1884 classic, *Origin of the Family, Private Property, and the State*, to leading "Freudo-Marxists" like Wilhelm Reich and Herbert Marcuse—as well as a new group of dialectical feminists—the close ties between patriarchy, capitalism, and statism seem clear. And Frantz Fanon, as a young psychiatrist and black revolutionary, laid bare the link of empire to each of these three cornerstones of civilization.[8]

As I read (and share) this point of view, the more or less autarchic natural communities placed on their members just a light load, a loose net, of governing mechanisms and sexual inhibitions. Such open, far from centralized forms of rule and sex met the old community's small needs and wants in terms of either goods or war. It is only as wealth and the making of war grew by leaps and bounds that loose ways of rule and sex gave way to what we call civilization: repressive, coercive rule by a few on top.

With civilization, in short, a state took the place of community. In turn, this state interacted with and enforced three other hierarchies of civilization: privately owned wealth that in the end turned into capitalism, an ever more fragmented and psychically repressive nuclear family, and no end of war and colonial conquest.

None of these hierarchies of civilization would mix wtih modern self rule, with a conscious community. For all of them tend to sap the desire and skill people need to run their own lives in a world as complex and intertwined as ours. That holds true in terms of the psychic twists and waste imposed by civilization on the individual. It holds true as well in terms of the resigned submission to authority from the top down that the state and capitalism and empire breed most of the time in most of us.

No wonder all-out pessimists have such a field day in our times!

Yet I share the view that civilization brought us more than just evil, and that in a better soil its best fruit can help us reap a rich harvest. More than that, for a modern kind of self rule we need to draw not just on the best fruit of civilization, but on those that fall between the best and the wost.

Mixed Blessings

Among the mixed blessings that a new life of self rule will have to make its peace with is one world; for better or worse, people now crowd this globe cheek to jowl. And we may see still more crowding in times to come. Plus all the strain and drain of a closeknit planet, most of it still far from affluent.

Just as Yugoslavia in the last generation tackled face on its national strife and uneven development in the midst of a Balkan tinderbox, we would need to do the same on a world scale to make a new self rule both conceivable and worth it.[9]

Likewise, we need to make our peace with a grand science and technology. Right now, both the systematic search for knowledge and its application to daily needs add up to a Frankenstein's monster. They serve far more the needs of those on top than the rest of us. That holds true when it comes to either meeting daily needs or being the sacred cow that the few in charge push to make a case for centralization, bureaucracy, inequality, and all the rest. To put it another way, those few serve up science and technology as both the end and the means for an intentionally wasteful capitalism, ever more bloated governments, imperial loot, and the channeling of private life and pleasure.

Needless to say, science and technology need not be a Frankenstein's monster. Nor need they be as huge and costly as now, made so by our whole bent for giantism and by the vastness of the "civilized" hierarchies that turn science and technology into their pawns.

A mixed blessing, too, comes to us from two big chunks of

civilization: mass-produced goods and regional or global cultures.

A positive aspect of mass-produced goods consists of the presumed ability of each conscious community to rely upon other communities to produce some of the goods it needs. In other words, the conception of self rule in no way supposes autarchy or complete self-sufficiency. On the negative side, as we see it here and now, artificially created needs drive us to consume whatever is made available. But where communities are free to make decisions about what to produce and what to consume, the availability of mass-produced goods from outside would be less a threat than an option.

When we turn to global or regional cultures as a mixed blessing, the positive aspect here once more is the wide range of choices a self-ruling community gains from being integrated into a larger universe. The negative side has to do with who makes the choices. Choice by anyone but this or that face-to-face group —no matter how wise or noble a choice—would bring us right back to the elitist vanguard that Marx and Bakunin leaned to. Once more, Yugoslavia's partial try at self rule shows us how people on the spot can feel free to make their own choice, be it good or bad.[10]

A Better Home for Individuality

Compared to that mixed blessing, I find the next one a lot more subtle and hard to deal with. I have in mind the whole realm of individuality, of the theory and practice of personal autonomy, of the rights of privacy, idiosyncracy, dissent.

As we now know it, individuality bloomed and came into its own only with civilization. True, natural community made for a great deal of individual distinctiveness and leeway. Anthropologists have found that to be much more so than a negative view of primitive life would lead one to think. And yet, all the same, the rich and at times wild kinds of personal autonomy civilization brought forth and let bloom show no counterpart in what we know of natural community.

What makes our kind of individuality a mixed blessing is not this rich choice of ways of life we at least talk of. For me, a wide range of personal autonomy is very much part of how I conceive of modern self rule, of conscious community.

Something else makes individuality a mixed blessing. For that, Herbert Marcuse used two apt terms: repressive tolerance and repressive desublimation.[11]

The powers that be use dribs and drabs of tolerating dissent as well as individuality as one more way to hold back people from changing life as a whole. And the same holds in the realm of sex: these days you can let go of more and more erotic inhibitions and prohibitions, you can take your pick of all sorts of sex, as long as you don't give trouble to those in charge. On both planes, Marcuse was right to claim, we find repression gains in this way.

Yet that is not the end of the tale, as Marcuse at times seems to feel. For he himself saw and said at other times that neither tolerating individuality nor desublimating the urge for sexual play and joy stops just where the few on top want them to. Here I see a close analogy to science and technology.

In each case, civilization has wrought both a grand gain and a Frankenstein's monster, a tool for its worst side. This link need not last for all time, any more for individuality than for science and technology. To write off these hard-won gains makes no sense.

Where does all this leave civilization if we view it as a bridge from the old natural community to a new conscious one? As the title of this section asks, does self rule need to move civilization from core to fringe just as I claimed it does both scarcity and industrialism?

Here I give a far more mixed answer. To wit:

1. The side of civilization that means its worst hierarchies, linked to one another but each autonomous from the rest—sexual repression, huge states, capitalism, colonies at home and abroad—would make the idea of self rule unintelligible.

2. The side of civilization that means global or regional cultures and mass-produced goods requires that self rule use the best of both. A world with conscious communities at its core cannot rule out by fiat any of their mixed blessings; it *will* aid people to try out more local, more autonomous and authentic options.

3. The side of civilization that means a crowded and inter-

Self Rule or 1984

acting single planet also gives us no choice but to make the best of it. A global scale of life lies as far as can be from small, face-to-face communities. But since few have tried, in practice or even in theory, to delve into ways to self rule in one world like ours, pessimism makes no more sense than optimism.

4. Lastly, the side of civilization that shows its grand gains—individuality and science and technology—makes our task conceivable as well as clear. We need to find a new home for these grand gains, a home in self rule as against civilization at its worst. As I say in the rest of this chapter and in the next, right now a host of groups and moves aim at just this change.

In sum, we need not leave civilization behind for self rule. On the contrary, parts of it can serve us as a model just as can parts of the primary, "primitive" life of old.

What we need to add in the short run to primitive and civilized to make self rule conceivable is not clear yet. Near the end of this book, I note that in the long run, too, we can never count on full clarity: the very possibility of self rule rests on our leaving the choice to each time and each place, to each generation and each community.

V. ORIGINAL ACCUMULATION OF COMMUNITY

How will the shifts I singled out take place? How will a core of humanity move away from scarcity, industrialism, and the worst parts of civilization?

Here Marx, our great theorist of revolution, gives us two opposing modes of posing and answering the question.

Original Accumulation versus Agents of Change

When he wrote of the birth of capitalism, the rise of the bourgeoisie, Marx looked for the dynamic of the initial accumulation of social, cultural, and material ties before the new form of life took full shape. Marx shows that dynamic of accumulation well in his longest and best developed statement on how he views history—a notable fragment in *Grundrisse*.[12]

At other times, when he turned from capitalism to communism, he no longer spoke of a long march, of the slow process of original accumulation. Instead, he stressed the flash point of a classic revolution, a swift political coup to take state power in hand. Here the industrial factory workers he put on a pedestal turned into "agents of change": the warlike vanguard, battalions, and armies of a political coup.[13]

In terms of my conception of self rule, on the other hand, revolution means a range of much slower shifts that in time makes self rule as the core of a new form of life much more intelligible and conceivable than it is in the world we live in now. Hence we need to shift our gaze to a wide range of people, and how they produce and reproduce their lives from day to day. Only there can we find the agents of change or, in the more suitable mode of Marx, the dynamic of original accumulation of community.[14]

In this juxtaposition between original accumulation as a whole and agents of swift political change, I see only 1984 gaining if we treat revolution as mainly a shift in political power. That would hold true whether 1984 came wrapped in the revolutionary colors of communist red or anarchist black, or in patriotic colors like our own red, white, and blue.

To see basic change as original accumulation fits well here a changed historical setting.

In high or competitive capitalism, alienated labor stood out. Now, with late or monopoly capitalism, we turn to alienated life as a whole, to how the social order separates most things people do from what they could or want to do.

The very spread of domination to every nook and cranny of people's lives likewise moves opposing historic tendencies and social struggles far beyond the classic realm of work, of the core clash between capital and labor in the one realm of industrial production. Hence we must not look just to the working class of manual factory workers, as did Marx, or to Bakunin's people at the fringe of that same early industrialism—nonindustrial laborers and petty proprietors. Many more spheres of life, and many more kinds of working people, now come into play when we try to conceive of basic, overall change of our form of life.

At this point, I can spell out in brief my grounds for treating self rule as a possibility in our time and place. As my grounds, I offer nothing less than a chain of grand shifts. The coming of these shifts is problematic, of course. So is the coming itself of self rule, at this point the underdog as against the prime contender, 1984. But the historic trends I cite may make the shifts I speak of no more improbable than either our status quo or 1984.

The grand shifts, sketched in this chapter, run all the way from the spread of a post-scarcity, postindustrial focus of life to the decline—in the end a withering away—of a patriarchal nuclear family, of a false democracy run by the few who control wealth-producing capital, and of a huge state enforcing imperial as well as economic and sexual domination. Not least, I ground my conception of self rule in a process of accumulation similar to that which Marx laid bare for capital.

No more than capital will conscious community spring forth full blown, like Venus on a shell. On the contrary, the path is a long one: through millennia of natural community, through many centuries more of civilization, and then to conscious community.

For conscious community, original accumulation gains shape and speed with late capitalism. Just what the accumulation adds up to people will know when that form of life does take full shape. For now, we can do no more than infer from a conception of the end goal how a prior accumulation of new means may make sense in this case.

The Fringe of a Form of Life

In the *Grundrisse* fragment on original accumulation, Marx notes more than once how "primitive" capitalists—artisans, merchants, money changers—lay at the fringe of precapitalist society. Their own new ties and ways took shape at the fringe of earlier forms of life and not at the core. Nor were they always held in high regard—for they opposed many of the old, feudal ways. Their emergent new mode of production and form of life thus did not, in a strong sense, flow from the bowels of the old.

As I see it, that aspect of original accumulation plays a key role in our own time as well.

Class elements at the fringe of late capitalism, it should be clear, show no sign that they will lead or even staff either big industry or big government as we now know it. The same goes for seizing and holding on to the commanding heights of contemporary society by means of swift political revolution or coup. If we look to them to do so, as Marx looked to the proletariat, then class elements at the fringe of late capitalism fail the test.

So, to be sure, did the proletariat Marx looked to—if you do not count a counter-elite of revolutionary intellectuals, as Bakunin was among the first to note. Only these claimants to power could conceivably run a contemporary society, for the bulk of the industrial workers could not.

Once this side of original accumulation comes to be clear, its stress on class elements on the fringe of late capitalism should make more sense. For conscious community does not presuppose the skill or will to lead or staff all of contemporary society. Just the reverse. It presupposes class elements that could and would turn their backs on the status quo. In its place, they would fit in well with a quite different form of life.

What does it mean, in this view, to look for how people in late capitalism produce the original accumulation of community? It means to look for a process by which people in this form of life not only reproduce the status quo (and the conception of Order) but also create new, strong foes of it (with a new conception like Self Rule).

Just as Marx gave no end of praise to high capitalism, we need to do the same for late capitalism. Next to the loose-knit, spotty starts of Marx's Europe, what we see today is all the more impressive in its worldwide growth, might, drive, sweep, loot—and contradictions. In both gains and troubles monopoly state capital goes far to round out the trends launched by competitive capital. First and last, the clash between its productive genius and the profit motive grows day in and day out. Each day, capitalism hobbles still more the great potentials it sets free itself.

Between Scarcity and a Possible End to It

For most of human history people neither met nor could meet their main felt needs. That still held true for high capitalism.

Self Rule or 1984

In our own day and for the first time ever, as I have stressed, living without dire scarcity came up as a possibility. Spurred on by late capitalism, human creativity and productivity made that possibility real. Yet the same form of life blocked a full shift from scarcity to affluence. For even more than overpopulation and a ravaged environment, late capitalism's own contradictions (not least its need for ever more consumption of ever new commodities) lead it to push to the brink of affluence and then pull back to scarcity.

The U.S. slump of the 1970s makes that all too clear.

In our slump we see fierce cuts in jobs, human services, and all of the public sector. At the same time, the monopoly sector tries to make up abroad for its troubles there and at home. It does so through multinational conglomerates, the sale of arms, and runaway industries in satellite and neocolonial dependencies. In this way, worldwide looting does not slow down, while production and marketing at home become still more monopolized and hence costly. Rather, the loot flows more to the rich and less to the rest of us. And adequate subsistence fades as a hope while scarcity sets the tone once more.

The contradiction between dire scarcity and the possibility of ending it, then, marks late capitalism. New in human history, this clash in turn acts as presupposition. It acts as presupposition for the process by which this form of life makes the original accumulation of community "possible, sensible, conceivable" in the first place.[15]

Let me now ask more specifically: just how does the clash between dire scarcity and the possibility of ending it act as presupposition, or as warrant, for self rule?

True to the dynamic of a historical dialectic, our form of life breeds not just strength. It breeds its own troubles as well. Quite a few trends lend strength to relative affluence and cast doubt on the need for scarcity. In the sight of such a possible change, who can tell us that we need to cling to scarcity?

As the rich get more rich, the poor still more poor, it comes to be hard to treat blocked growth as a given. As the hope of adequate subsistence leads the world to fight a streamlined colonialism all the more, people in imperial America doubt for the first time their bloated felt needs for things, for possessions and conveniences. As science and technology point to smallness no less than bigness in how to make things best, monopoly and bureaucracy make less sense than they did in times of swift growth through just bigness. As more and more people learn of the world at large, of how to run what and who now runs it, antiestablishment feeling spreads in the form of grass-root populism and hate of war.

Socialization and routinization and legitimization—what the sociologists of Order dwell on—all of these notions of the status quo don't make any better sense of it than their opposites. These opposites the sociologists of Order put down as deviance or anomie or alienation or downward mobility by individuals. Yet these opposites tell us of hosts of working people who now live and act at the fringe of ever more mechanized, dehumanized ways of producing and reproducing capital. In other words, if the status quo manipulates and absorbs many of us much of the time, some of the time at least as many people may now make a life that late capitalism will find hard either to manipulate or to absorb.

A Shift of Balance

Here the balance between scarcity and a possible end to it shifts. As our form of life sets free more human potentials, more working people of all sorts make ties not with the status quo but outside of it. That of course lends strength to the pull of a newly intelligible choice in place of scarcity. This strength flows not just to social alienation but at the same time to its main alternative now, social unity and self rule.

Still more specifically, we see the gains and sweep of late capitalism make not just for the shades of 1984, the ultimate we can imagine of separation between those in charge and the rest of us, but for the very reverse of 1984. The whole fabric of social organization shifts as a new choice seems to rise up next to scarcity.

A work ethic, core of the industrial sociology of scarcity, gives way to low productivity, malingering, a host of strife. Unless they use 1984 to do so, big business or big labor or big government may not be able to stop this trend.

Still more striking is a strong shift from the politics of public life to the politics of private life. Electoral struggles and reform of government touch people far less these days than do all the troubles on the home front. Most of all, the family of old fails to change in step with the times; new ways to make and keep close ties are starting to take shape now. For more and more people, the face-to-face personal struggles in this realm crowd out the impersonal mass politics of the public realm.

In the same vein, the industrial sociology of scarcity fails to account for the mass of college graduates who now flow into routine jobs in large private and public organizations—engineers and computer technicians, teachers and social workers, and of late nurses and police officers. For them, as for youth in shops, work turns out to be false promises. The same goes for school and college. At each step, the old dream of individual upward mobility brings less to them. Hence it speaks to them less.

The hold on people by big business, big government, big labor, big science, and big police still runs deep. Yet it now lives side by side with an opposite trend. Few of us fail to see a drop in work ethic, in traditional politics and home life, in faith in the state and the American Dream.

None of this adds up to a struggle for social unity and against social separation. We need to note this—and to stress it. At least that lack of clear, intelligible struggle holds true in the old terms, of grand social change and millenarian goals. Even in those terms, though, the new clash between scarcity and a possible end to it shows necessary if not sufficient grounds. Without all the shifts just sketched, no struggle at all would make sense in our time. In any terms, most of the struggle lies ahead. But now our form of life, late capitalism, produces the grounds for this particular struggle.

Class Elements at the Fringe

In that light, how might class elements now at the fringe of late capitalism serve as the original accumulation, or as presupposition, for conscious community?

Here the answer is far from clear. But if we look at class elements with the fewest ties to our present form of life, at least some of them make sense as potential builders of conscious community.

In the United States, for one, a large underclass of unemployed and underemployed shows weak ties to the economy, culture, and polity of late capitalism. At the same time, this underclass by means of ghetto riots, Third World struggles, and bonds to community control went of late beyond the anomie and alienation that sociologists of Order stress.

The same holds for the large new class element of déclassé, or underemployed, college graduates tracked into routine jobs in large private and public organizations. Whether they get or seek or hold on to such jobs, these new workers with college degrees show no more ties to our form of life than does the underclass. These new workers may not take part in antiestablishment struggles. Yet they and their juniors in college and high school tend to share a counterculture a good deal closer to Self Rule than to Order.

We find the same counterculture, and the same weak ties to our form of life, in quite a few young factory workers. These working youth open doors—swinging doors, to be sure, that can open both toward conscious community and toward all the more consumerism and passivity. They do so through their weak faith in a work ethic and the American Dream of individual upward mobility. The same swinging doors open with their shift from mass culture to their own popular culture and personal politics, and the closeness of these to the counterculture of rock, drugs, open sex, and antiestablishment feeling.

To these large class elements at the fringe of late capitalism we should add newly aroused groups that lie between the fringe and the core of our form of life. I have in mind all those well off economically or educationally, but now tied to organized or endemic struggles for sexual equality, for a revolution in sex roles. Those drawn into struggles against racism, war, police state, prison, pollution, and urban rot fit in here as well.

In all, these class elements add up to quite a dynamic potential for accumulation of conscious community. So do all sorts of working people (manual and mental labor, old working class and new) whose main ties to our form of life now fit less and less the bourgeois-proletarian clash of old. Of course, it remains to be seen if and how each of them joins a struggle between social unity and separation. For now, we need to look at one more question: what process, what ongoing theory and practice, might make sense as presupposition or warrant for conscious community?

Here, too, one can be sure only in retrospect. But conscious community rules out some ways and points to others.

In short, it rules out—at the core of a new form of life—modes of centralization, bureaucracy, monopoly, and bigness that shape late capitalism. The ban is simple and clear. At the core, no rule will do other than self rule in the sense spelled out here. No other way lets groups of people consciously run their own lives.

No change bodes well if it takes a set group of leaders to make it. For self rule, the one good elite is no elite.

That holds for "in" elites and "out" elites, for saints and sinners, for children of light and children of darkness, for efficiency-minded technocrats and humanitarians who stress people's goodness and fulfillment. It holds whether it takes place under state capitalism or state socialism, with or without private control over means of production, with or without constitutional liberties. It holds for revolution and reform, for each and every kind of social democrat and communist, for counter-elites that work within the status quo and others who claim to be our vanguard.

A short step takes us from this ban to the process of original accumulation. First and last, the emancipation of working people must in truth lie in their own hands. So must their whole lives. Coordination, administration, leadership, authority—with self rule all these start and end within human-sized groups.

Human scale means here a group not too large to manage all its own affairs jointly. Internally, all jobs rotate. Externally, groups tie in with each other through a web of voluntary and loose federations along territorial and functional lines. With these means, self rule makes sense at the core of even a most complex kind of society and world.

In terms of what we now live with, this presupposition calls for no end of change. Bigness rules our form of life. Self rule calls for the reverse. Human scale means nothing if it does not give primacy to smallness. Here and there, to be sure, people may choose to settle for bigness. But with conscious community that would be a carefully limited exception and at no time the rule.

Human scale and no bosses stand out, then, in what the original accumulation of community presupposes in our time. Just what does that mean, here and now?

Neither the anticapitalist conception of Critique nor the procapitalist conception of Order pays heed to this question. But of late some new theory and practice does. Informed by an anticapitalist conception of Self Rule, this set of little-known answers shows quite a few gaps and weak spots. Still, we can now say more on possible specifics than most of us realize.[16]

Key Realms of Original Accumulation

Self rule leads me to speak of the possible specifics in terms of three key realms of original accumulation: workplace democracy, neighborhood power, and personal liberation.

The place of work still ranks first in the social order. That is where the main power of late capitalism lies. That is the main place where it keeps up an industrial sociology of scarcity, where it makes people do things from day to day with little or no say. And that is where most people earn their bread and serve the rest of us.

Right now, trade unions play a key role in the original accumulation of workplace democracy. At one and the same time they both aid workplace democracy and hold it back no end.

Big labor, in the form of a huge union structure, now eagerly accepts a binding trade-off with big business and big government. In return for a contract, dues check-off, and a stabilized businesslike existence, unions vouch for the very opposite of workplace democracy. They pledge no strikes and no militancy during the life of a contract. They vouch for a quiet, disciplined work force.

They promise no rank and file participation in settling grievances.

If by all this unions hold back workplace democracy, their very existence makes it possible as well just because workers of all sorts fight big labor a great deal. Each rank and file insurgency, each unauthorized work stoppage or slowdown, each wildcat strike serves as an all-important school for workplace democracy. It shows plain people how to cut bosses down to size in their place of work. Each struggle of this kind breeds a bit of social unity from below. Each cuts down a bit the separation from above in which unions play a full part in late capitalism.

In the workplace, too, original accumulation deals with the problem of technology, of the tools and ways with which we get things done.

In our form of life a mammoth technology—ever more mechanization and hence dehumanization of work—helps a few people rule the rest of us. Huge machines make for undemocratic, closed-door decisions by bosses—leaders, officials, executives, and experts. Through this, and the vast costs involved, they convince many people they can't run their own lives and communities. In short, a big technology makes people small—and feel small.

The last five or ten years saw the start of a change. Next to big technology, new foes of it launched a search for a small, human-sized technology. A range of studies and movements now show how a small technology can feed, house, and keep us as well or even better. Workplace democracy gains a lot when people search and fight for whatever best takes the place of a technology that helps to keep all of us down.[17]

At the core of the workplace lies the politics of it, the control and management by whoever runs it. The industrial sociology of scarcity treats it as natural that a few people run things. Self rule makes that conception of Order problematic.

Here accumulation takes the form of workers' control or self-management. To control means to supervise or check what others —the bosses—do. In terms of conscious community, self-management means a great deal more; it means to initiate and run a wide range of steps on your own. Here and there, one now finds examples of both workers' control and self-management. But late capitalism is slow to yield where its main strength lies. And while most people feel sure they can get their own work done best on their own, they doubt so far if a whole firm or public agency could run with no boss.

If people earn their bread and do things for the rest of us where they work, in their neighborhoods they live and play and learn as well as work. To control your own neighborhood means to have a strong say in all this. In our form of life, most people have no such say in running the institutions that serve a neighborhood the most: schools, hospitals, social services, courts, police, not to speak of "public" utilities or any other businesses.

In the United States, the struggles of the 1960s taught people a great deal about neighborhood power, about its possibilities and limits. Most of all, those struggles let some people move from the formal democracy of faraway legislatures, parties, and elections to democracy on a human scale. By this I mean control of institutions right where people live.

A strong urge for local power lives on in all sorts of neighborhoods. The urge runs all the way from Third World ghettos and upper suburbia to suburbs as well as near ghettos where some white workers cling to ethnic ties. While people doubt workplace democracy a lot, fewer doubt neighborhood power—the possibility of a neighborhood's self-determination and self-development.[18]

Neither workplace democracy nor neighborhood power stands a chance on its own. Most of all, neither stands a chance as long as people act as masters or servants in their face-to-face relations. Personal liberation, a third and last specific for accumulation of community, comes in here.

In ways subtle and not so subtle, our form of life breeds master-servant relations in our most intimate ties and our most sacred ideals. Next to some freedoms and human potentials, late capitalism breeds inequality and domination. It makes us treat as a given, as part of nature or Order, that we boss and get bossed all the time.

Men learn to dominate women, people with lighter skins to oppress people with darker skins. Educational "haves" learn to exploit educational "have nots," the skilled, the unskilled. Adults learn to control children, middle-aged people, the old. Heterosexuals learn to put down homosexuals, and straight people, the dissenters and freaks. And so it goes . . .

In the 1960s, personal liberation moved to the fore. It gave birth to a host of struggles for much more equality and autonomy in face-to-face relations. Even when defused and watered down, these struggles came to be part of our culture. Now, too, they touch a lot more people than most of us think.

Of these struggles, feminism—the struggle for equality between women and men—may well touch people the most. It goes to the root of key human ties, all the way from work and power to love and sex, from property and laws to child-rearing and homemaking. It brings to the fore problems and possibilities that shake people up. It hints at great shifts—shifts from Possessive Individualism to untried and much more fluid and open ties. Most of all, feminism puts in doubt the family, the main bond in society as we know it.

By this chain of breaks with the past, plus a stress on equality, a revolution in sex roles adds a lot of strength to self rule.

Less large or central is another ongoing search for personal liberation, another child of the sixties. I speak of communes. A whole movement now seeks to build and keep up all sorts of joint, group arrangements for living, for working, for child-rearing, for serving people or nature or gods. The movement made a splash in the public eye at first, but now works at the fringe and in the shade. For people who live at the fringe, though, it gives a space to try out new ways—most of all, like feminism, as a challenge and alternative to life and love within our traditional family. At each step it shares a strong tie to conscious community. Hence communes cannot help but play a role in personal liberation—and in accumulation.

Our form of life splits and rules people in terms of class, of sex and race, of age and schooling. Only by and by, as people turn to workplace democracy and neighborhood power and personal liberation, will social unity from below push back social alienation from above. At the fringe of our form of life, the original accumulation of community aids precisely this process, this struggle.

In summary, this notion of original accumulation lets me account for the grounds of what I treat here as self rule. In this chapter, I tried to display half a dozen such underlying assumptions. Here I presuppose that the negation of what I speak of—scarcity, industrialism, patriarchy, statism, capitalism, and empire—constitutes these grounds. Together, all these grounds for change—interacting and yet not at all a single whole—may make self rule conceivable in our time and place.

What makes any such list conceivable as constituting a "game" like self rule is an added presupposition, stressed at the start of this chapter. This presupposition grounds self rule in people themselves producing a new form of life in the course of everyday change and struggles—the original accumulation of community—as against a seizing of political power most modern liberals as well as radicals take for granted.

* * *

In the end, let me come back to the title I gave this chapter, "Self Rule or 1984."

The prospect of self rule would seem to make some sense in our historically specific form of life. Still more, alas, does the spectre of 1984.

In the twentieth century, the high noon of capitalism gave way to its dusk. Now a new contradiction, between scarcity and a possible end to it, pits all of social alienation from above against social unity from below. This changed struggle of opposing tendencies, in turn, produces two no less opposing conceptions of a possible future. Now separation from above forms the auspices or grounds for 1984. The opposing tendency, social unity from below, does the same for self rule.

Other possible futures face us as well—such as more of the same, or still more social rot and drift. In our time of troubles, though, we would do well to pay heed to both self rule and 1984.

NOTES

1. See my Introduction and chapters one and two.
2. Roslyn Wallach Bologh, "Dialectical Phenomenology" (Doctoral Dissertation in Sociology, Graduate Center, City University of New York, 1976, to be published in 1979 as a book with the same title by Routledge & Kegan Paul of Boston and London); chapter two of this book. The concept of late capitalism I draw from the works of critical scholars in Europe: Juergen Habermas, Ernest Mandel, Claus Offe.

   As the third section of chapter one brings out, grounding order in a dominant form of life should not be confused analytically with the order people themselves achieve (and change all the time) in the course of daily life and struggles. Rather, the order mainstream sociologists assume fits well the normative (or great power) view stressed in chapter two, section I.
3. *Bakunin on Anarchy*, edited by Sam Dolgoff (New York: Knopf, 1972), brings out the worth of Bakunin's thought much more than did E. H. Carr's classic biography, *Michael Bakunin* (1937, reissued with minor alterations in 1975 by Macmillan & Co. of London). For the rest, the Dolgoff collection in large part bears out Carr. On Marx, see his most wide-ranging and self-revealing work of theorizing, *Grundrisse* (New York: Vintage, 1973) and Bologh, "Dialectical Phenomenology" (note 2).

   I also found useful two other works. In an extensive preface to *Bakunin on Anarchy*, just cited, Paul Avrich links Bakunin to our own time. Norman Levine, in *The Tragic Deception* (Santa Barbara, California: Clio Press, 1975), spells out the view that treats not Marx but Engels as the prime source in marxism of mechanistic materialism and social positivism.
4. All three of these very different views of postindustrialism carry weight in our time. Daniel Bell speaks for the first

view in *The Coming of Post-Industrial Society* (New York: Basic Books, 1973). The second view, of no growth, is backed by Robert Heilbroner in *An Inquiry into the Human Prospect* (New York: Norton, 1974). (Left critiques of Heilbroner's dour view will be found in *Dissent*, Summer 1978.) Herbert Marcuse, *Eros and Civilization* (Boston: Beacon Press, 1955), and Stanley Aronowitz, *False Promises* (New York: McGraw-Hill, 1974), spell out the third option. So do Murray Bookchin and Ivan Illich. Bookchin speaks of "eco-communities" minus capitalism in *Post-Scarcity Anarchism* (New York: Pantheon for Ramparts Press, 1971); "Open Letter to the Ecology Movement," *Liberation*, January 1974; and *The Limits of the City* (New York: Harper & Row, 1974). Illich makes a case for a human-sized, individualized technology (and society) in *Tools for Conviviality* (New York: Harper & Row, 1973).

5. Rousseau draws this line, according to Marshall Berman in *The Politics of Authenticity* (New York: Pantheon, 1970). Lawrence Krader holds the same for Marx, in his *Works of Marx and Engels in Ethnology Compared,* introduced and edited by him (Hague, Netherlands: Mouton, 1973). Freud probably speaks the most of the civilized versus the primitive in *Totem and Taboo* and in *Civilization and its Discontents*.

6. I drew this threefold scheme out of Marx by way of chapters 3 and 4 of the work by Bologh (note 2). As a rule, Marx puts capitalism where I speak here of civilization. Bologh applies to the old versus new community the same distinction Marx made for an early as against a later working class: a group just IN itself when unconscious, and FOR itself once it becomes conscious.

7. Stanley Diamond, *In Search of the Primitive* (New York: E. P. Dutton for Transaction Books, 1974), especially chapter 4; Muriel Dimen-Schein, *The Anthropological Imagination* (New York: McGraw-Hill, 1977), chapters 5 and 6; Lawrence Krader, *Formation of the State* (Englewood Cliffs, New Jersey: Prentice-Hall, 1968). Two books newly trans-

lated into English take up the link between civilization and the state: Pierre Clastres, *Society Against the State* and Norbert Elias, second volume of *The Civilizing Process*. Urizen Books of New York put out both translations, the first in 1977 and the second in 1978.

Through an essay on the book by Clastres that I cite in this note, Michael E. Brown gives a critique both of anthropology in general and of critical anthropology: *October* magazine (New York), No. 6, Summer 1978.

In four striking novels, Chinua Achebe offers an inside view of how empire mediates the shift from natural community to civilization. Fawcett Publications of Greenwich, Connecticut, put out *Things Fall Apart* and *No Longer at Ease*. *Arrow of God* and *A Man of the People* came from Doubleday in New York.

8. Wilhelm Reich, *Sex-Pol: Essays 1929-1934*, edited by Lee Baxandall (New York: Random House, 1972), especially a book-length piece of 1931, "The Imposition of Sexual Morality"; Herbert Marcuse, *Eros and Civilization* (note 4); Natalie J. Sokoloff, "Women in the Labor Market" (Doctoral Dissertation in Sociology, Graduate Center, City University of New York, 1978), chapters 5 and 6. The main works by Frantz Fanon are *Black Skin, White Masks* (New York: Grove, 1967), and *The Wretched of the Earth* (New York: Grove, 1963).

9. Of this side of the scene in Yugoslavia, Bogdan Denitch gives a plausible view in *Dissent*, Summer 1978. See also his book, *The Legitimation of a Revolution* (New Haven: Yale University Press, 1976).

10. Denitch (note 9).

11. Marcuse in *A Critique of Pure Tolerance* (Boston: Beacon Press, 1965) and in *One-Dimensional Man* (Boston: Beacon Press, 1964), chapter 3. See also C. B. MacPherson, *The Political Theory of Possessive Individualism* (New York: Oxford University Press, 1973).

12. *Grundrisse* (note 3), pp. 459-515. An earlier translation of the same fragment, with an introduction by Eric J. Hobs-

bawn, can be found in Karl Marx, *Pre-Capitalist Economic Formations* (New York: International Publishers, 1965).
13. E. P. Thompson in *The Making of the English Working Class* (New York: Random House, 1966) gives us a close-up view that shows some likeness to the proletariat of Marx: working people as often as not informed and linked up, group conscious and militant, both democratic and capable of high discipline, wretched but with faith and zeal. Yet Thompson speaks of the turn of the nineteenth century, a generation before Marx launched his scheme. And Thompson notes that the new urban wage slaves he speaks of had as a rule just left lives as peasants and small town artisans and laborers. By the 1830s they had lost a good deal of the revolutionary traits they gained more from the unique British past of social and religious strife and liberty than from the industrialism Marx dwelled on.

For his own time, Marx did not go all the way either in his view of the new industrial workers. As Marshall Berman shows in an essay in *Dissent,* Winter 1978, he failed to apply to this chosen people of his the dark, all-deforming side of capitalism that he saw so well when it came to middle-class life and work. Thus in the heart of the *Communist Manifesto* Marx said of modern bourgeois society as a whole: "All that is solid melts into air . . . ." Yet he exempted the proletariat from this glum "modernist" truth, as if one group could stand free of the social rot he spotted all around it.

Together, Thompson's point and Berman's cast further doubt on assuming one group to be the sure agency of change yet to come.
14. Even the least orthodox or dogmatic marxists, including the critical, dialectical or neo-marxists I touch on in the Introduction and in chapters one and two, find it hard to go past the grounds of Marx's own conception: industrialism, proletariat, takeover of the state as the climax of revolution, science as a sacred cow, capitalism as the one main scourge.

We can see this in two marxist textbooks of quality that take opposing views of marxism. A college textbook in sociology is very orthodox: Albert Szymanski, *The Capitalist State and the Politics of Class* (Cambridge, Massachusetts: Winthrop, 1978). The other textbook, in economics, shows little orthodoxy: Raymond S. Franklin, *American Capitalism* (New York: Random House, 1977). Yet both stay wed to the main themes of Marx I list here.

15. Peter McHugh et al., *On the Beginning of Social Inquiry* (Boston: Routledge & Kegan Paul, 1974).
16. In *Anarchy in Action* (New York: Harper & Row, 1974), Colin Ward looks at theory and practice in these realms: neighborhoods, voluntary organizations, decentralized public services, planning, housing, schools, play, work, welfare, family, and laws.
17. Bookchin, chapter on Liberatory Technology in *Post-Scarcity Anarchism;* Illich, *Tools for Conviviality* (both cited in note 4).

Radical Technology, edited by Peter Harper, Geoffrey Boyle, and the editors of *Undercurrents* (London), (New York: Pantheon, 1976), brings out the current stage of this search. The large tome singles out food, energy, shelter, autonomy, materials, communications. At the end, the book speaks of Other Perspectives: Women's Page, Mysterious Energies, 19th Century Utopian Communities, Intermediate Technology, India, Chile, China. This last list of concerns goes against a widespread view on the left, that a stress on Alternate Technology or Small is Beautiful must perforce turn out a fad, ethnocentrically Western, and easily absorbed ("coopted") by the status quo.

We find other evidence to the contrary in the first words of *Radical Technology*:

This is a book about technologies that could help create a less oppressive and more fulfilling society. It argues for the growth of small-scale techniques suitable for use by individuals and communities, in a wider social context of humanized production under workers' and consumers' control (p. 5).

We tend to think that an autonomously evolving technology makes for more and new forms of social control. Two notable case studies point to the reverse. In the main it has been the historically specific wish of those who run industry —to raise their control over those who work for them— that leads each time and place to pick or slight the technology it did. Both case studies will be found in the Summer 1974 issue of *Review of Radical Political Economics*: Catherine Stone, "The Origin of Job Structures in the Steel Industry" and Stephen Marglin, "What Do Bosses Do?" All the more reason, in the term I use in chapter one and in the fourth section of chapter six, to treat technology no more a sacred cow than we should treat science.

18. Milton Kotler, *Neighborhood Government* (Indianapolis: Bobbs-Merrill, 1969); David Morris and Karl Hess, *Neighborhood Power* (Boston: Beacon Press, 1975). See also the last section of my chapter four.

ACKNOWLEDGMENT

My thanks to Stanley Aronowitz, Isaiah Berlin, Paul Berman, Roslyn Wallach Bologh, Michael E. Brown, Bogdan Denitch, Alexander Erlich, William DiFazio, Celene Krauss, Carol Lopate, Dennis Sullivan, Rudi Supek, and to all members of my City University Doctoral Seminar in the spring of 1978. And special thanks to Colette Amoda for helping me revise and edit this chapter and also the Introduction and chapter six.

SIX

FUSING MEANS AND ENDS

Self rule makes little sense so long as a form of life imposes or takes for granted authority from above—be the hierarchy that of state or empire, patriarchy or capitalism. More and more of a drop in this kind of unquestioned, outside authority lies at the heart of all ways to self rule as I see that goal: modern people themselves in the course of everyday change and struggles producing a direct, participatory democracy that starts and ends with free individuals and face to face communities in all spheres of life.[1]

How do we move toward some such self rule? What ways make sense? Which ones don't?

Doubts on this score come up all the time these days. People deal with these doubts in three main ways:

1. *Sectarians* dwell so much on pure means that it becomes irrelevant how much closer what they do brings them to their goals.

2. *Opportunists* accommodate both their means and their ends to what they feel can get done here and now.

3. In between, many people choose *neither a sect nor opportunism*. They refrain from either extreme. More than anything, they fear that in fact sectarianism means inaction or passivity, while opportunism means absorption or cooptation by The System. Yet all sorts of people see no third choice for how to move toward a goal like self rule.

Parts of the last two sections of this chapter are drawn from same paper as chapter five; the rest I wrote in 1978 for this book.

As a way out—and a key way to self rule—I point to fusing means and ends in place of either extreme, in place of both passivity and cooptation. Transcending this usual choice makes sense of some other ways to self rule. All these ways I treat in the form of five recipes: Beyond a False Choice, Both Individuality and Community, A Mixed System, No Sacred Cows, and Risking a Bad Choice. For each but the first recipe, I draw on one or more top writers on self rule. Some of the writers come from marxism, some from anarchism.

I. BEYOND A FALSE CHOICE

I see the choice between sectarianism and opportunism as a false choice. Hence the first recipe calls for transcending that false choice. All of my other recipes rest on this one.

The false choice I speak of comes from making an equally false distinction between the present and the future. We tend to assume that we can find some one right way to move from an imperfect present to a perfect future. So we think of what we do now (the means) as in a totally different time period from what we want to achieve (the end). Then we torment ourselves because no action seems to bring the leap to this great future. And eventually we feel forced to sacrifice either our means or our ends if we are not to give up on taking any action at all right now.

The choice will be seen as false if we start from the premise that life is an ongoing process without any break between yesterday, today, and tomorrow. With this changed starting point, the relation between means and ends becomes a continuing interaction. This continuing interaction takes place between the actions we take now, the effects they have, and the actions we then choose to take in the somewhat different conditions we ourselves helped to create.

We cannot break off our actions from their consequences, in other words, whether intended or unintended. Nor can we walk away from those consequences, for they are the new "present" in which we act. Whatever actions we take *or fail to take,* in effect, constitute our means to an end. Likewise, whatever consequences

Fusing Means and Ends

there may be to our actions constitute the ends, whether they are what we were trying to achieve or not.

To come back to my theme for this chapter as a whole, I presuppose that we fuse our means and ends in the process of moving to self rule. I see them as inseparable in all the ways one might choose.

To say that the ends are the means is to say that we display what we want to achieve in every effort we make to bring self rule closer. We practice the principles of self rule in those actions. Our means cannot betray our ends if we keep to this.

By the same token, to say that the means are the ends is to say that the actions we engage in now are important for themselves. We value them for what we experience in them: nothing but partial achievements will bring us closer to a world of self rule. Our ends cannot induce us to improper means if we keep to this.

Thus my conception of self rule assumes that there exists no such thing as perfection or an end to history. It assumes that nothing we ever accomplish can be perfect. We try for the best, we get part of the way there. To get that far, to succeed for a while and then find the success dissipate, doesn't mean we have failed or been coopted.

In large part, our dread of cooptation flows from our national genius so far: the long leash. One percent of America's population, say, runs the rest of us by means of lots of leeway in private life and at the fringe of work and public life.

Let me call to mind, however, a built-in clash that helps us account for how people deal with life from day to day. The built-in clash pits what we take for granted against the fresh problems we face all the time. It pits against each other old and new, actual and possible, the feared and the hoped for, what we "know" for sure and what we only sense or guess at. And this clash in daily life goes on and on. That's why even the genius of our long leash has not saved the United States from a stormy history of ever new contradictions, critiques, and struggles.

Even if the powers that be think that they have cleverly used our energies to their ends, we can know that we are just another step closer to where we want to go. For our partial steps make that job easier in two ways. They give us good moments and small successes to make life a little easier now and boost our morale. And they change bit by bit The System in which we will undertake our next struggle.

Hence I see no good grounds to stick to the false choice between sectarianism and opportunism, between passivity and cooptation. The very dynamic of daily life and struggles lets us fuse ends and means.

II. BOTH INDIVIDUALITY AND COMMUNITY

If the prospect of 1984 looms large in our minds and in much of what we hear and read, self rule often seems far away and unreal. And yet right now, in our own day and age, people do run much more of their lives with little or no imposed, outside authority than most of us can tell.

As a critic puts it, "The fact is that while there are thousands of students and teachers of government, there are hardly any of non-government." In countless moments, the critic tells us, society holds together by the cement of human solidarity alone. "Yet you don't find them discussed in the texts of social psychology and you don't find them written about by the historians."[2]

In the groves of academe one now comes across a trickle of exceptions. On the whole, traditional academics and even critical ones go on to dwell on how rule from the top down works and not on what there is of self rule right now. Not by chance, then, both the critic I quote and the two writers I now turn to work and write in the main outside the Ivory Tower, outside established higher learning.

Community at Work

We see that well in the case of C. L. R. James, a septuagenarian black marxist of uniquely broad gauge.

Born and still active in the Caribbean, James played quite a role too in the struggles of Africa and in the left of both Britain and the United States. At the same time, he put out a stream of books and pamphlets. Best known of these are *The Black Jacobins* (1938), on the remarkable Haitian war of independence at the time of the French Revolution, and *Mariners, Renegades and Castaways* (1953), a view of industrial America as a whole by way of thoughts on Herman Melville and *Moby Dick*. And a host of past works now sees the light of day once more in the form of three volumes of selected writings.[3]

In his book *Facing Reality*[4] James finds an informal individuality and community in the realm of work. For him, in both the capitalist world and the communist countries, workers wield considerable control over what they do at work and how they do it, far beyond anything most people have grasped. And far beyond what workers themselves put into words, still less into whole schemes of tactics, strategy, or theory.

James speaks of China and Russia, Hungary and Poland, Britain and France. And he speaks of the new nations of the Third World. He finds self rule of this kind most often, though, in the United States. He grounds this in the view that "the much lauded know-how of American management is a myth. . . ." More than that, "The realities of life inside the American factory drive relentlessly to one overpowering conclusion. This conclusion is that management and supervision have now become as much an anachronism as a feudal landlord or a slave driver on a cotton plantation."

On these grounds, how does the author see workers gaining both individuality and community? For James, the answer seems clear:

> Under the conditions of modern industry, production holds no mystery for the worker. Cooperation rather than competition is in the nature of the work itself. Because of the rhythm with which he is working, he is able to devise and perfect a work and social schedule of his own.

Naturally, he adds, management counterattacks at every opportunity. The result is a "gigantic, disruptive, and unceasing conflict." Yet, he adds, American workers, like workers everywhere, are not dominated by the desire not to work. Instead, "the cooperation and discipline that have been instilled into them by large-scale machinery have been turned into bitterness and frustration by the capitalist nature of production." For now, they engage not in attack but in resistance—most often in the form of a wildcat strike.

With all this, the author claims, the industrial working class has wrought, if not a whole philosophy, at least the basis of a philosophy of life of its own: ". . . that it can manage production, that to do so is its inalienable right, that the secret of a happy life is mastery over machinery and production, and that the rest can be easily managed."

Here James makes quite a claim, of course, for a way to self rule. He does so with the same terms—capitalism, industrialism, and factory workers—Marx used. A second author makes no less a claim, but shifts it from an informal individuality and community at the workplace to individuality reviving through communitylike new groups.

Individuality through Small Groups

Bruce Brown sees individuality growing here and now in alienated people with the help of a host of new small groups.

This author grounds his claim in what he calls a convergence of marxism and psychoanalysis. To Brown, early Freudo-Marxists like Reich and Marcuse launched this convergence in the thirties. To them, the repression of the individual brought out by Freud served to account for the energies capitalism channeled into the social repression and alienation Marx sang of. The New Left of the 1960s—for which Brown speaks—made this convergence a part of daily life by means of small groups. In turn, these small groups saw what they did in terms of participatory democracy and counterculture.[5]

Small groups play a key role since they can serve two tasks at the same time. They stand outside of the very form of life that represses and fragments individuality. And they can at the same time be both subversive and therapeutic. In the author's own

Fusing Means and Ends

words, a small group as a current way to self rule "must be capable of undermining the triple pillars of hierarchy, specialization, and noncommunication by which the system maintains the individual in a state of passive subordination; and it must be capable of facilitating the crystallization of new, self-confident, and integrated personalities capable of subjective autonomy."

It was to meet this need—to liberate the individual psyche in a context that supports rather than exploit and destroy it—that the New Left singled out small groups. At the time, such groups took the form of affinity groups, collectives, communes, microsocieties, consciousness-raising groups, and the like. By now, a decade later, some of these gave way to a host of new ones. They run from food cooperatives and neighborhood health clinics to others I touch on earlier in this book.

In making a case for small groups, Brown at the same time anticipates criticisms, from both right and left, of our time as a Me Decade.[6] He notes the close tie between the growth of various schools of group dynamics and the stress big business puts on what it calls industrial relations. He notes, too, that the huge energy people store up in the course of a repressed, sublimated life can turn them as much to passivity, madness, or what current critics call a mindless narcissism as it can to a newly autonomous, liberating life through small groups.

All the same, this author holds out for small groups as a key way to self rule. With numbering and paragraphs added, let me quote in sum the flow of his argument:

1. A new praxis . . . begins with the individual's personal experience of oppression and of the fragmentation of experience which makes authentic experience impossible for her or him;
2. it leads from the discovery of this alienation to the individual's refusal of it through a process which is best described as the *politicization of oneself* [italics by author] and which aims at retotalization of the individual's experience;
3. it develops further through the individual's collision with the inertia of an oppressive social reality in his or her search for authenticity;

4. with this recognition of the social sources of the individual's malaise, it leads to the inauguration of a radical contestation of existing institutions on the level of everyday life carried out by small groups and collectives, and extended through their spontaneous multiplication as micro-social centers of resistance. . . .

What C. L. R. James and Bruce Brown point out as ways to self rule are not close to the core of what people read or talk of these days. Yet both informal kinds of individuality and community on the shop floor and the spread of individuality through more and more types of communitylike small groups are among the continuing big trends in our time and place. More than that, they point to our great advantage when we put faith not in either individuality or community by itself, but in the two of them together.

III. A MIXED SYSTEM

Few things mark, and mar, movements for a good life as much as does millenarianism, the hope and faith in a heaven on earth: all things bad and all things ambiguous and hazy, too, will give way to some pure, set, clear form of life. By the same token, few calls for basic change speak of a mixed system, a form a life that (as in the past) will bring with it something old as well as new, bits of this and bits of that.

Yet if people are in truth to run their own lives in full, one way to self rule must let them opt for just such a mix. Or it must let some people opt for one thing and others for quite another.

To be sure, I myself have through much of this book made the point that self rule as a form of life means that conscious community must lie at the core of all a society does. That view still makes sense to me. For example, if we fail to move scarcity, industrialism, and the worst of civilization to the fringe of a new form of life, I don't see how people can run their own lives. By definition, conscious community must move to the fore, and set the tone, as a new form of life takes shape.

This is not to say, though, that a turn to community rules out a mixed system. It does not. It rules out such a mixed system neither en route to a new form of life nor once self rule comes to be the core.

So when I speak of self rule, the reader should note, I do not have in mind a world of either/or, of all or nothing. On the contrary, I neither can nor want to see a future in which our world, varied and mixed in no end of ways, comes to fit some one scheme. That does not seem to be a bit plausible. Or, for that matter, at all desirable.

Only within this proviso do I see self rule as what in years to come might and could add up to the core of a new form of life—but not the whole of it. In short, a mixed system.

An American Voice

Paul Goodman (1911-1972) stands as our main voice for self rule with (and through) a mixed system.

A prolific poet and novelist, literary and social critic, therapist and sexual gadfly, Goodman saw himself as a disciple of Peter Kropotkin, the Anarchist Prince. The two shared a Proudhon-like faith in a natural modern bond to mutual aid and economic cooperation from the ground up. Going beyond Proudhon, both also stressed communal planning and environmentalism. They shared, too, a faith in a reasoned, plain, low-key discourse; in this, their mode was of course not at all like the hard sell we get from Bakunin and Marx.

At the same time, Goodman failed to rule the state or capitalism out of court altogether, as did both Kropotkin and Bakunin. Nor did he dwell on science, to which Kropotkin bowed still more than Marx.

A few quotations show how Paul Goodman saw a mixed system as a way to self rule:

> Since all actual societies are, and have to be, mixtures of socialism, market economy, etc., the problem in any society is to get a more judicious mixture, and this *might* be most attainable by tinkering [italics by author].

> The idea of a Mixed System is a proportioning among types of enterprises so that they in fact influence one another pluralistically and if necessary can check one another....
>
> A mixed system would allow various types of motivation and organization to do what they do most appropriately and cheapest.
>
> A mixed system would re-open opportunities for people to choose the way of working and living that most suits them, and would thus re-create the possibility of engagement.[7]

A Call from Yugoslavia

Another call for a mixed system as a way to self rule comes to us from Eastern Europe. A range of antiauthoritarian marxists there argue for various combinations of free market, self-management by workers and communities, and accommodations with this or that mode of socialism.

As a leading example, let me cite Rudi Supek. An old Croat intellectual and revolutionary, Supek is the heart and soul of the international journal of antiauthoritarian marxism (*Praxis*) that Yugoslav officials closed down a few years back.

With self-management in Yugoslavia in mind, Supek makes points such as these (emphasis mine) in favor of a mixed system:

Pluralism in self-management:

> Thus we can speak of a *pluralistic* model of self-managed organizations with respect to their socioeconomic relations.

Change from participation to self-management:

> The development of *various* forms of participation [will] by creating an awareness of the naturalness or necessity of such a qualitative change ease the transition to self-management.

A community neither autonomous nor run from outside:

Fusing Means and Ends 225

Between these two extreme forms, the free association attempts to find a *compromise* that represents the most favorable solution in view of the concrete conditions of the given social system.

Antiauthoritarian marxists like Supek share the view that economic self-management lies close to the heart of any nonauthoritarian social structure. But for Supek not capitalism but only socialism of a nonauthoritarian marxist kind stands as the one sure base for self-management. More than that, to Supek economic self rule requires political self rule too. That is why he speaks not of management but of government: self-*governing* socialism. Full self rule means the whole polity and not just the economy. It means nothing less than "the organization of society as a federation of workers' and citizens' councils..."[8]

Supek, like Goodman, puts faith in trying out such combinations whenever possible. And—coming from a land that sits astride the three worlds of Western capitalism, the Soviet bloc, and the emerging nations of the southern hemisphere—Supek puts a great deal of weight on mixed systems that open new ways for self rule for people in all of these regions. For him, mixed systems must and can fit the most varied roots and needs of self rule in each part of the globe.

Local, Regional, Global

Let me stress, too, that a mixed system does not stop with the local, the small, the face to face. While my conception of self rule treats people's primary ties as the start and end of how they would run their own lives, this conception does not leave out the rest of the world. On the contrary, I assume at each step a much fuller and better integration than now by means of a host of "topless" federations.

Here any conception of self rule gains from anarchist thought on statelessness versus reliance on centralized authority, the state. For that current holds that life with no state at all can work in a complex society like our own.

To show how statelessness would do so, some anarchists draw on new work in anthropology and in cybernetic theory. They hold that this work backs in full the anarchist view that harmony flows not from concentration but from a complex sort of fragmentation.

True complexity means here no single centers but a linked web of highly varied, autonomous, and labile coordinating groups. Cybernetics and anthropology lead less orthodox anarchists to speak now in terms of complex self-organizing systems ("fission rather than fusion") plus feedback. Feedback takes the form of "topless" federations without any set authority at all. Stateless kinds of integrating bodies serve global and regional needs as well as local ones.[9]

The Problem of Autonomy

To see a mixed system as basic to self rule does not stop with a theory or practice of diversity or pluralism or flexibility for its own sake. The call for a mixed system speaks to a gap in past schemes for self rule, a gap we have yet to fill. I have in mind the central problem of autonomy—of conceiving of more than one social base, and each base autonomous from the rest, in both private and public spheres of life.

From ancient times to modern, we find that minorities, dissenters, and popular rule take root only insofar as they could rest on just such an autonomous base. As Hermann Hesse's main novels of Central Europe show well, often that base took the form of inherited private property, or of rights traditionally vested in religious, municipal, collegiate, and like institutions and endowments.

No one realm—be it material, legal, political, or cultural—constitutes or assures autonomy. All the same, any conception of self rule without a mixed system would deny this problem.

As in all social life and change, the actual solutions to a problem take the form of ongoing achievements in the course of daily life. So we cannot "solve" the problem ahead of time or for sure. As a recipe, a mixed system does call to mind the need to conceive of self rule in terms of the age-old problem I speak of. At each step of the way, we need to ask: what kinds of autonomous social base, if none of them were at hand, would make self rule unintelligible or implausible altogether?

IV. NO FETISH, NO SACRED COWS

Sacred cows, all views or things we treat as a holy of holies, block choice and hence conscious community. In our own time, two such sacred cows seem to me to block self rule the most. One is science, as against other modes of knowing oneself and life. The other is need, as against desire and satisfaction.

Science as Creed

Science, in the sense of systematic factual knowledge and a methodical search for it, stands out as the great creed of our time. People must go to school so as to gain the fruits of science. They can learn of other ways of knowing—the esthetic, the metaphysical, the psychic, the traditionalistic—only if they do so through the prism of science.

This prism, the Swiss philosopher and scientist Paul Feyerabend tells us, means nothing less than the tyranny of science.[10] As an anarchist, he speaks against such tyranny on two counts. It makes our mental life authoritarian, with its ways set down on high. And the great faith we put in science boosts all sorts of authoritarian ways in the rest of our lives. Feyerabend calls on people to end the tyranny of science. We must treat science as no more than one of a host of ways to know life, and to learn of it. We must treat science not as given but as something we ourselves choose and shape.

Each time and place takes for granted some way of knowing life. That way of knowing serves as its map, guide, mind's eye. It comes to stand outside and above what people do in their own lives.

When that takes place, conscious community can't make sense. Conversely, conscious community means being able to make an established truth problematic. It means to free people to choose how to learn and know, and not be ruled by an established mode such as science. To be sure, at all times people will want to take some parts of life for granted. No group can question and re-examine each thing it does or thinks. Community stops making sense, though, once people are no longer conscious that the choice is in fact theirs. As soon as people fail to keep that in mind, they start to act as objects. And for self rule the key lies with people as subjects versus people as objects.

In this light, we can read history as permanent struggle between taking one way of knowing for granted and people making a conscious choice between ways of knowing—or leaving the choice open. In our age, science lies at the heart of this struggle: people now make a fetish out of science.[11]

As a fetish, science now gains much strength from a classic view that runs deep in our form of life and goes far back in our past. I have in mind duality, or dualism as the theory and practice of duality. This means, of course, to treat all not as a single whole but as made up of (split into) two parts.

We come to take dualism for granted as we take part in the human appropriation of nature (Man versus Nature), the search for what's sure and what we can count on (the Known versus the Unknown), earning a living (Work versus Own Time), and all of the divisions of life and labor (by rank and power, by class or wealth, by sex, by creed and ethnicity and race, by schooling and skill, by age). In a word, I see our splitting the whole of life into the "mere" human or everyday versus something superior—be it the divine or the scientific or those on top on this or that scale.

As long as we treat such duality and dualism as a given, we treat some people or things as superior, sacred, untouchable, unchangeable. Or, in the terms of Marx, fetishized, eternalized, reified. In plain words, we put a large part of our lives out of our own reach.

In such a split view, self rule and conscious community would seem an unlikely form of life. That form of life assumes that people do feel and act as full masters of their fate. The dualism I speak of helps people assume just the reverse.

All we learn and see and do in the here and now makes an end to the dualistc split appear just as hard as to jump out of one's own skin. Yet we need to do that in realms like science, where these days people feel we lack a choice. As and when real choice gains primacy, science could change from a superior force out of our reach to a human-sized part of self rule.

Our View of Need

Next to science, I see our view of need as a sacred cow that blocks self rule. Whether we juxtapose need here to desire or to satisfaction, the outcome is the same. In our form of life, late capitalism, treating need as a holy of holies stands in the way of self rule. We should grasp this need in its historically specific sense: a ubiquitous obsessive consumption and hence "scarcity" of ever new and ever more commodities.

A leading anarchist, Murray Bookchin, sets off need from desire. An academic marxist, William Leiss, sets it off from satisfaction. By quite distinct routes, the two writers bear out how I see our view of need.

In the end piece of his well-known *Post-Scarcity Anarchism*, Bookchin starts with a credo:

> The Revolution that seeks to annul Need
> must enthrone Desire for everybody.
> Desire must become Need!

By need, he means the need to survive, to secure the bare means of existence. He means a religious credo of renunciation. Or a republican credo of virtue. Or the reality principle of Freud's theory. Desire stands for play, sexuality, and sensuousness. It stands for the sensibility of poets and the pleasure principle.

Bookchin then takes up an issue raised and stressed here already, that of a possible end to dire scarcity. He sees in our time the "enthronement of Desire as Need." That enthronement, he holds, is "nourished as a *public* issue [his italics] by the productivity of modern industry and by the possibility of a society without toil."

As of now, this chance to move beyond scarcity spells trouble. It shows "the irrationalities of modern affluence." What makes it irrational to Bookchin is that "the revolutionary growth of modern technology has brought into question every historical precept that promoted renunciation, denial and toil." Yet when those on top shift Desire from a privilege of a few to a task for all of us, they seem to have in mind no more than the postwar American Dream of consumption, work by rote, and suburbia.

That sort of Desire leaves people cold, though. While it might serve their social interest, it fails to touch what Bookchin calls their social libido. By social libido he means, for example, "the anarchic, intoxicating phase that opens all the great revolutions of history. . . ."

What seems to trouble this critic is that, when all is said and done, Need still rides high in late capitalism. The need to consume and conform, now called Desire, brings with it no more meaning than egotism and "vicious nihilism." To Bookchin, authoritarian marxists or leninists are just as bad. For they too, like late capitalism, show no care for real change, for full human liberation.

The book's last piece ends, as it starts, with a credo:

Our Being is Becoming, not stasis.
Our Science is Utopia, our Reality is Eros,
Our Desire is Revolution.[12]

When we turn from Desire to Satisfaction, and from an anarchist to an academic marxist, the tone shifts. A brief prose poem gives way to a long, grave case. Yet the two authors differ more in style than they do in what they say of need as a sacred cow that stands in the way of self rule.

To Leiss as to Bookchin, the need to consume the unprecedented outpouring of commodities strips people of a real choice. People can't gain satisfaction because this need to consume blocks out the view of anything else they might need, want, or enjoy.

Fusing Means and Ends

With late capitalism in mind, the author speaks of "the high-intensity market setting of contemporary industrialized societies." He paints a grim picture:

> This setting promotes a lifestyle that is dependent upon an endlessly rising level of material goods. I have tried to show that, within the social process which enshrines this lifestyle as the highest goal of human endeavor, individuals are led to misinterpret the nature of their needs and to misunderstand the relationship between their needs and the ways in which they may be satisfied.

A key point here has to do with a terror that this familiar process brings with it. The terror stems not from actual but from anticipated scarcity. And the terror grows in direct proportion to the massive, ever-growing accumulation of wealth.

But not all is grim or lost. On the contrary, like Bookchin, Leiss sees hope in the human condition. People, he holds, can move from a single need to a range of satisfactions, from no choice to a choice:

> The possibilities for satisfaction that might be drawn from different forms of productive activity and of our relationship to non-human nature, and that are now so deeply suppressed, can minister to our needs far more effectively than can any new assortment of goods. In orienting ourselves toward these suppressed possibilities we can discover some of the abundant sources of satisfaction that have lain untapped for so long.[13]

V. RISKING A BAD CHOICE

As the last one of a few ways to self rule that I single out, I want to come back to an age-old theme. The theme harks on the ups and downs of change, the ebb and flow that leave no soul or thing in the same place for long. What goes for all of life goes for self rule in particular.

A grasp of that may seem simple. Yet much of the doubt on the score of a new form of life, and the pain in the course of struggle, comes from an old, deep hope that—this one time—the flow won't stop, no ebb will come. Yet flow means ebb, just as day means night—and life means death.

In that light, self rule should not be seen as a prize that people gain and then keep for a long time to come. In no way does self rule mean the end of history. While Marx at times said the same, both he and Bakunin gave people a sense that for them the end goal of communism in fact meant an end to history. At least history would end as we have known it, and something like a millennium would takes its place.[14] I take the opposite view. I see conscious community as no more than one of a range of historically specific possibilities.

Each generation will choose from these ever-changing possibilities. Each will work out its own mix. It will do so in line with its own felt needs, and not those of a past generation.

True, all of the past tracks and molds the choices people can make. The stress on people themselves producing self rule in the course of everyday change and struggles means all the more, though, that self rule makes sense only as part of a struggle between contradictory options and trends. People will go back and forth between felt needs that self rule fits and others that self rule fits less well or not at all. We must expect the quantity and quality of conscious community to change all the time. We can see this from how it fares here and now.

All this means, first and last, that self rule brings with it a big risk. It brings the risk of people free to choose using that freedom to make a bad choice—bad, that is, in terms of their own self rule.

A Utopia Makes a Bad Choice

We find a utopia full of self rule facing in time, by and by, just that risk of a bad choice. And at some time making a choice in truth bad for a conscious community.

The utopia comes from Ursula LeGuin, an anthropologist and a leading writer of science fiction. In a well known work, *The Dispossessed,*[15] LeGuin paints a whole utopia of conscious com-

Fusing Means and Ends 233

munity. She shows in rich hues how a leader launched an anarchist community on a barren planet. LeGuin shows, too, how the leader —later made a goddess—laid down rules to make sure that people would run their lives on their own.

The tale tells of a great scientist in that community who finds out that it will not let him do the new work he has chosen. This roadblock takes the form of both popular ill will and the acts of work coordinators. At first the community set up these work coordinators as no more than administrators of things. But in time their role grew and they came to run people and not just things.

So a once conscious community falters due to the fetishism of established ways on the one hand and on the other the rise of some people from equals to masters. Forced to leave the community to get on with his work, the scientist in the end comes back and leads a revolt against the loss of self rule.

In the face of all the plans of its founding mother, how did this utopia go wrong? In short, the freedom to make a bad choice led to just that.

The answer helps to sum all of my conception of self rule: of scarcity, industrialism, and the worst of civilization (patriarchy, statism, capitalism, empire) giving way step by step to conscious community at the core of a new form of life.[16] For LeGuin's utopia lacks quite a few of these presuppositions.

It lacks, for one, a possible end to scarcity and industrialism. The anarchist pioneers in the tale had no choice but to launch their community on the least well-off planet in sight and to focus on mechanized mass production. The fetishization of the founding mother meant creating a boss, and hence giving up some self rule. So did the rise of an elite out of what was meant to be a small technical service. Not least, the utopia lacked human scale. In place of a loose web of self-managing small groups, all of a large land and population formed a single unit that in the end worked more like a state than a community.

Next to all this, and most important in terms of risking a bad choice, is a side of self rule not stressed till now. I have in mind the presupposition that a conscious community will need to make its choice to stay as such anew with each and every generation. The founding mother of LeGuin's utopia, and the people who first came to set up a new form of life on a planet of dire scarcity, chose of their own free will to do so.

Their children did not, though. Nor did the children of those children. For them the new form of life came down from their parents and elders as a given, as a sacred cow. No wonder they chose to turn their backs in time on some key parts of the scheme. Just that forms the risk that we must keep in mind when we look for ways to self rule.

In place of risking a bad choice, Mao spoke in the sixties of a permanent cultural revolution. Each generation would struggle and change to stay true to the core creed and ways of a form of life. Mao's scheme lacks a prime feature of self rule and conscious community; he saw the form of life as by and large a given—and a given made safe from the top down.[17] No truly conscious community could or would saddle its heirs with any of these chains.

Does the conception of self rule display an alternative to Mao's kind of paternalism? Yes, insofar as it assumes that as people produce conscious community as a new form of life, they will in the process create a new type of person and a whole new culture.

From this key assumption we can infer that in the new form of life self-transformed people—much more liberated and integrated than we are—would not be apt to choose or hold out for ways or things that hurt other people or other communities. On the other hand, self rule in no way presupposes the end of struggles and contradictions within or between conscious communities or whole federations and regions. Once more, the ways to self rule cannot save us or our heirs from the risk of a bad choice.

EPILOGUE: HERE AND NOW

Self rule promises no superhuman change or heaven on earth. On the contrary, each generation may well lose ground and see a gain once more for outside authority—institutionalized domination, structured inequality, hierarchy of all sorts. That holds true for our generation, of course, in spite of a dynamic of original accumulation of community by which we might change life at this

Fusing Means and Ends

time. The conception I put forth brings to mind how slow self rule is to grow. For such growth, people as a whole need to take part. This means that each step links up with people's doubts, their splits, their ties to things as they are.

So each generation can do no more, for self rule, than make some gains it cares for. In our own time and place, we will do well if we push back the shades of 1984, our specter of a state that wields all-out force to keep us tied to social alienation and material scarcity. To push back 1984 means to meet at last some felt needs for self rule: workplace democracy, neighborhood power, personal liberation.

How?

Here my recipes display a few clear "rules of the game" to makes conceivable self rule. All the recipes point to fusing means and ends, as against a false choice between sectarianism (or passivity) and opportunism (or cooptation). The recipes point not to just individuality or just community, but to both. They point not to capitalism but to a mixed system. Not to sacred cows but to active choice. Not to elites but to experiments, and other risks of people free to choose.

A few words sum up well the ways to self rule as I see them:[18]

> The important thing is to work on all fronts at once, the home, the neighborhood and the workplace. Such a balance is the essence of utopian strategy. Likewise we must be realistic *and* full of fantasy, attend to public needs *and* individual consciousness, create a balance of mental *and* manual work for everyone, a measure of city *and* country life, focus on immediate problems *and* build for the future, live in earnest *and* just for fun, confront *and* compromise. Have our cake *and* eat it? Why not?

NOTES

1. Liberal political theorists give views in favor of direct democracy, as against our representative one, in Carole Pateman, *Participation and Democratic Theory* (New York:

Cambridge University Press, 1970); *Participation in Politics, Nomos Yearbook XVI,* eds. J. Roland Pennock and John W. Chapman (New York: Lieber-Atherton, 1975); and C. B. McPherson, *The Life and Times of Liberal Democracy* (New York: Oxford University Press, 1977). On the same plane of analysis, we get a radical brief from Peter T. Manicus in *The Death of the State* (New York: Putnam, 1974). Both less academic and less systematic is a collection of left views, *The Case for Participatory Democracy,* edited by C. George Benello and Dimitrios Roussopoulos (New York: Grossman, 1971).
2. Colin Ward, *Anarchy in Action* (New York: Harper & Row, 1974), pp. 13, 35.
3. *The Black Jacobins* was reprinted in revised form by Vintage Books of New York in 1963, and *Mariners, Renegades and Castaways* the author published himself in New York in 1953. The author titles his new selected works, put out by Lawrence Hill in Westport, Connecticut, *The Future in the Present, Spheres of Existence,* and *At the Rendezvous of Victory.*
4. First published by C. L. R. James, Grace C. Lee, and Pierre Chaulieu, in 1958; reprinted in 1974 by a small publisher: Bewick Editions, 1443 Bewick, Detroit, Michigan 48214 ($1.50 a copy). I draw here most of all on chapter 2 of *Facing Reality.*
5. Bruce Brown, *Marx, Freud, and the Critique of Everyday Life* (New York: Monthly Review Press, 1973). I quote from the last part of the book, chapter 7.

The norms and goals of both individuality and community come to us not only through the shopfloor's natural community or the New Left's conscious one. Through a back door, if you will, our own form of life does its share to hold high some such goals and norms. All else aside, we can see this in a range of film hits of the mid-seventies.

In the end, each hit of this kind leaves you with the point that The System is all-powerful and all-absorbing; to resist it or stay out of it is futile. Yet first, to make a tale ring true, it shows bits of life in the raw. That means to show The System can rob and crush people—and how people don't like, and at times fight, The System and its breach of the Promise of America. I have in mind such varied hits as *Billy Jack, Blue Collar, Chinatown, Dogday Afternoon, Jaws, Network, One Flew Over the Cuckoo's Nest,* and *Saturday Night Fever.*

In terms of another mass medium, Peter Dahlgren treats this dynamic of late capitalism in "Network TV News and the Corporate State," Doctoral Dissertation in Sociology, Graduate Center, City University of New York, 1977.

6. Tom Wolfe, "The Me Decade," in his *Mauve Gloves and Madmen, Clutter and Vine* (New York: Farrar, Straus, and Giroux, 1976); Christopher Lasch, "The Narcissist Society," *New York Review of Books,* September 30, 1976.

I see the narcissism of the seventies as I do the rise and fall of the youth revolt in the sixties. Both strike me as spontaneous, strong, and hence very significant reactions to the social rot all around us. Insofar as my view makes sense, to put down out of hand one or both—as quite a few critics do now—makes no sense at all. The same holds true of a host of brief, local, wildcat strikes by rank and file workers, housing tenants, consumers, and farmers that mark our time.

In each case, the dynamic of struggles between things as they are and people negating them might slam shut this or that door but pry open quite different doors. The youth revolt of the sixties suggests that dynamic on a large scale. Together, its rise and fall helped to touch off feminism, Third World movements at home, workplace struggles by younger wage earners and professionals, new brands and forms of the Old Left and of populism and electoral politics. By the same token, I think the narcissism of the seventies by the very depth and limits of its reaction may lead people involved to turn to further, but changed, reactions to the status quo.

These days many waver between that potential and the loss (or forgetting) of it. Still more than competing or hustling within The System, a loss of the potential tends to take the shape of narrow, passive individualism: the conforming and the driven consuming of lone people our form of life makes for. Further negation, on the other hand, could well point to something like my recipe here: to link up broad, active individuality with community of a self-determining, self-developing sort. In turn, to make that link plausible in the world at large is what revolutionary reformism seems to me all about now.

In terms of the spontaneous reactions against the status quo I speak of, at least the more visible, organized part of the left in the United States shows little of the compassion plus candor that a Eugene Debs and a Malcolm X did. Or an Eleanor Roosevelt. That helps a lot to account for the left's own isolation and lack of appeal. For other Americans of course find The System as hard to take as does the left, and could be its natural allies if not recruits. So radicals need to show much more compassion plus candor for the struggles—flaws and all—by a wide range of people outside their own cause or group.

(In this book, I tried to do just that in the last section of chapter four, on neighborhood populism. That piece and the last point made here owe much to Ezra Birnbaum.)

7. The first paragraph quoted comes from Paul Goodman, *New Reformation* (New York: Random House, 1970), p. 205. The rest comes from his *Drawing the Line* (New York: Free Life Editions, 1977), pp. 201-2. This last book is part of three volumes of essays—a volume each on politics, literature, and psychology—that came out at the same time under the editorship of Taylor Stoehr. Goodman also speaks of a mixed system in *Utopian Essays and Practical Proposals* (New York: Random House, 1962), and *People or Personnel* (New York: Vintage, 1968).

8. *Self-Governing Socialism,* edited by Branko Horvat, Mihailo Marković, and Rudi Supek (White Plains, New York: International Arts and Sciences Press, 1975), vol. 2, pp. 9, 51, 52, and Preface. See also various books by Supek available in German or French but not yet in English.

9. Ward, *Anarchy in Action* (note 2), chapters 4 and 5.

Richard Sennett in *The Uses of Disorder* (New York: Random House, 1971) makes a case for a mixed system in our cities. Suburbs, he argues, still aim at sameness. To give people a chance at the individuality and community they want, urban neighborhoods need the opposite. They need ethnic and economic diversity—plus lots of autonomy to work out problems on their own.

10. Paul Feyerabend, *Against the Method* (New York: Humanities Press, 1975). See also chapter one of this book.

In the last section of chapter one I speak of the fetish of science, and at the start of chapter two of the fetish of sociology. I linked both, as I do the sacred cows singled out here, to the fetishism of commodities Marx laid bare in *Capital*, vol. I, in the key last section of chapter one.

11. As long as we hold high scientism, or science as a fetish, this scientism can serve as the grounds for authoritarian forms of life. Millenarian elitism is a case in point. We can see this well in a piece by Louis Menashe on Lenin, which he calls "Vladimir Ilyich Bakunin" (*Socialist Revolution*, no. 18, vol. 3, no. 6, November-December 1973).

Displayed in this article we find in full form the same millenarian elitism, based on scientism, that we only glimpse in Marx and (with some doubts) in Bakunin. In Marx we find next to his Scientific unmasking and predicting (as I note in the Introduction and in chapters one and two) a much less authoritarian kind of Dialectical critique: most neo-marxists come nowhere near leninism in their emphasis on scientism. In each case scientism does prevail, a self-styled vanguard claims to fuse revolutionary intellectuals with a true science of society. That claim makes sense only when people treat science as a sacred cow.

A self-styled revolutionary vanguard with a large following, in turn, tends to become a counter-elite. Such a counter-elite seeks to gain traditional power and then uses that power just for itself.

Max Nomad bears out this point in his accounts of the

lives and careers of dozens of ex-marxists and ex-anarchists in Europe and the United States over the past century. Nomad, a prodigious left biographer and researcher (1881-1972), wrote a handful of books on well-known and obscure revolutionaries. He gives the background for his case in the Preface and chapter 1 of his *Aspects of Revolution,* Introduction by Edmund Wilson (New York: Farrar, Straus, and Cudahy, 1960), and in his autobiography, *Dreamers, Dynamiters and Demagogues* (New York: Walden Press, 1964). Nomad also wrote "The Evolution of Anarchism and Syndicalism, A Critical View," in *European Ideologies,* edited by Feliks Gross (New York: Philosophical Library, 1948), and "The Anarchist Tradition," in *The Revolutionary Internationals, 1864-1943,* edited by Milorad M. Drachkovitch (Stanford: Stanford University Press, 1966).

12. Murray Bookchin, *Post-Scarcity Anarchism* (New York: Pantheon for Ramparts Press, 1971), pp. 271-86.
13. William Leiss, *The Limits of Satisfaction* (Toronto: University of Toronto Press, 1976), Preface and p. 130.
14. Isaiah Berlin tells us a good deal about millenarianism and what he calls historiosophy. See two of his works: *The Life and Times of Moses Hess* (Cambridge, England: Heffer, 1959), and *Four Essays on Liberty* (New York: Oxford University Press, 1970). In the first of these works (p. 8), Berlin speaks of historiosophy as "the attempt to make history do the work of theology or speculative metaphysics."
15. New York: Harper & Row, 1974.
16. Chapter 5.
17. See fourth section of chapter 4.
18. Peter Harper, in *Radical Technology,* edited by Peter Harper, Geoffrey Boyle, and the editors of *Undercurrents* (London), (New York: Pantheon, 1976), p. 296. Emphasis in original.

INDEX OF NAMES

Abzug, Bella, 159
Achebe, Chinua, 211
Against the Grain, 23-25, 153-54, 169-71
Albert, Stew, 170-72
Alinsky, Saul, 175
Alligerville, New York, 23, 149
American Civil Liberties Union, 168
Andrade, Rebecca, 173-74
Arutiunian, Iu. V., 81

Badillo, Herman, 159
Bakunin, Michael, 23, 178, 181-86, 188, 189, 190, 193, 196, 198, 209, 223, 239
Banfield, Edward, 151
Beame, Abraham L., 176
Bell, Daniel, 31, 34, 151
Bendix, Reinhard, 31
Bensman, Joseph, 32
Berlin, Isaiah, 11, 24, 240
Berman, Marshall, 212
Birnbaum, Ezra, 238
Birnbaum, Norman, 151-52
Blau, Peter, 130
Blum, Alan F., 28, 69-70, 90-91, 94, 97-100
Bobker, Michael, 175
Bologh, Roslyn Wallach, 210
Bookchin, Murray, 22-23, 229-32
Boudon, Raymond, 148
Brooke, Edward L., 176
Brown, Bruce, 220-22

Califano, Joseph, 176
California, 110, 111
Campbell, Angus, 31
Carnegie Commission on Higher Education, 111, 113, 129, 135-36, 143
Carter, Jimmy, 176
Chickering, Arthur W., 130
China, 163-68, 219
City University of New York (CUNY), 13-14, 17, 21, 110, 117, 131, 141-42, 149, 159-62
CNT (labor federation of Spanish syndicates), 23
Coleman, James S., 152
College of Public and Community Service, University of Massachusetts (Boston), 108, 127, 129, 130, 132
Colfax, J. David, 96
Commission on Non-Traditional Study, 111
Columbia University, 12, 21
Converse, Philip W., 31
Critical anthropology, 190, 211

Daley, Richard J., 175
Danziger, Kurt, 31
Debs, Eugene V., 238
Dewey, John, 124-125, 139
Dibble, Vernon K., 31, 32
Dixon, Marlene, 91-94, 101
Douglas, Jack D., 104
Durkheim, Emile, 31

Index of Names

Empire State College, State University of New York (SUNY): Metropolitan Regional Learning Center (Manhattan), 108, 118, 119, 127, 129, 130, 132, 138-40
Engels, Frederick, 84, 191, 209
Etzkowitz, Henry, 94-95

Fanon, Frantz, 191
Farber, Jerry, 150
Feyerabend, Paul, 74, 227
Fischer, Bertha Markoosha, 12
Fischer, George (works), 18, 20, 26, 69, 73, 103, 108-10, 125, 149
Fischer, Louis, 12
Fischer, Mark, 149
Fischer, Sara, 149
Flacks, Richard, 91-92, 94
Fowler's Modern English Usage, 71-72
Frankfurt school of critical sociology, 84
Freire, Paulo, 95
Freud, Sigmund, 190
Friedman, Milton, 151
Friedrichs, Robert W., 82, 87-88

Gaff, Jerry G., 143
Garfinkel, Harold, 28, 52, 53
Geertz, Clifford, 31, 34, 37
Glazer, Nathan, 31, 151
Goldman, Emma, 23
Goode, William J., 34-35
Goodman, Paul, 22, 223-24, 225, 238
Gordon, Leonid A., 81
Gotbaum, Victor, 158, 161
Gould, Samuel B., 111
Gouldner, Alvin W., 90, 92, 94, 96-97, 107
Governors State University (Chicago), 108, 118, 120, 127, 129, 130, 132, 136, 139

Gramsci, Antonio, 84
Grundrisse (Karl Marx), 196-97
Grushin, Boris A., 81

Habermas, Juergen, 21, 31, 96, 209
Halpern, Ben, 31, 33-34
Harper, Peter, 235
Harrington, Michael, 159
Harris, Patricia, 176
Hegel, G. W. F., 84
Hesse, Hermann, 226
Hodgkinson, Harold, 130, 146
Hollywood, 236-237
Horton, John, 76
Hostos Community College (South Bronx), 161
Hutchins, Robert M., 124-25, 139

James, C. L. R., 218-220, 222
Javits, Jacob, 176
Jencks, Christopher, 148

Kakalek, Joseph, 174
Kautsky, Karl, 84
Kerr, Clark, 111
Klopov, E. V., 81
Koch, Edward I., 176
Kon, Igor S., 81
Kotler, Milton, 174-76
Kristol, Irving, 151
Kropotkin, Peter, 23, 223
Kuhn, Thomas S., 35, 51

Lazarsfeld, Paul F., 81
LeGuin, Ursula, 23, 232-33
Leiss, William, 229-32
Lenin, V. I., 20, 84, 90, 164, 239
Lichtheim, George, 31
Lindsay, John V., 176
Livingston College, Rutgers University (New Brunswick, New Jersey), 108, 128, 130, 131, 137, 139, 140, 143
Lukacs, Giorgy (Georg), 84

Index of Names

Madian, Alan K., 31
Makhno, Nestor, 23
Malatesta, Errico, 23
Malcolm X, 238
Mandel, Ernest, 209
Mannheim, Karl, 26, 30, 31, 36-39
Mao Tse-tung, 24, 47, 162-68, 234
Marcuse, Herbert, 21, 57, 191, 194, 220
Marglin, Stephen, 214
Marx, Karl, 19, 21-23, 31, 69-70, 74, 76-77, 84-86, 88, 90, 99, 101, 105-6, 107, 120, 178, 181-86, 188, 189, 190, 191, 193, 195-98, 209, 210, 212-13, 220, 223, 228, 239
Mayer, Martin, 117
McClure, Helen Margaret, 26
McGovern, George, 148
McHugh, Peter, 28, 52, 90-91, 94, 97-100
Melville, Herman, 219
Menashe, Louis, 239
Merton, Robert K., 30, 72, 81
Messinger, Ruth, 175
Mills, C. Wright, 30
Minnesota Metropolitan State College (Twin Cities), 108, 126-30, 136, 139
Monteith College, Wayne State University (Detroit), 108, 116, 118, 128-131, 139, 140
Moscow, 11-12, 19-20
Moynihan, Daniel Patrick, 151, 176
Mueller, Claus, 30
Mulkay, Michael, 35

National Association of Neighborhoods (NAN), 174-76
National Congress of Neighborhood Women, 175
Neighbors of Greenpoint and Williamsburg, 175
Newark, 172-77

New Left Review, 31
Newman, Frank, 111, 122, 124
Newton, Isaac, 90
New York, 11, 153-59, 172-76
Nisbet, Robert, 151
Nixon, Richard M., 55
Nomad, Max, 239-40

O'Connor, James, 148
O'Dwyer, Paul, 159
Offe, Claus, 209
O'Neill, John, 95

Parsons, Talcott, 31, 32, 81, 151
People's Development Corporation (South Bronx), 175
Plato, 99
Proudhon, Pierre-Joseph, 23, 223
Proxmire, William

Reich, Wilhelm, 62, 191, 220
Richardson, Charles, 174
Riesman, David, 143-44
Roosevelt, Eleanor, 238
Roszak, Theodore, 170
Rousseau, Jean Jacques, 190

Scanlon, Laura Polla, 175
Schurman, Franz, 32
Schutz, Alfred, 28, 41-44, 49, 53
Sennett, Richard, 239
Shanker, Albert, 158-59
Shaughnessy, Mina, 142
Shils, Edward, 31, 32-34, 73-74
Shubkin, Vladimir N., 81
Skokie, Illinois, 24, 168-72
Smith, Dorothy, 32, 69-70
Socialist Register, 31
Socialist Scholars Conference, 18
Soviet Union (USSR, Russia), 12, 17-18, 20, 59, 62, 76-81, 163-64, 171, 219
Stalin, Joseph V., 19-20, 84, 164

Stone, Catherine, 214
Strauss, Anselm L., 32
Supek, Rudi, 224-225
Sutton, Francis X., 31

Task Force on Higher Education, 111
Taylor, Gerald, 175
Third World, 184, 206, 211, 213, 219, 225
Thompson, E. P., 105-6, 212
Thompson, Victor A., 32
Tito, Josip Broz, 163-64
Tolstoy, Leo, 170
Trotsky, Leon, 84

United States of America, 12, 13, 17-18, 20, 21, 25-26, 30, 58-59, 62, 75-81, 132, 155-59, 188, 199-202, 206, 217, 219, 238

Velikovsky, Immanuel, 62-63

Ward, Colin, 23, 213, 218
Willingham, Warren W., 109
Wobblies (IWW: Industrial Workers of the World), 23
Wolff, Kurt H., 30

Yugoslavia, 21, 163, 192-93, 224

LIBRARY OF DAVIDSON COLLEGE

Books on regular loan may be checked out for **two weeks.** Books must be presented at the Circulation Desk in order to be renewed.

A fine is charged after date due.

Special books are subject to special regulations at the discretion of the library staff.

JAN 0 8 1992			